Published under the auspices of
THE CENTER FOR JAPANESE AND KOREAN STUDIES
University of California, Berkeley

THE POLITICS OF LABOR LEGISLATION IN JAPAN

The Politics of
Labor Legislation
in Japan

National-International
Interaction

EHUD HARARI

University of California Press
Berkeley, Los Angeles, London

UNIVERSITY OF CALIFORNIA PRESS
BERKELEY AND LOS ANGELES, CALIFORNIA
UNIVERSITY OF CALIFORNIA PRESS, LTD.
LONDON, ENGLAND
COPYRIGHT © 1973 BY
THE REGENTS OF THE UNIVERSITY OF CALIFORNIA
ISBN: 0-520-02264-5
LIBRARY OF CONGRESS CATALOG CARD NUMBER: 72-78945

To My Parents

Contents

Preface

This study of Japanese labor policy examines the interrelationship of politics at the local-provincial, national, and international levels. It focuses on Japan's ratification of International Labor Organization Convention 87 (Freedom of Association and Protection of the Right to Organize) and related domestic legislation.

Research on public policy making in Japan has been a hard challenge indeed. A non-Japanese can overcome the language barrier with self-discipline and perseverance. However, a great number of participants are involved, and secrecy surrounds some of the processes; consequently, considerable humility is called for in making assertions and setting the level of expectations in a study of this magnitude.

This book is a revised and updated version of my doctoral dissertation submitted to the Department of Political Science of the University of California, Berkeley, in 1968. Most of the research was conducted in Japan under the auspices of the Institute of Social Science of the University of Tokyo, from November 1965 to September 1967. The study was completed at the Center for Japanese and Korean Studies of the University of California, Berkeley, and at the Tel-Aviv University.

It would have been impossible for me to have undertaken this endeavor without the intellectual stimulation, guidance, help, and patience of many people at its various stages. Unfortunately, I cannot adequately express my indebtedness to everyone. My heaviest obligation is to Professor Robert A. Scalapino, who continuously provided me with a generous combination of the above forms of assistance. I am greatly indebted to Professor Chalmers A. Johnson for his keen interest in this study and for his encouragement and criticism. I also wish to express my appreciation to Professor Ernst

B. Haas for invaluable suggestions and criticisms. Furthermore, the comments and suggestions of the anonymous reviewers of the University of California Press have been very useful. In Japan, my deepest debts are to Professor Ishida Takeshi and his associates at the Institute of Social Science of Tokyo University, for sponsoring my research and providing me with invaluable insights; to Dr. Hanami Tadashi of Sophia University and of the Japan Institute of Labor, and to his associates at the institute for warm support and advice on many matters; Dr. Hanami read the entire manuscript and offered very useful suggestions for improvement; to Shimodaira Hiromi of Tokyo University for painstaking tutoring in the Japanese language, including a patient introduction to the jargon of Japanese labor economics and politics, for assistance in translating part of the Japanese sources, and for interpreting during my first interviews; to Dr. Takahashi Takeshi, Chief of the Research Department, ILO Tokyo office, for extensive information and numerous suggestions; to Professor Fujita Shozō of Hōsei University for deepening my understanding of Japanese political philosophy during long hours of intermittent conversations; to Theodore Cohen, formerly the head of SCAP Labor Division, for information, explanations, and corrections; and to Professor Kataoka Hiromitsu of Waseda University. I am grateful to Judith Bernstein for research assistance; to M. Iverson for editing an early draft: to Lew Golan of Tel-Aviv University for editing the manuscript; to Gladys Castor for the final copy editing; and to Kikue Epstein for the glossary's calligraphy. To my wife, Ruth, I owe a great deal for helping me in many ways.

Among those not mentioned are party leaders and workers (especially of the Democratic Socialist party, the Japan Socialist party, and the Liberal Democratic party); union leaders, secretaries, and rank and file members; newspaper reporters; government officials; officials of the Japan Federation of Employers' Associations; and my neighborhood barber, who offered his explanations of Japanese politics far beyond the call of duty.

For financial assistance, I am grateful to the Center for Japanese and Korean Studies of the University of California, Berkeley, whose grants facilitated my graduate studies, and the writing and revision of the dissertation; to the Japan Society for the Promotion of Science, whose Foreign Research Fellowship facilitated my research in Japan from November 1955 to August 1967; to the Faculty of Social Sciences and the Institute of Labor and Social Studies, Tel-Aviv University; and to the Peretz Naftali Foundation, Tel-Aviv. The sources of assistance have been numerous; any errors can have sprung from only one source—myself.

Abbreviations

DSP	Democratic Socialist Party
ICFTU	International Confederation of Free Trade Unions
IFFTU	International Federation of Free Teachers Unions
ILO	International Labor Organization
ITWF	International Transport Workers Federation
JCP	Japan Communist Party
JNR	Japan National Railways
JSP	Japan Socialist Party
LDP	Liberal Democratic Party
LPELRL	Local Public Enterprises Labor Relations Law
LPSL	Local Public Service Law
NPSL	National Public Service Law
OECD	Organization for Economic Cooperation and Development
PARC	Policy Affairs Research Council (LDP)
PCNELRL	Public Corporations and National Enterprises Labor Relations Law
PTTI	Postal, Telegraph, and Telephone International
SCAP	Supreme Command Allied Powers; Supreme Commander Allied Powers
WFTU	World Federation of Trade Unions

1
Introduction

During the 1957 International Labor Conference in Geneva, Haraguchi Yukitaka,[1] Japan's workers' delegate, appealed for the International Labor Organization's support in a conflict between the authorities and two national union organizations of Japanese railways workers. This event ushered in nine years (1957–1966) of extensive interaction between the ILO and various political actors in Japan.

The appeal was followed by a formal complaint against the Japanese government; this was filed jointly by Sōhyō (General Council of Japan's Trade Unions), Japan's largest trade union center, and Kirō (Locomotive Engineers' Union). The complaint was supported by the International Confederation of Free Trade Unions (ICFTU) and one of its affiliates, the International Transport Workers Federation (ITWF).

The complaint centered on two major problems. The first concerned the eligibility of public employees for union membership and union leadership. In Japan, union membership and leadership were restricted *by law* to employees of the particular ministry, municipality, or public enterprise; upon their discharge for whatever reason, employees thus became ineligible for union membership and leadership. The second problem was alleged police interference in union affairs.

The Japanese government was accused of violating ILO Convention 87 (Freedom of Association and Protection of the Right to Organize, 1948), which Japan had not ratified. Presumably, the problems raised by the complaint could have been solved had

1. Throughout the book I have followed the Japanese convention of writing the last name first and the first name second.

Japan ratified the convention immediately. Indeed, the ILO pressured the Japanese government to ratify the Convention, and the government in turn expressed willingness to do so.

However, the government's intention to ratify the convention had actually broadened the cleavage between the unions and the authorities instead of solving the problems. Zentei (Japan Postal Workers' Union) and then other unions, encouraged by the liberal spirit of the convention about to be ratified, intensified the severity of their struggle against the authorities. In response, the government introduced new restrictive legislation together with the bill for the ratification of the convention, in order to safeguard against union excesses under the protective wings of the convention.

Gradually, the issue assumed larger proportions and grew more and more complex both domestically and in the ILO. The original complainants to the ILO, Sōhyō and Kirō, were joined by other Japanese unions in the public sector. The latter were also supported by the ICFTU and several of its affiliates.[2] Furthermore, the complainants raised new problems in addition to the original subjects of eligibility for membership and police interference. Finally, in addition to violating Convention 87, which Japan had not ratified, Japanese labor policies and practices were charged with violating Convention 98 (The Right to Organize and Collective Bargaining, 1949), which Japan *had* ratified in 1953.

As the issue evolved and the Japanese government seemed incapable of settlement, the ILO Committee on Freedom of Association increased the intensity and severity of its pressures. In January 1965, after securing the agreement of the Japanese government, the Governing Body dispatched its Fact-Finding and Conciliation Commission to Japan; in 1966 it published a report of the commission's frame of reference, activities, findings, and recommendations.[3]

Finally, a compromise was reached in 1965 among the ruling Liberal Democratic party (LDP), the Japan Socialist party (JSP), and the Democratic Socialist party (DSP); the Diet ratified Con-

2. These were the Postal, Telegraph, and Telephone International (PTTI), the Public Service International (PSI), and the International Federation of Free Teachers Unions (IFFTU).

3. International Labor Office, "Report of the Fact-Finding and Conciliation Commission on Freedom of Association Concerning Persons Employed in the Public Sector in Japan." Hereafter cited as the Dreyer Report.

vention 87, eliminated from the existing laws those provisions admittedly in clear violation of the convention, and passed the least controversial of the government bills.

The more controversial bills were shelved for a year pending their examination by the Advisory Council on the Public Personnel System (Kōmuim Seido Shingikai). The Advisory Council, which was newly established for this task as well as for the reexamination of the whole system of labor relations in the Japanese public sector, failed to reach a consensus on the shelved bills. After one year it recommended, by majority vote, that all the bills be accorded automatic validity except for one, the enforcement of which was postponed for an additional six months. The government obliged, and the bills became laws.

Significance

The appeal of the Japanese unions to the ILO and the subsequent interaction among the ILO, the international labor movement, and various Japanese actors were significant in several ways.

In the ILO, the issue, known as Case 179 (Japan), became the organization's most instructive case in the area of freedom of association, having set in motion *all* the instruments of its supervisory machinery. The case was related to two of the most ratified conventions, 87 and 98,[4] the only ones having *permanent* and *standing* machinery for complaints against a member government as embodied in the Committee on Freedom of Association.[5] For the first time in the history of the ILO, the case involved a visit to a defendant country by the Fact-Finding and Conciliation Commission after all other available instruments of supervision had been exhausted. Judging by the length of time required for its settlement, and by the intricacies of the procedures involved, Case 179 seemed problematical. Yet, of the eighty-seven countries whose labor policies became subject to complaints by 1968, Japan was the most responsive to ILO pressures.

The appeal (and especially the ILO's favorable response) facilitated, in Easton's terminology, the conversion of union *demands* into a political *issue* involving authoritative consideration of realistic alternatives to the current policy.[6] Since 1948, when a series of

4. K. N. Dahl, "The Role of ILO Standards in the Global Integration Process."
5. E. B. Haas, *Human Rights and International Action*, p. 26.
6. D. Easton, *A System Analysis of Political Life*, pp. 140–49.

restrictions had been initiated, the unions had been unable to bring about a serious reexamination of the current labor legislation. Once recognized, the issue became the longest continuous issue in the Japanese Diet; it involved a variety of individuals, groups, and institutions in several styles of conflict.

Case 179 (Japan), then, was both a domestic issue and an international issue. Actors, institutions, and processes at the level of Japanese domestic politics interacted with their counterparts at the international level. Several actors figured prominently at both levels, such as leaders of national union federations who also served as members of ILO committees. Therefore, for those concerned with bridging the academic fields of *comparative* politics and *international* politics, the evolution of the issue serves as an instructive illustration of what J. N. Rosenau called "national-international linkage politics." [7]

The national-international linkage in this case raises three major questions. First, what confluence of circumstances internationalized the Japanese domestic problem, thus making it both a *domestic* issue and a *foreign policy* issue? Second, why did the internationalization of the issue last so long? And third, what was the feedback of the internationalization in both Japanese labor politics and the system of the ILO? Let us elaborate on these questions.

Internationalization

ISSUES. A political issue may break into the public arena with meteoric suddenness and brightness as a result of a spectacular event. More often, however, issues develop during extended periods of incubation.[8] Certain needs are created by technological or social changes, or as a result of public policies. However, demands for the satisfaction of these needs do not necessarily gain immediate recognition by the political elites as legitimate public issues; and some demands may never reach the *open* arena of

7. Concerning the evaluation of the concept of "linkage politics," see J. N. Rosenau, "Pre-theories and Theories of Foreign Policy"; K. W. Deutsch, "External Influences on the Internal Behavior of States"; and Rosenau, "Toward a Study of National International Linkages." For a more elaborate model and its skillful application to a country's foreign policy, see M. Brecher, *The Foreign Policy System of Israel.*

8. N. W. Polsby, "Notes on Policy Initiation in the American Political System."

politics under the scrutinizing eye of the communications media and, hence, the attentive public.[9]

Why do issues finally surface at a certain point in time? Several, sometimes contradictory, possibilities have been suggested. According to one source, in a pluralistic society with a low degree of cleavage (such as the United States) where groups and individuals ordinarily cannot dominate each other, bargaining takes place constantly behind the scenes. Needs and demands become issues when, out of weakness, certain groups lose their bargaining effectiveness and "socialize" the process in order to mobilize adequate support.[10] Another source argues that as long as certain groups are weak and lack the resources to compel those in power to recognize the legitimacy of their demand, an issue cannot surface.[11] Still another asserts that an issue surfaces when a variety of groups, of which some are in competition with others, becomes conscious of certain needs and of the necessity to adopt a new policy to meet the needs (although they differ as to what policy should be adopted).[12] A pioneering study of a Japanese foreign policy issue related to the Soviet-Japanese negotiations indicated that the issue surfaced in Japan as a result of an input from an external source—the Soviet Union.[13]

In the case of Japanese unions, restrictions on their freedom of association were imposed as early as 1948. Why did they surface only in 1957? To answer this question, we should trace the evolution of the various points of contention. As issues do not evolve in isolation but rather tend to cluster in issue-areas, we should, therefore, explore the issue-area of freedom of association of Japanese unions in general and freedom of association in the public sector in particular. Specifically, what was the role played by the unions in Japanese politics? How much access did they have to public policy makers? Could they press for the recognition of their demands domestically without appealing to the ILO?

9. P. Bachrach and M. Baratz, *Power and Poverty;* "Decisions and Non-Decisions: An Analytical Framework"; and "Two Faces of Power"; see J. W. White's treatment of this argument in the Japanese context in his "The Sōka Gakkai: Implications of a Mass Movement for Democratic Society."

10. R. Dahl, *Who Governs?*

11. Bachrach and Baratz, *Power and Poverty.*

12. A. K. McAdams, *Power and Politics in Labor Legislation.*

13. D. C. Hellmann, *Japanese Foreign Policy and Domestic Politics,* pp. 32-35.

GOVERNMENT ATTITUDES. Formally, membership in international organizations is voluntary. Governments are motivated to join international organizations by the perception of their interests. Presumably, they weigh the expected rewards to be gained by international cooperation against the resulting limitations on their freedom of action and their "sovereignty"—or against the possible penalties for refraining from cooperating. ILO membership imposed (at least formally) such limitations not only on obviously *international* matters, such as the treatment of international migrant workers, but also on matters commonly considered *domestic*, such as unions' freedom of association and their participation in their country's policy making. Therefore, what motivated the Japanese government to join the ILO? What rewards did it expect to gain? What penalties did it want to avoid? When the appeal to the ILO was made, why was the government ready to subject itself to the organization's supervisory machinery instead of considering ILO's measures to be illegitimate interference in Japan's internal affairs?

UNION EXPECTATIONS. Having decided to involve an international organization in their conflict with the authorities, what opportunities within the ILO did union leaders expect to harness? Did they expect the organization to pressure, or even *force*, the government to comply with union demands? Did they hope only to embarrass the government into providing for meaningful union participation in domestic labor policy making? On what was based their image of ILO's *responsiveness* to union demands and *effectiveness* in pressuring member governments?

ILO RESPONSIVENESS. The responsiveness of an international organization to complaints against member governments may be determined by several factors: its structure, its ideology, and its current programs. These factors may determine not only its general responsiveness, but also its tendencies toward selective responsiveness, depending on the characteristics of both the complainants and the governments concerned. Since its formation in 1919, the structure, ideology, and various programs of the ILO have undergone several changes.[14] These were related to the evolution of international politics (the organization's environment) and to the

14. The most systematic and thorough studies of these changes are E. B. Haas, *Beyond the Nation State*, and *Human Rights and International Action*.

interactions of governments, labor organizations, employees associations, and top officials of the International Labor Office within the various institutions of the ILO.

These changes influenced the desired scope of freedom of association, the measures for promoting it in various countries, and the complaints procedures. When Japanese unions appealed for assistance, at what stage of development was the issue of freedom of association? What was the propensity of the organization to respond to complaints against member governments? What actors within the ILO were most influential in determining ILO responsiveness to appeals for assistance? Were they selective in their responses?—that is, were there certain reasons which conditioned their response to *Japanese* unions compared with unions in other countries?

Solution Processes

THE ILO. Having chosen to take up a case, the organization can follow several formal procedures. Moreover, the organization's procedures ordinarily allow its institutions a wide range of discretion: (1) in the manner in which evidence is collected; (2) in the length of time devoted to the collection of evidence; (3) in whether the evidence or the organization's response—when it is critical—should be made public prior to its solution; (4) in the timing for increasing the pressures on the defendant government before dispatching the Fact-Finding and Conciliation Commission and publishing its report. How did the ILO exercise its discretion in the Japanese case? What were the informal pressures exerted on the Japanese government by various actors within the ILO system?

DOMESTIC POLICIES. A government's acceptance of the ILO's *legitimacy*, by recognizing the organization's right to be concerned with the country's labor problems, may not necessarily be coupled with the government's acceptance of the organization's *authority* to impose compliance with its rules.[15] A government may choose to join the ILO without being ready to subject itself to the organization's pressures; or it may choose to subject itself to the organization's pressures without intending to change its own domestic

15. For the distinction between *legitimacy* and *authority* in the context of international organizations, see Haas, *Human Rights and International Action*, pp. 48–55.

policies in response to these pressures; or it may respond selectively to these pressures by changing some policies and retaining others. How effective were the various external pressures in prodding the Japanese government into compliance with ILO conventions? [16] How did the actors and the institutions [17] perceive the issue? How much power did they have? What styles did they use? How did their interaction with external actors and institutions affect their participation?

Feedback

Participants in social processes have certain expectations regarding the consequences of these processes. The consequences may be *intended,* that is, they may fit the expectations; but often they are *unintended.* Whether intended or not, consequences may condition future expectations and actions through feedback and learning. How did the ILO's contribution to the solution of Case 179 affect the future of the politics of labor legislation in Japan? How did the participation of the various Japanese actors in the internationalization of the issue affect their attitudes toward similar action in the future? How did the ILO's contribution affect the propensity of the organization to employ its supervisory machinery against "delinquent" governments? Did it affect other governments' attitudes toward subjecting themselves to this machinery—in particular, to a visit of the Fact-Finding and Conciliation Commission?

In this study we sought to combine a narrow policy-making approach, exploring who did what and when, with a macro view associated with the systemic approach.[18] The study of any issue-area and any social system should be investigated as far back into

16. For general, comprehensive studies of this question, see E. A. Landy. *The Effectiveness of International Supervision,* and Haas, *Human Rights and International Action;* see also K. N. Dahl, "The Role of ILO Standards."

17. Rosenau lists the actors as executive officials, legislative officials, civilian bureaucrats, military bureaucrats, political parties, interest groups, and elite groups. Institutions, in his formulation, include executives, legislatures, bureaucracies, military establishments, elections, party systems, communication systems, and social institutions. "Toward a Study of National International Linkages," p. 52.

18. On the desirability of this combination, see T. J. Lowi, "American Business, Public Policy, Case Studies, and Political Theory"; and E. C. B. Schoettle, "The State of the Art in Policy Studies."

their histories as possible.[19] The legal provisions figuring in the Japanese issue—primarily the abrogation of the right of public employees to strike and to bargain collectively, and the limitations on union membership—were adopted during the American occupation. These followed an initial, liberal stage during which American, New Deal-type concepts and policies were largely transplanted into the Japanese system, laying the foundation of Japanese labor law. However, the consensus among Japanese and non-Japanese scholars has been that an understanding of labor politics in the presurrender era is indispensable to a proper grasp of postsurrender developments.[20] Specifically, it is significant because the "political memory" (that part of the political culture based on personal experiences of the individual or of his associates [21]) of the participants in Case 179 was replete with values, policies, and events of the pre-1945 era. Those memories were related, in part, to linkages with the external environment, including Japan's interaction with the ILO. We shall, therefore, devote the next two chapters to the discussion of the ILO and Japan in the presurrender era.

19. For elaborations, see, for example, Polsby, "Notes on Policy Initiation"; and J. D. Singer, "The Global System and Its Subsystem: A Developmental View," p. 22.

20. For example, R. A. Scalapino, "Labor and Politics in Postwar Japan"; S. B. Levine, *Industrial Relations in Postwar Japan;* I. F. Ayusawa, *A History of Labor in Modern Japan;* Hanami Tadashi, *ILO to Nihon no Danketsuken;* and Ōkōchi Kazuo, *Sengo Nihon no Rōdō Undō.*

21. S. Verba, "Conclusion," in L. W. Pye and S. Verba, *Political Culture and Political Development,* p. 552; the tendency of decision makers in a crisis situation to supplement objective information with memories acquired in the process of "social learning" was found to be significant by Paige, in *The Korean Decision,* proposition 2.4., p. 295.

2

The Road to the ILO

In 1919, for the first time, Japan became a member of an international body concerned with protective labor legislation. She was one of the original members of the International Labor Organization, which was established following the Paris Peace Conference. Efforts to create formal international machinery for protective labor legislation had been made for over seventy years prior to the establishment of the organization. However, neither the Japanese government nor nongovernmental actors from Japan participated in these efforts.

The advocates of international protective labor legislation were motivated by both humanitarian and economic considerations. They were strongly moved by the plight of the industrial workers, whose wretched labor conditions were detrimental to their physical and mental health and threatened a possible decrease in labor efficiency. Those advocating an international, binding labor policy were also concerned with "unfair" competition in international trade; they sought to equalize labor conditions in order to equalize the cost of labor. Hence, *protective* labor legislation had a dual benefit: for the individual worker, and for a national industry.[1]

The participants in the process leading to the formation of the ILO were international socialist and trade union organizations; labor movements in several countries, especially the United States and industrially advanced countries in Europe; groups of social

1. The following account is based on J. T. Shotwell, *The Origins of the International Labor Organization;* E. B. Haas, *Beyond the Nation State;* K. N. Dahl, "The Role of ILO Standards in the Global Integration Process"; and Kaite and Toda, *ILO: Kokusai Rōdō Kikan.*

reformers; international groups of experts on labor legislation; and national governments.[2]

International action took several forms. There were political publications in about 1840, and an intergovernmental conference in Berlin in 1890, which led to the formation of the International Association for Labor Legislation, consisting of delegates from fourteen European countries. A bilateral treaty of reciprocity was signed by France and Italy in 1904, granting equal protection to the workers of both nationalities. In 1906, an intergovernmental conference in Berne resulted in treaties that provided for binding labor legislation.

During this period Japan was not a party to any of the bilateral or multilateral labor treaties. In 1905, when the International Association for Labor Legislation adopted two international conventions (Respecting the Prohibition of the Use of Yellow Phosphorus in the Manufacture of Matches, and Respecting the Prohibition of Night Work for Women in Industrial Employment), Japan was invited to accede to the first. The Japanese government, while acknowledging the gravity of the hygienic situation in the match industry, rejected the invitation (which was partly motivated by apprehension about Japanese competition on the part of several European countries). Until 1921, the Japanese government refrained from any action.[3]

Similarly, Japanese labor was not part of the First Socialist International; it had a very limited part in the Second International; and it was not active in the International Federation of Trade Unions (IFTU).[4] On several occasions, Japanese labor leaders attended meetings of the Second International and labor conventions in the United States. However, they either played a passive role or were active in other areas—such as protesting the Japanese government's role in the Russo-Japanese War.[5] When the Peace

2. The role of a number of individuals, while important, would carry us too far afield.

3. Kaite and Toda, *ILO*, p. 14; J. W. Follows, *The Antecedents of the ILO*, pp. 162–63, 167.

4. The formal participation of Japanese unions in a noncommunist international trade union organization began only in 1929 when the Japan Seamen's Union joined the International Federation of Transportation Workers. G. O. Totten, *The Social Democratic Movement in Prewar Japan*, p. 270.

5. I. Ayusawa, *A History of Labor in Modern Japan*, p. 32; Watanabe Tōru, *Gendai Rōdō Undō Shi Nenpyō*; R. A. Scalapino, "The Japanese Labor Movement," chap. 2.

Conference drafted the ILO Charter in Paris in 1919, Japanese government representatives participated in the deliberations of the Commission for Labor Legislation. They did not, however, play a positive role in the founding of the new organization. Rather, their duty was to safeguard their government's interests in an international organization being established by others.

What were the reasons for the absence of Japanese among the actors leading to the formation of the ILO? Why did the Japanese government join the organization despite this absence?

From the middle of the nineteenth century to the end of World War I, the Japanese political system and its relationship with the international environment had undergone major changes; despite these changes, however, a strong element of continuity persisted. In 1853, Japan was forced open by the naval mission of Commodore M. C. Perry of the United States, after having been a voluntarily secluded nation under the rule of the Tokugawa family for more than two hundred and fifty years. Japan was subsequently transformed into a "penetrated" state,[6] having been pressed to sign the Unequal Treaties with the United States, Russia, England, France, and Holland; these provided for extraterritoriality, reduction of import duties to 5 percent, and elimination of almost all restrictions on foreign trade.

In 1868, the Meiji Restoration abolished the Tokugawa rule and replaced the decentralized feudal system with an imperial system. This eliminated the old class distinctions and privileges, as well as the relative autonomy of the several feudal domains (*han*). The real power was concentrated in the hands of a small group of determined young ex-samurai from southern and western Japan, who were aided by centralized civilian and military bureaucracies. Political centralization was facilitated by the cultural homogeneity of the Japanese (which had been strengthened during the long period of seclusion), an advanced network of communication, and a high degree of social integration. The last was achieved through the leaders' manipulation of two traditional values: group loyalty, and the identification of the Japanese nation as an extended family headed by the emperor.[7] These values were incul-

6. This is another term coined by Rosenau, in "Toward a Theory of National International Linkages," p. 46.
7. R. N. Bellah, "Continuity and Change in Japanese Society."

cated through a centralized educational system and through the army (which was based on general conscription).

To the Japanese leadership and public, the Unequal Treaties were a source of intense resentment. The Meiji oligarchs were committed to advancing Japan both economically and militarily in order to strengthen her demand for the abolition of the treaties. The key element in the drive to achieve this goal was rapid industrialization; this was initially financed—and later aided and controlled—by the central government.[8] By the end of World War I, the net output of the country's secondary industry almost equaled that of her agriculture.[9]

The treaties were abolished in 1894; extraterritoriality ended in 1899, when a new Japanese civil code came into effect. Other stepping-stones in Japan's drive for security, influence, economic expansion, and international prestige were her victory in the Sino-Japanese war (1894–1895); her participation in the military intervention in China during the Boxer rebellion; the Anglo-Japanese Alliance of 1902; her defeat of Russia in 1904–1905; and her participation in World War I.

Political centralization and military aggrandizement were not the only trends during this period. The former was countered by social forces advocating a more liberal form of government—one that allowed wider participation in politics and elected party governments rather than oligarchic extraparliamentarian rule. The latter was countered by pressures for a peaceful diplomacy in Asia, since Japanese *economic* expansion backed by force was antagonizing prospective customers in the area.

At the end of World War I, Japan was satisfied with the new international status accorded to her for her military prowess. At the same time, the prevailing domestic forces supported a peaceful international system based on collective security through the League of Nations.

The demands for the formation of a representative government were expressed by a "popular rights" movement (*Jiyūminken Undō*) and the formation of two political parties: the Jiyūtō (Liberal party) in 1881, and the Kaishintō (Progressive party) in 1882. The Meiji Constitution was promulgated in 1889, and the first Diet (legislature) convened a year later. As chambers of com-

8. H. Rosovsky, *Capital Formation in Japan*, pp. 21–36.   9. Ibid., p. 11.

merce and associations of agricultural and industrial interests were
formed, they demanded a voice in policy making. However, the
powers of the Diet were limited by the constitution, and the
extent of popular political participation was still minimal; suffrage was limited by property-tax criteria to around three million
male citizens in 1919.

The Japanese press developed rapidly in terms of circulation
and political orientation. While only about one person in six
hundred read a newspaper in 1875, readership grew to one in ten
by 1924.[10] Politically, the press was first encouraged by the oligarchy in return for political loyalty. Later, it became a tool of the
opposition during the "popular rights" movement; its struggle
against the government invited suppression. Throughout, the press
was strongly political, but the government encouraged the advocacy of only those opinions congenial to its own policy.

The political parties themselves were organizationally weak, and
depended on contributions from the industrial interests. The
parties were elitist in character, despite their claim to liberalism;
significantly, they had to vie for power with an entrenched combination of an informal council of elder statesmen (*genrō*), officials
of the Imperial Household, the Privy Council, the civil and military bureaucracies, and a nonelective House of Peers of the Imperial Diet. Political pluralism did not develop in Japan, despite
the emergence of new social groups as a result of rapid industrialization and increasing urbanization. A semblance of pluralism
existed, but only at the thin upper layer of the social pyramid.

From the point of view of labor policy, the timing of the Meiji
Constitution was very significant. It solidified an elitist (and, to a
large extent, closed) political system *before* the emergence of a
labor movement. When a labor movement emerged, the road to
participation in power was firmly blocked. Frequent cleavages
within the ranks of labor were caused by the complexity of its
ideological structure, the social origin of its leadership, the personal rivalries among its leaders, and the dearth and fluidity of
support among the public and the rank and file; these combined to
make labor's attempt to penetrate the political system prior to 1919
all the more difficult. By 1919 the Japanese labor movement had

10. For a discussion of the Japanese press, see S. Kato, "The Mass Media," in
Ward and Rustow, *Political Modernization in Japan and Turkey*, pp. 236–54.

passed through two such periods: from the Sino-Japanese War of 1894–1895 to 1910, and from 1912 to 1919. Both periods started with "pure" trade unionism, strongly emphasizing harmony, mutual aid, and education of the workers; the ranks then split into two main streams: parliamentary socialism on one hand, and anarcho-syndicalism on the other. In order to put these developments into proper perspective, following are descriptions of the prevailing *labor conditions* in Japan, the characteristics of the *labor force,* and the characteristics of *labor relations* in Japanese industry at that time.

The oligarchs' policy of rapid industrialization, which was continued by subsequent party governments, was financed mainly by taxation of the agricultural sector.[11] Mobilization of the country's available resources was also of strategic importance in setting the foundation for the government's labor policy (or, in effect, the absence of labor legislation). Industry was expected to surge ahead without such disruptions as absenteeism or strikes. Men, women, and children were required to work long hours for minuscule pay. Conditions of work were determined not by law but by the employers; they were expected to contribute to harmonious relationships with the workers in the spirit and practice of paternalism. In many establishments, paternal relations were indeed prevalent; in many others, the system amounted to despotism.[12]

The wretched conditions of Japanese labor did not result in widespread alienation among the workers. Their sacrifices were exalted by the government and the employers as indispensable contributions to the well-being and prestige of their country. No less important, however, was the nature of the Japanese labor force, termed by Professor Ōkōchi *dekasegigata.*[13] It was an im-

11. Rosovsky and Ohkawa, "The Role of Agriculture in Modern Japanese Economic Development."

12. For a pioneering study employing a distinction between "despotic" and "'patriarchal" types of Japanese management, see S. B. Levine, *Industrial Relations in Postwar Japan,* pp. 35–41.

13. Professor Ōkōchi Kazuo, former president of Tokyo University, has been the leading labor economist and historian in Japan. His disciples form a respectable segment of the leading labor scholars in Japan. His theory has been discussed by every author writing about Japanese labor. For a sample of his writing in English, see *Labor in Modern Japan,* and "Traditionalism of Industrial Relations in Japan," pp. 124–41. For a survey of the labor theories by Japanese scholars, see M. Tsuda, *The Basic Structure of Japanese Labor Rerations* (sic); and Ujihara Shojiro and Rōdō Mondai Bunken Kenkyūkai, eds., *Nihon no Rōdō Mondai,* especially pp. 58–110.

permanent, uncommitted labor force that hailed primarily from
the agricultural sector, and maintained close ties with kindred
groups in the rural community. Members of the labor force either
returned to the rural areas after short periods of employment in
industry or intended to return as soon as possible. The workers
could rely on family support in the rural areas in times of industrial unemployment: this served not only as a shock absorber to
facilitate smoother development of Japanese industrialization, but
also as an obstacle to the process of unionization inside or outside
the place of employment.[14] Another important factor in the imper-
manence of the labor force was the numerical dominance of young
girls employed in the textile industry, a major and growing industry. And the employers' paternalism, though often despotic,
was a potent factor in curbing workers' alienation. The pattern of
Japanese social relations, constituting a framework of mutual obligations based on a familial type of structure of authority and
compliance, was extended to the place of employment.[15]

Despite these mitigating factors, however, disruptions did break
out in Japanese industry. Some of them were spontaneous; others
were instigated by labor unions. The institution entrusted with
the handling of labor disputes was not a Ministry of Labor or a
similar agency, but the police, who contributed a great deal to the
centralization of control and internal stability throughout the
country.

From the dawn of Japanese industrialization and the emergence
of the labor movement, the ruling elite identified labor problems
as problems of internal security. The first time that labor problems
were treated legally on a national level was in 1900, when the
Public Peace Police Law (*Chian Keisatsu Hō*) was enacted. As
suggested by R. A. Scalapino, articles 17 and 30 of that law were

14. See also Maruyama Masao, "Patterns of Individuation and the Case of
Japan," pp. 528–29.
15. See a detailed discussion on this respect in J. C. Abegglen, *The Japanese
Factory: Aspects of Its Social Organization.* For a criticism of the Abegglen theory
for overemphasizing the social aspects and neglecting the impact of supply and
demand fluctuations, see Taira Koji, "The Characteristics of Japanese Labor
Markets," pp. 150–68. For a study of Japanese paternalism based on data collected
during the occupation, see Bennett and Ishino, *Paternalism in the Japanese Economy.* For a recent criticism of the Abegglen theory, see Robert E. Cole, *Japanese
Blue Collar.*

interpreted as prohibiting strikes and union organizations, and became the "death-knell of the Meiji labor movement." [16]

Since the "liberal" parties were actually elitist in character and not really committed to social reform, organized efforts to ameliorate labor conditions had to originate elsewhere. These efforts involved three types of actors: political parties, labor unions, and liberal intellectuals; the last were associated with universities (primarily Tokyo University), segments of the national bureaucracy, and business.

SOCIALIST PARTIES. Early attempts to organize socialist parties in Japan were fruitless. The parties faced a shortage of funds, and their "natural" constituency support, the workers, were denied the right to vote. Moreover, suppression by the police nipped in the bud any serious attempts to organize effectively. The forerunner of the socialist parties was the Oriental Liberal party (*Tōyō Jiyūtō*), formed by Ōi Kentarō in 1892. The party's purpose was concretely expressed by the founding of three organizations: the Greater Japan Labor Society, the League of Petition for Universal Suffrage, and the Committee on Investigation of Tenancy Regulation.[17] The party functioned for a short while and then was disbanded; the Social Democratic party (Shakai Minshutō) had an even shorter career, having been disbanded by the police on the day of its foundation (May 20, 1901).[18] After that, no socialist party was founded prior to the enactment of the Universal Suffrage Act in 1925. During this period, one attempt was made by a socialist to run in the general elections as a socialist candidate; he drew only 32 out of the 16,000 ballots cast.[19]

UNION ORGANIZATIONS. At its initial stage, Japanese unionism was strongly influenced by foreign ideas and practices. These were imported to Japan by intellectuals who identified themselves with the workers and sought to provide leadership, and by workers who had experience with trade unionism abroad, primarily in the United States. Together, they founded the Association for the

16. "The Japanese Labor Movement," chap. 2.
17. R. A. Scalapino, *Democracy and the Party Movement in Prewar Japan*, p. 316, n. 34.
18. Ibid., p. 318; Ayusawa, *History of Labor*, p. 67; Totten, *Social Democratic Movement*, p. 23, 26–27.
19. Totten, ibid., p. 289.

Establishment of Labor Unions (Rōdō Kumiai Kiseikai) in 1897. They were disposed toward organizing the workers for self-improvement and depending on persuasion to get the employers to cooperate. They found American-style trade unionism, Christian humanism, and German theories of social reform most promising for the Japanese setting. They appealed to liberal officials and Diet members for protective labor legislation; temporarily, the organizational drive looked promising, but no favorable legislation was forthcoming. On the contrary, the government's reaction to the trade union movement (and to the strikes associated with it) was the enactment of the restrictive Public Peace Police Law.

By the turn of the century, the organizational drive had lost its momentum, and most of the remaining organizations gradually faded. This trend, compounded by police repression, triggered a radicalization of the union movement throughout the Meiji era (i.e., until 1912). Study groups intensified their activities, and the number of publications dealing with labor problems increased. The prevailing arguments reflected disillusionment with Japanese-style parliamentarianism—which had created a backlash that strengthened the appeal of the imported ideology of anarchism.

Anarchism was associated with a modified doctrine of trade unionism. "Direct action" was to be carried out by a thoroughly *decentralized* movement comprising the smallest units of production. The process of politics was to be bypassed.

The issue of parliamentary socialism versus "direct action" was heatedly debated in the leftist literature of the time, and by the multiplicity of study groups. Still, the workers who were expected to figure prominently in the realization of either ideology were unresponsive, for the reasons enumerated earlier. In 1910, the debate was concluded in a manner reminiscent of "the end of a Japanese tragedy." [20] In the aftermath of the Kōtoku Affair—the alleged attempt on Emperor Meiji's life by anarchist leader Kōtoku Denjiro—the police cracked down on radical union leaders.

The crackdown represented one side of the official policy toward labor. Whenever possible, the government used both a whip and a carrot simultaneously; the other side of the coin took the form of two carrots. In 1911 the Factory Act was finally enacted; although

20. Ōkōchi Kazuo, *Reimeki no Nihon Rōdō Undō*, p. 155.

it afforded the workers very little protection, and its enforcement
was postponed until 1916, it was a conciliatory act on the part of
the ruling oligarchy. In the following year the formation of a moderate trade union organization, the Yūaikai (Friendly Love Society), was tolerated by the government. The Yūaikai was under
the leadership of Suzuki Bunji, an intellectual turned unionist,
who had intimate ties with business and bureaucratic ties through
his former classmates at Tokyo Imperial University. It sought
"harmonism" with management through labor education and
mediation rather than class conflict and confrontations.

By 1919, however, the Yūaikai, too, had shifted to radicalism,
because of a number of factors. The Yūaikai had labored to bring
about the repeal of the Public Peace Police Law and the enactment of laws that would bestow official recognition on labor
unions. It had also been active in the movement for universal
suffrage. But these efforts were frustrated by the ruling elite, and
the situation was aggravated by economic difficulties following the
end of World War I (when the rapid wartime expansion had to
be readjusted to the new, postwar conditions). The change in the
composition of the Yūaikai was also an important factor, especially
following a large influx of young university graduates under the
influence of radical ideology. Its radicalization was symbolized by
the change of its name from Friendly Love Society to Great Japan
Trade Union Federation (Dai Nippon Rōdō Sōdōmei—Sōdōmei
for short).

NON-LEFTIST LIBERALS. This group of people concerned with protective labor legislation consisted of university professors, liberal
businessmen, and bureaucrats who refrained from direct participation in the labor movement. Socially, they did not belong to
the working class; they had been graduated from prestigious universities and held reputable positions. They were all intellectuals,
each in his own way—having been concerned with social problems
and having made his contribution to Japanese culture. They were
all well versed in social conditions abroad; at the least, they were
interested in foreign developments and cultivated a particular
image on the basis of information they were able to gather. They
were familiar with the miserable effects of industrialization abroad,
and feared the replication of these in Japan. However, they were

also aware of national welfare policies (especially in Germany) that were designed to alleviate the situation and to prevent alienation and rebellion.

As they had all been integrated in Japanese culture, in which the concept of the state was couched in familial terms, it was natural for them to believe that social reform had to be undertaken by the state. Inspired by this idea, a small, informal group formed the Social Policy Academic Association (Shakai Seisaku Gakkai [21]) in April 1896. They defined their program positively, advocating humanitarianism, and negatively, rejecting laissez faire and socialism. In their first convention they portrayed social legislation as the dike that would stem the tide of socialism in Japan.[22]

THE BUREAUCRATS. The attitude of the members of the national bureaucracy concerned with labor problems was most significant because of their direct influence on policy making. Prominent among them were the officials of the Home Ministry. They were concerned less with the rights and well-being of the individual workers than with internal stability and labor efficiency for the sake of rapid industrial development. The same ministry that had employed the police to fight subversion and handle social unrest also advocated protective legislation to uproot the causes of social unrest. The interplay of these two themes in the attitudes of that ministry's officials was reflected in two different organizations they sponsored, the Kokusuikai (National Essence Society) and the Kyōchōkai (Harmonization Society).

The National Essence Society (and other groups with similar programs) advocated labor legislation that harmonized the interests of labor and capital.[23] Its active membership included a great number of builders, foremen, labor contractors, and gangs of workers. The organization was founded in October 1919, a little over a year after the Rice Riots of August 1918 had made the work of the police extremely difficult. The Kokusuikai was intended to be an auxiliary body to reinforce the police.

The Harmonization Society was created with the same aims, but in a more constructive way. The Home Ministry proposed an organization of representatives from business, labor, and government;

21. Totten, *Social Democratic Movement*, p. 25.
22. Kishimoto Eitarō, *Nihon Rōdō Seisaku Shoshi*, pp. 29 ff.
23. R. Storry, *The Double Patriots*, pp. 26–29; Scalapino, *Democracy and the Party Movement*, p. 352.

it would conduct research on labor problems and make policy recommendations to the government. This was the first attempt by the government to co-opt a major segment of the labor movement. The home minister, Tokonami Takejiro, its chief proponent (and the main sponsor of the Kokusuikai), succeeded in gaining political support for the proposed organization. However, the Yūaikai rebuffed this initiative at its Seventh General Convention in 1919, which reflected the advanced degree of radicalization. The proposal was rejected as meaningless and untimely because it gave no indication of legislative reforms, and the vaguely defined methods of mediation were suspected of having suppressive intent. Moreover, Suzuki Bunji, Yūaikai president, resented the name Harmonization Society; he preferred the name Social Policy Association (Shakai Seisaku Kyōkai).[24]

While the Harmonization Society did not include organized labor and did not perform all the tasks for which it was originally designed, it did evolve as an institutional mechanism for identifying or defining labor issues. This was achieved through serious research supported generously by the government and private donations. Its direct role in legislation was limited, but its research provided reliable data oriented toward policy formulation. Research carried out by the society also had international repercussions when a respectable part of the ILO's report on Japanese labor was based on the society's publication.[25]

EMPLOYERS' ASSOCIATIONS. Economic associations appeared about ten years after the Meiji Restoration of 1868, in advance of both labor unions and agricultural associations. Employers' associations did not spring up as a direct response to a challenge from the labor movement, nor were they denied official recognition. On the contrary, they were initiated, encouraged, and regulated by Meiji governments, for the purpose of mitigating wasteful competition and improving the quality of production.[26] However, with the

24. Scalapino, "Japanese Labor Movement," chap. 3.
25. The publication was *Industrial Labor in Japan*. The same year, *Ōhara Shakai Mondai Kenkyūjo*, a nongovernmental research organization dedicated to the study of industrial relations and related subjects was established. See C. A. Johnson, *An Instant of Treason*, pp. 37 ff.
26. Morita Yoshio, *Nihon Keieisha Dantai Hatten Shi*, pp. 31–32. For a detailed discussion of the emergence of Japanese economic associations, their leadership, and their relationship with the government, see Nagata Masaomi, *Keizai Dantai Hatten Shi*; and ILO, "Industrial Labor in Japan," pp. 73–76.

progress of industrialization and the increasing participation of businessmen in politics (notably through contributions to the evolving political parties and personal ties with the extraparty aristocracy), these associations gradually pulled away from government control and took on a growing degree of independence. Moreover, while government-sponsored organizations were the prevailing norm, more associations began to emerge spontaneously. The most important of these was the Japan Industrial Club (Nihon Kōgyō Kurabu), founded in 1917. The club was financed by membership dues, including handsome sums from the Mitsui and Mitubishi combines; [27] its effectiveness won it a reputation as the "central power representing the interests of capital and the industrialists in regard to labor problems." [28]

Employers' associations played a prominent role in defeating attempts to enact liberal labor laws. They pressured the government to postpone the enactment of the Factory Act and, subsequently, to postpone its enforcement.[29] Their reaction to the Paris Peace Conference deliberations on international labor legislation was swift and unequivocal: the Japan Industrial Club cabled the Japanese representatives to express apprehension about undesirable consequences due to the immaturity of Japan's industry. They insisted on special treatment for Japan and essentially reinforced the position of the representatives themselves.[30]

Japan participated in the Peace Conference as one of the victors in World War I. The question of international labor legislation was not a major preoccupation of the Peace Conference. The participating governments were concerned with French security against another German attack, reparations, the Shantung issue and Japan's claim to the German Pacific islands north of the equator, the disposition of German colonies, the annexationist claims of Italy, and of course the basic issue of the creation of the League of Nations. As Haas has suggested, the governments' preoccupation with other issues facilitated the establishment of the ILO.[31]

Japanese interests also focused on other issues. Japan had joined

27. Nagata, ibid., pp. 81–82.   28. "Industrial Labor in Japan," p. 82.
29. Azuma Mitsutoshi, *Rōdō Hō*, p. 10; R. P. Dore, "The Modernizer as a Special Case," p. 440.
30. Morita, *Nihon Keieisha Dantai Hatten Shi*, pp. 132–33.
31. *Beyond the Nation State*, p. 143.

what was initially a European war in order to strengthen her foot-
hold in Asia. In Paris, therefore, she was mostly concerned with
extending her leases on Port Arthur, Talien, and the South Manchurian Railway, as well as with inheriting German possessions in
the Far East.[32] But even though two Japanese representatives
joined the Commission for Labor Legislation in Paris, deliberations and decisions in the commission were dominated by the
American, British, French, Italian, and Belgian representatives.[33]

The European governments were obligated to their labor movements for the latter's participation in the war. This obligation was
made "an urgent political necessity by the success of the Bolshevik
Revolution and the imminence of kindred outbreaks in the
West."[34] Moreover, labor's participation in the political process
in those countries was an established fact. In Britain, labor was even
co-opted into the government. Hence, the participation of labor
in a tripartite international organization was not as offensive as it
might have been before. Finally, vague notions as to the course the
ILO would take blunted whatever misgivings the governments
had concerning the participation of their countries; they probably
had no idea that the ILO would limit their freedom of action on
internal matters.

The Japanese government was not motivated by any of these
factors. Japan's participation in the war did not necessitate a commitment to labor, since the Japanese military forces were based
primarily on peasant conscripts nourished by the ideology of
loyalty to the emperor and the nation. In addition, the scope of
Japanese military operations had been relatively limited. Domestic industries boomed as Japan's former competitors engaged in
a war which taxed their resources.

Labor in Japan was not recognized as a legitimate participant
in the political process. The possible influence of the successful
Bolshevik Revolution was regarded as a threat, and some attempts
were made to co-opt a segment of Japan's labor movement. How-

32. Japanese claims, supported by Britain, France, and Italy, in conformity with
secret agreements between these countries, Czarist Russia, and Japan, en-
countered the stiff resistance of President Wilson. See R. W. Curry, *Woodrow
Wilson and the Far Eastern Policy, 1913–1921.*
33. Haas, *Beyond the Nation State*, p. 539, n. 3.
34. Ibid., p. 140. For the circumstances making it indispensable to the European
governments, see L. L. Lorwin, *The International Labor Movement*, pp. 35–60.

ever, the attempt failed, and the government response was thorough suppression.

Japan joined the ILO, despite these factors, for the same reason that she joined the League of Nations. Japan approved of the international system that seemed to emerge with the League, and of the status she was accorded within this system. True, the Japanese government had some reservations about the outcome of the Paris Peace Conference; it resented the failure to have an article on racial equality included in the Covenant of the League of Nations, and the fact that the German islands in the northern Pacific were not handed to Japan for annexation, but were only mandated to her. However, Japan was recognized as a major power, and achieved a marked degree of international recognition and respectability, which she had coveted for over forty years. Japan was given permanent membership in the Council of the League of Nations, and the prestigious permanent membership in the Governing Body of the ILO.

Joining the ILO was perceived by the government as a necessary and a tolerable nuisance—tolerable for two reasons. The first was the "special countries" clause, which the Japanese representative succeeded in incorporating in Article 405, Paragraph 3 of the Peace Treaty: [35] "In framing any recommendation or draft convention of general application the conference shall give due regard to those countries in which climate conditions, the imperfect development of industrial organization, or other special circumstances make the industrial conditions substantially different and shall suggest the modifications if any, which it considers may be required to meet the case of such countries." The second reason was that compliance with ILO standards was voluntary; when it came to imposing serious sanctions, the Council of the League of Nations—not the ILO—was the ultimate authority.

This readiness to accept undesirable aspects of a desirable system had a remarkable precedent in Japanese history. Thirty years earlier, following the Meiji Restoration, the Meiji oligarchy had adopted a policy of borrowing from the West in order to meet the challenge of Western imperialism on its own terms and to turn Japan into a rich and strong nation. In a society based on respect

35. T. Hanami, *ILO to Nihon no Danketsuken*, pp 61–64; Ayusawa, *History of Labor*, p. 179–80.

for hierarchy and on skillfully cultivated loyalty to the emperor (and through the emperor to the Japanese nation), parliamentarianism and popular participation seemed out of place to the oligarchs. However, these were important parts of the system they chose for emulation. Hence, under the spur of mounting domestic pressure, a form of parliamentarianism was incorporated in the Meiji Constitution of 1889. In practice, however, the oligarchs used constitutional and extraconstitutional measures to maintain a tight hold on the centralist political system they were forging.[36]

The Japanese government did not expect the ILO to affect its domestic policies. The leadership of organized labor pinned high hopes on the organization. But the evolution of the ILO resulted in certain consequences that were not anticipated by either Japanese labor or the government.

36. E. O. Reischauer, *The United States and Japan*, pp. 35–60.

3

The ILO and Japan:
The Prewar Experience

The ILO constitution included a general outline of a program
for universal peace and social justice and set up the formal structure of the organization. It provided for several organs, prominent
among which were the Governing Body, the International Labor
Conference, and the International Labor Office headed by the director general.

Once inaugurated, the organization's evolution was determined
by the composition of its membership, the degree of commitment
to the organization of the three categories of delegates—governments, workers, and employers—and the ideology and strategy of
the director general. These were connected with international
developments. Throughout the period ending in World War II,
certain characteristics of the organization persisted, though others
changed significantly in the early 1930s.

Persistent Characteristics

At first, the ILO was a "club" consisting of only forty-four
states.[1] By 1945, the number had increased to sixty-one. The high
quotient of industrial-democratic countries continued, as did the
disproportionate representation of Europe and North America
over Afro-Asian states.

The only group unreservedly committed to the ideology and
program of the organization was that of the workers. The employers played a defensive role, trying to prevent the adoption of any
extreme policy that might jeopardize industrial growth. At first,

1. K. N. Dahl, "The Role of ILO Standards," p. 318.

governments were mostly ambivalent toward the program; later, when they adopted concrete policies, they were more concerned with using the ILO for political purposes than with the program itself.

Between 1919 and 1939, sixty-seven conventions were adopted. Ratification by member states, however, did not necessarily result in automatic adjustment of domestic policies to the provisions of the conventions. The organization did not have the power to force a reluctant government to accept its norms; neither did the directors general attempt to marshal such power, as they did not wish to alienate the reluctant government and jeopardize what authority the organization did have.[2]

PHASE ONE. The government delegates were not prepared to present definite programs for international labor policy. This cleared the way for the director general, Albert Thomas, a French labor leader, to set the tone. The object of his program was to raise and equalize labor standards through conventions that would gradually evolve into an International Labor Code. Such a program was to be created, not through the unilateral benevolence of governments, but through a pluralistic process of international bargaining in which labor was to be a major participant. His emphasis on labor participation provided the stimulus for concerted action by a country's organized labor; in those countries where there were no labor organizations, this approach encouraged the formation and rapid growth of such bodies.

PHASE TWO. World depression, in addition to nurturing the emergence of fascist regimes, gave rise to governmental policies of economic nationalism. These were expressed by protectionism, a search for autarchy, and attempts by leading nations such as Great Britain, Germany, and Japan to preside over economic blocs. Hence, ILO emphasis shifted from *labor standards* to *economic planning.*[3] Under these conditions the principle of universality of membership became overriding; consequently, the new director general was forced to overlook the significant changes in the regimes of Italy, Germany, and Japan, in order to prevent their withdrawal from the organization.[4] Despite his change of attitude, Germany and Italy withdrew from the ILO

2. E. B. Haas, *Beyond the Nation State*, pp. 146–48.   4. Ibid., p. 150.
3. Ibid., pp.148–51.

immediately following their withdrawal from the League of Nations. Japan, however, continued her membership in the ILO even after her withdrawal from the League.

The League System, Japanese Diplomacy, and the ILO

During the 1920s, successive Japanese governments were able to adopt foreign policies in conformity with the spirit of the Paris Peace Conference and the League of Nations. There were, of course, certain disadvantages involved in such participation. Of major importance were (1) the limits imposed on Japan's freedom of action, including the prohibition of ultimatums and secret treaties; (2) the possibility of being drawn into a dispute un-related to Japanese interests through the principle of collective security; and (3) the relatively heavy financial burden of Japan's share in the League's budget and related expenses, compounded by the distance between Geneva and Tokyo.

Still, the advantages of Japan's participation in the League were overriding. It ensured continued recognition of the Great Power status of Japan, although the status was not as great as Japan would have liked. Japanese diplomats resented Great Britain's refusal to renew the Anglo-Japanese Alliance (which, since 1902, had served Japan well in her emergence as a world power); still, they found it to be in Japan's interest to bow to the inevitable and accept a less desirable substitute in the form of the Four-Power Pact at the Washington Conference of 1921. Although striving for a more favorable ratio, they accepted the 5:5:3 ratio of capital-ship tonnage assigned to Great Britain, United States, and Japan—after they were satisfied that a viable collective security system could be established in the Pacific. As late as 1930, at the London Naval Conference, the Japanese government was still able to surmount the growing opposition of its navy and army, and once more accepted inequalities in naval armaments in order to maintain the system in the Pacific.

Japanese respresentatives participated actively in the Council of the League of Nations, at times presiding over discussions on important questions. Japanese officials held key positions in the secretariat of the League, and Japanese jurists were appointed judges of the Permanent Court of International Justice; one of them even became president of the Court. Most Japanese who were involved with international activities, including members of the Foreign Ministry, were inclined toward the perpetuation of the League system. Since the ILO was an integral part of the League, Japanese governments took their participation in it for granted despite embarrassing criticism leveled at their country.

When militarism eliminated the democratic elements in Japan, and Japan embarked on an aggressive policy abroad, the League of Nations reacted negatively to Japanese moves in China. The Japanese government considered the League's actions to be infringements on Japan's sovereignty, and withdrew from the League. But while Germany and Italy withdrew from the ILO immediately after withdrawing from the League, Japan continued her membership in the ILO until 1938, utilizing its stage for maintaining communications with her opponents and defending her policies.

Because of the prestige involved, the Japanese sent the largest delegation to the first International Labor Conference held in Geneva in 1920. The delegation of sixty people, including advisers and the press, had one of the longest journeys to get there.[5] While Japan maintained its membership, it never missed even one session of the International Labor Conference (unlike some other countries).[6] The Japanese government maintained regular communication, both formal and informal, with the International Labor Office. In addition to participating in annual conferences, Japan established an Imperial Office in Geneva for continuous contact with the League and the ILO. Within the Japanese bureaucracy, liaison with the ILO was entrusted to the Home Ministry.

Japan's willingness to participate in the ILO proceedings did not imply readiness to abide by the organization's norms. The Japanese record of ratifying conventions was poor, since the government took advantage of the "special country" clause in the ILO Charter. Only two out of the forty conventions completed by 1933 were promptly ratified by Japan and inspired respective legislation;[7] another was ratified after domestic legislation had al-

---

5. J. T. Shotwell, "Recollections on the Founding of the ILO," *Monthly Labor Review* 82, no. 6 (June 1959), cited in Hanami, *ILO to Nihon no Danketsuken*, p. 64.

6. T. Landelius, *Workers, Employers, and Governments*, p. 25.

7. Conventions 2 and 9: Employment Exchange Act of 1921, and Seamen's Exchange Act of 1922, respectively.

ready been promulgated prior to the adoption of the convention by the ILO.[8]

The government's attitude was reinforced by what it had learned about ILO authority. Japanese surveys of the performance of other nations, and of the response of the organization, indicated that participation in the drafting and adopting of conventions did not necessarily imply an obligation to comply with them. For example, the Japanese Privy Council rebuked the cabinet in 1936 for voting in Geneva in support of a convention without emphasizing that Japan could not possibly ratify it in the near future. In reply, the government mustered statistical evidence to prove that it was indeed possible to act this way without losing international confidence. This may be a partial explanation of the fact that, despite Japanese sensitivity about Japan's sovereignty, it refrained from defying the ILO outright. Instead, it defended its position by emphasizing its adherence to ILO principles while pleading the special circumstances of its society and economy, or by indicating that the allegations were unfounded.

Japanese Employers' Associations and the ILO

Japanese employers were influential in determining the attitude of the Japanese government toward the ILO. They expressed suspicion of the ILO, both as individuals—because of the highly personalized style of Japanese politics [9]—and through their associations. Their behavior in the organization in the 1920s was primarily passive, although various associations expressed interest in certain proceedings and published statements. Those associations seeking the election of their leaders as the Japanese employers' delegate had a direct interest in the themes of the various conferences. This was especially true of the textile industry; it employed the largest number of women and children and presented the most acute problems of long hours and night work. The Japan Industrial Club, the largest and most representative of Japanese employers' associations, gave its approval to the respective selections and attached its signature to various state-

8. Conventions 24 and 25 (Factory and Agriculture) of 1927: Health Insurance Act of 1922 (revised in 1926) and Health Insurance Special Account Act of 1926. See Ayusawa, *History of Labor*, pp. 204–16.

9. R. E. Ward, "Japan: The Continuity of Modernization"; Ishida Takeshi, "Interest Groups in Japan."

ments, but it did not show interest in sending its *own* representatives to Geneva. The International Organization of Employers (IOE) was formed in 1920 to consolidate the position of the employers vis-à-vis the workers in the ILO; however, the Japanese employers' delegate, Mutō Sanji, joined the IOE in his capacity as president of the National Spinning Association (Dai-Nihon Bōseki Rengō Kai), not as a representative of Japanese employers' associations in general. Mutō urged Japanese employers to form one comprehensive organization for participation in the ILO, but his efforts proved fruitless.[10]

In order to improve its image and win the cooperation of the Japan Industrial Club, the International Labor Office sent the head of its Liaison and Information Department to Japan in 1924. Enlisting the assistance of the ILO Tokyo branch, opened the year before, he tried to sell the organization to the club's leadership.[11] He failed, however, and the active participation of the most powerful Japanese association was delayed until 1930; at that time, the National Federation of Industrial Associations (Zensanren) was formed in response to the serious challenge of a trade union bill favorable to Japanese labor. The Japanese employers' representatives remained adamantly against replacing paternalistic labor relations with what they considered a culturally foreign, impersonal system that was bound to lead to discord, disruption, and industrial backwardness.

As the ILO became the only forum advocating international trade, the employers intensified their activities with the organization. However, they remained critical of the work of the ILO. In 1937, a year before Japan's withdrawal from the ILO, the Japanese employers' delegates openly expressed the following criticisms: (1) that conventions were adopted in an overly hasty manner; (2) that their provisions had been too detailed and rigid, leaving little leeway for circumstantial differences; (3) that the method of voting did not reflect the degree of interest of the various countries in a particular convention; and (4) that the ILO had been overly European-centered.[12]

10. Morita, *Nihon Keieisha Dantai Hatten Shi*, p. 144.
11. Ibid., p. 134.
12. ILO, *"Record of Proceedings,"* 23rd session, International Labor Conference, 1937, pp. 211–12.

Japanese Labor and the ILO

Japanese labor had a varied and complex attitude toward co-operation with the organization and the extent of effective ILO support it expected for domestic political action. The attitude differed in accordance with attitudes toward politics and the legislative process. These attitudes reflected the cleavages within the ranks of labor; the divisions, in turn, were influenced by external ideologies, government policies, and the ILO's responsiveness and effectiveness.

The establishment of the ILO had drawn the interest of a large segment of Japan's labor leaders, who had high expectations for its support. Their resentment was all the more intense, therefore, when the ILO failed to offer any effective support during the first four years of its existence. However, when the ILO finally demonstrated a semblance of effectiveness on the issue of the Japanese workers' delegate, the leaders renewed their support for (and expectations of support from) the organization.

After the formal division of the Japanese trade union movement in 1925 and the subsequent splits and realignments of the movement into Left, Center, and Right, the attitudes toward the ILO followed a virtually uniform pattern. The Right, supporting parliamentary socialism in general, and protective labor legislation in particular, cooperated actively with the ILO. Its leaders, as workers' delegates from Japan, persistently attempted to bring about the adoption of an international instrument regarding freedom of association of labor unions. They seemed to be close to their goal, but the approaching storm of World War II was instrumental in shelving the issue.[13]

The Left was under the strong influence of international communism, having been affiliated with the Profintern and the Communist-sponsored Pan-Pacific Trade Union Conference; it was consistently against participation in the ILO, holding fast to its image of the organization as an international "harmonization society." The Center adopted an internationally neutral position; most of its unions refrained from participation in ILO activities.[14]

13. For details concerning these efforts, the wordings of the resolutions, and the circumstances surrounding their deliberations, see Hanami, *ILO to Nihon no Danketsuken*, pp. 69–84.

14. R. A. Scalapino, "Labor and Politics in Postwar Japan," pp. 677–78; ILO, "Industrial Labor in Japan," pp. 104–12.

Unlike the Left, which participated in Profintern activities, the Right was not officially affiliated with the socialist International Federation of Trade Unions (IFTU), although ideologically it felt a close affinity to it. This was partly due to the lack of energy shown by the Amsterdam International in its activities in Asia, which one source attributed to lack of funds.[15] It was also due to the Japanese preference for an *Asian* organization, which could not materialize because of internal disturbances, first in China and then in India in the 1930s.[16]

As the period prior to Japan's withdrawal progressed, members of the Left were thrown into jail for alleged subversive activities; the Center and the Right drew closer together in efforts to bring about labor legislation and further Japanese labor interests in cooperation with the ILO. Cooperation included efforts by Japanese delegates to form an ILO branch organization devoted specifically to Asian labor problems and to promote the adoption of an instrument regarding freedom of association. Together with Indian labor leaders, they appealed to the ILO director general; from 1931 on, they presented formal resolutions on these matters to every annual International Labor Conference, but no concrete action was taken.[17]

The Issues

The following examination of the interaction of the ILO and the Japanese political system focuses on three issues. We shall identify the values that are involved in each issue, what initiated them, who participated, what means were used, the reasons for the outcome, and the outcome itself.

SELECTION OF THE WORKERS' DELEGATE. Article 389 of the ILO Constiution states that representatives shall be "chosen in agreement with the industrial organizations, if such organizations exist, that are most representative of employers or workpeople (as the case may be) in their respective countries." The Japanese government was opposed to labor's free participation in an international process of bargaining within the ILO. It considered Japanese labor to be immature for such a role. As early as the deliberations that preceded the adoption of this provision, the Japanese govern-

15. L. Lorwin, *The International Labor Movement*, p. 171.
16. Scalapino, "The Japanese Labor Movement," chap. 4; John Price, *The International Labor Movement*, p. 136.
17. Kaite and Toda, *ILO: Kokusai Rōdō Kikan*, p. 273; Hanami, *ILO*, pp. 69–84.

ment delegate to the Paris Peace Conference inquired into the
selection procedure planned for countries where properly representative worker (or employer) groups did not exist. His apprehensions were dispelled when an understanding was reached: although this scheme was designed to encourage the development
of industrial organizations, the governments in those countries
lacking even elementary forms of organization would have the
right to appoint the delegates.[18]

The two labor organizations most qualified to represent Japanese workers were the Yūaikai (Friendly Love Society), under the
leadership of Suzuki Bunji, and the Shinyūkai (Printers Union
Fraternal Society).[19] The government, however, insisted that the
workers' delegate ought to represent not only *organized* workers
but *all* Japanese workers.[20] Therefore, it devised an elaborate procedure that resulted in the selection of a man who did not represent *any* of the Japanese workers: Masumoto Uhei, a chief en-
gineer at the Kawasaki Dockyards, who thus became the "workers'
delegate" to the First International Labor Conference in Washington in 1919.

The initiative for raising the issue at the conference was taken
by Suzuki Bunji. He enlisted the help of Samuel Gompers of the
United States, who was influential with the workers' group although he was unable to participate directly in the proceedings
because of his government's refusal to join the organization. Suzuki was joined by other union leaders in Japan who disagreed
with the selection procedure, and by a group of Japanese socialists
staying in New York, who distributed petitions to the various
delegations. Among the official participants in the conference who
supported the Japanese unions' position were both the director
general and the leader of the Amsterdam International (who
served as the leader of the workers' group); representatives of
governments and employers did not intervene. By raising the
question in a plenary session, the workers' representatives succeeded in causing great embarrassment to the Japanese delegate.
Masumoto, having no diplomatic experience, was overawed by

18. It was incorporated in article 389 of the Peace Treaty.
19. The Shinyūkai was one of the descendants of the Seiyūkai and Konwakai
of the Meiji era. By 1920, its membership reached 1,500. Scalapino, "The Japanese
Labor Movement," chap. 3.
20. Ibid.

the atmosphere of the international conference. Instead of defending his qualifications, he delivered a speech that castigated the labor policies of his own government, which oppressed labor unions and tolerated slavelike labor conditions in Japanese industry.[21] Despite his speech, he was seated. His seating reflected the reluctance of the organization to alienate one of its major "clients" at its first international conference. Rejection of the Japanese workers' delegate would have automatically disqualified the Japanese employers' delegate as well, a blow considered intolerable for Japan.

The next conference was the Maritime Conference held in 1920 in Genoa; it marked a short interlude in the drama. Owing to the advanced stage of employer-worker cooperation in the maritime industry, Okazaki Kenichi, the president of the Seamen's Union, was appointed workers' delegate—this time in conformity with the official requirements of the organization. However, during the next three conferences the issue was again raised. On two of these occasions, those appointed by the government to represent the workers openly asserted their own disqualification; on the third occasion, the delegate joined the criticism directed at his government without insisting on his own disqualification.

In 1922 and 1923 Japanese labor did not limit its protest to written messages—it also sent one of its leaders to lobby. In 1922 the Credentials Committee did not disqualify the workers' delegate; it did, however, indicate dissatisfaction with the selection procedure, and it expressed the hope that a change would be forthcoming. In its 1923 report the committee intimated that if the practice continued in 1924, a rejection would be inevitable. Assessing the mood in Geneva at the time, Adachi Mineichiro, Japanese ambassador to Belgium, and Maeda Tamon, permanent government delegate to Geneva, urged Home Minister Mizuno to conform to the ILO Constitution in the selection procedure. The following year, partly in response to these pressures, the government changed the procedure to guarantee the selection of a member of a bona fide union organization; Suzuki Bunji of Sōdōmei (formerly the Yūaikai), was chosen.

Why did the Japanese government change the selection pro-

---

21. Ayusawa, *A History of Labor in Modern Japan*, pp. 125–26; S. S. Large, *The Yūaikai, 1912–1919*, pp. 167–70.

cedure? Was it only because of the embarrassment of the ILO?
Undoubtedly, the embarrassment was an important factor, and
permanent government representatives reported to the Home Ministry that pressures were unbearable. Maeda Tamon, for example,
seriously considered resigning if the policy were not changed.[22]
Nevertheless, domestic factors were just as important. They were
related to changes in the labor movement, to the social unrest
following the Kanto earthquake of 1923, and to the politics centering on the movement for universal suffrage. These factors were
all related to each other as well as to the issue of the labor
representative.

As was pointed out in the previous chapter, the radicalization of
the labor movement was due to the government's lack of response
to demands for labor legislation and universal suffrage. It was reinforced by imported ideologies of anarchism and communism. The
government's refusal to change its selection policy gave additional
force to the anarchists' contention that parliamentarianism was
a futile, delaying factor—that it tied the hands of the workers
and prevented immediate action that would simultaneously redress all social ills.

The position of those following the communist logic was also
strengthened by the government's intransigence. Their basic tenet,
however, was *political* action, centrally originated and coordinated, rather than spontaneous eruption of "direct action" by
uncoordinated groups as advocated by the anarchists. They considered both parliamentary and extraparliamentary politics to be
essential, depending on the circumstances.

The moderates continued their drive for universal suffrage,
having opted for parliamentarianism despite the government's
position. These efforts culminated in the formation of the National Labor League for the Attainment of Universal Suffrage
(Fusen Kisei Zenkoku Rōdō Dai-Remmei) in February 1920.[23]
However, in the Diet elections of May 1920, the Seiyūkai (the
ruling party), which opposed universal suffrage, won an absolute

22. Tōkyō Shisei Chōsa Kai, ed., *Maeda Tamon: Sono Bun, Sono Hitō*, pp.
37–38.
23. Sumiya Mikio, *Nihon Rōdō Undō Shi*, pp. 117–18; Ayusawa, *History*, pp.
139–40.

majority and doomed the movement to failure.[24] The moderates were disheartened, but not completely without hope.

An attempt was made in 1920 to unify the ranks of organized labor and the various splinters of the socialist movement. The Labor Unions Federation (Rōdō Kumiai Dōmeikai) was formed in May 1920, and the Japan Socialist Federation (Nihon Shakaishugi Dōmei) in December. The two organizations, composed of anarchists, socialists, and Bolshevists, were closely related: the leaders of the major unions of the Dōmeikai were active in the Shakaishugi Dōmei. Although the intense controversies among the various segments did not subside after unification, they did draft a number of positive programs for political action and appealed to industrialists and government officials for support. These efforts, however, were fruitless.[25] The centrifugal forces within the Dōmeikai were too strong, and it collapsed after the withdrawal of the moderate unions. It was dissolved by the police shortly thereafter.

The rising strength of the anarchists was short-lived. They took advantage of the economic recession in 1920 that followed the wartime prosperity, and launched violent labor disputes. The employers, however, took repressive measures, including widespread dismissals of union activists. The anarchists' tactics backfired, and their appeal declined sharply. Moreover, their objects of emulation, the anarcho-syndicalists in Europe, failed to produce a concrete example vindicating their philosophy and thus added to the disillusionment of Japanese labor leaders.[26] The murder in 1923 of anarchist leader Ōsugi Sakae and his wife by the Military Police (Kempeitai) and the arrest of his fellow anarchists inflicted a crushing blow to the movement in Japan.

The Bolshevists, on the other hand, had the successful model of the Soviet Union. Organizational efforts by Japanese Bolshevists had been discovered by the police as early as 1921, when Kondō Rizo was arrested as he returned from a mission to Shanghai

24. For a fuller discussion of the movement, see Ishida Takeshi, *Kindai Nihon Seiji Kōzō no Kenkyū;* for excerpts in English, see G. O. Totten, ed., *Democracy in Prewar Japan*, pp. 75–84.
25. *Nihon Rōdō Nenkan*, 1921, pp. 36, 38, cited in Scalapino, "The Japanese Labor Movement," chap. 4.
26. Scalapino, ibid.

(where he had established contacts with and received funds from the Far Eastern Bureau of the Comintern). Later that year, the police traced a group from Waseda University called the Men of the Dawn Communist party (Gyōmin Kyōsantō) as they distributed antimilitary handbills among Japanese troops in Tokyo. The Japan Communist party (Nihon Kyōsantō) is said to have been founded in July 1922 in accordance with Comintern instructions, following the First Congress of the Toilers of the Far East held in Moscow early in the year. The progress of Bolshevist influence was clearly reflected in the growing support within the labor movement for the pro-Soviet policies incorporated in Sōdōmei's program of 1922. The party operated underground to avoid police suppression; but in June 1923 the police conducted mass arrests after discovering the party's membership list and policy documents at Waseda University.[27]

The Japanese government was alarmed at the spread of Bolshevist influence and aware of the division within the ranks of labor between the radicals and the moderates. The government decided to help the moderates assert themselves within the movement, and thus stem the tide of radicalism. While chasing the anarchists and Bolshevists, the government changed the procedure for choosing the ILO workers' delegate and his advisers, in order to assure the election of moderates. The new system was based on voting units, each unit being composed of a labor organization having at least a thousand members. In addition, the government supported the organization of what were commonly considered to be "kept unions" in the navy and army arsenals and in transportation.

This procedural concession to the labor movement (which was not considered a formal recognition of freedom of association) was part of a conciliatory trend in Japanese politics. The trend was a reaction to the social unrest that followed the Kanto earthquake, and was symbolized by the government's promise of early enactment of a universal suffrage law. In this context, the vote of organized labor was still insignificant. Its members numbered only 104,412 in 1921 and 137,381 in 1922; then, following the abortive "direct action" and disillusionment of many workers, it dropped to 125,551 in 1923.[28] But despite the numerical weakness of orga-

27. Scalapino, *The Japanese Communist Movement*, pp. 18–19.
28. Suehiro Izutarō, *Nihon Rōdō Kumiai Undō Shi*.

nized labor, its potential increase under universal suffrage was not lost on the leaders of both "liberal" parties.

The policy of using a carrot was reminiscent of the circumstances surrounding the formation of the Harmonization Society following the Rice Riots of 1918. In 1924, however, the government was successful in winning the cooperation of the moderates. They collaborated in governmental relief programs to alleviate the miseries of the earthquake and served on government commissions on labor and economic affairs.[29] The impact of these changes was evident at the 1924 convention of Sōdōmei, where the moderates won the upper hand. It marked a clear shift from radicalism to "realism," from emphasis on revolution to emphasis on legal reforms.[30]

The Universal Suffrage Law was enacted in May 1925, increasing the electorate from three million to thirteen million. The stick followed a week later, when the government had the Diet pass the Peace Preservation Law (Chian Iji Hō), which prohibited "extreme" leftist political activities. Similarly, a year later, the Act for the Conciliation of Labor Disputes (Rōdō Sōgi Chōtei Hō), purporting to change the policy of outright repression and punishment to one of conciliation, was blunted by the Act Concerning Punishment of Violent Acts (Bōryoku Kōi nado ni kansuru Hōritsu).[31]

In an attempt to settle the issue of the Japanese workers' delegate, the ILO pressured the Japanese government; it did not, however, succeed in triggering a domestic movement of effective political bargaining by strengthening organized labor. The issue did stimulate some interest among workers, and a few organizational drives were undertaken to qualify for participation in the selection of the workers' delegate; but most union leaders at the time viewed the ILO as an international "Harmonization Society," neither *of* nor *for* Japanese labor.[32] The increase in the number of *organizations*—162 in 1919, 273 in 1920, 300 in 1921,

---

29. Totten, *The Social Democratic Movement in Prewar Japan*, p. 47.
30. Ōkōchi, *Labor in Modern Japan*, pp. 50–51; Sumiya, *Nihon Rōdō Undō Shi*, pp. 126–28; Hosoya Matsuta, *Nihon no Rōdō Kumiai Undō: Sono Rekishi to Genjō*, pp. 30–36.
31. Toru Ariizumi, "Historical Outline of the Judiciary in Industrial Relation," p. 219; Azuma Mitsutoshi, *Rōdō Hō*, pp. 16–17.
32. Scalapino, "The Japanese Labor Movement," chap. 4.

387 in 1922, 432 in 1923, and 449 in 1924 [33]—was accompanied by the above-mentioned decrease in the number of union *members*.

Regardless of whether the ILO intervention was the overriding factor in getting the Japanese government to change the selection procedure, both the International Labor Office and the Japanese unions (primarily the Right and the Center) claimed it was. This view was expressed by the office in its publications,[34] and by the Japanese unions through their active participation in ILO organs.

The issue was not instrumental in increasing ILO authority over freedom of association and the right to organize. Defiant authoritarian countries continued to send delegates who did not have the qualifications required by the ILO Charter. They were seated, however, because the office wished to avoid a clash with the regimes; their cooperation was essential to the success of policies and programs initiated in response to the world economic crisis of the 1930s.[35]

THE TRADE UNION BILL. Article 29 of the Meiji Constitution stated: "Japanese subjects shall, within the limits of law, enjoy the liberty of speech, writing, publication, public meetings and *associations*." [36] Article 17 of the Public Peace Police Law of 1900, which the unions were seeking to amend, apparently violated this article. Nevertheless, as the supreme authority of the emperor impeded the possibility of judicial review,[37] the law was not challenged in the courts. Although the framers of the Meiji Constitution may have anticipated a genuine sharing of power, it is doubtful whether they anticipated that freedom of association would include labor unions. Since the freedoms enumerated in article 29 were to be enjoyed "within the limits of law," only Diet legislation could have brought about the legalization of labor unions. Theoretically, the law could have been amended by an imperial ordinance; about three-fourths of all legislation under the Meiji Constitution came in the form of imperial ordinances.[38] In reality, however, this amendment was not possible because of

33. Suehiro, *Nihon Rōdō Kumiai Undō Shi*, cited in Ayusawa, *History of Labor*, p. 154.
34. "Japan," *Freedom of Association*, p. 414.
35. See E. B. Haas, *Beyond the Nation State*, p. 150.
36. Emphasis added. In the Japanese original: *kessha no jiyū*.
37. J. M. Maki, *Court and Constitution in Japan*, pp. 19–20.
38. SCAP, *Political Reorientation of Japan*.

the conservative bent of the extraparty, extraparliamentary institutions advising the emperor.

The initiative for liberal labor legislation was taken by members of the Japanese bureaucracy, a bastion of Japanese conservatism. The bureaucracy was characterized by a marked degree of uniformity and solidarity stemming from the common background of education and institutional status. However, it included some innovative elements, and sectionalism and functional rivalries were also evident.[39] It was the rivalry between the Home Ministry and the Ministry of Agriculture and Commerce that figured most prominently in labor legislation.

The Ministry of Agriculture and Commerce was entrusted by the Meiji oligarchs with the task of promoting and supervising rapid industrial growth. Although part of its official duties was the protection of workers, its primary occupation was to serve and protect industry by guaranteeing a sufficient, stable, and disciplined labor supply. It was this ministry that initiated the establishment of employers' organizations; it also designed and supervised the elaborate workers' delegate selection process that antagonized the unions and the ILO.

The Home Ministry, as we noted earlier in the context of the establishment of the Harmonization Society, had developed more sensitivity to the social aspects of industrialization. This was because of its responsibility for the welfare of the country, and because of the close relationship between these problems and public safety that was brought into sharp relief during labor disputes.[40] The Home Ministry was willing to accept the existence of a labor movement as an integral part of industrialization as long as it was cooperative and could be kept under constant surveillance and prevented from threatening a well-integrated Japanese "national polity" (*kokutai*).

In February 1920 a cabinet advisory organ, the Temporary Committee for the Study of Industry (Rinji Sangyō Chōsakai), was asked to review the country's labor policy. The Ministry of Agriculture and Commerce and the Home Ministry presented the

39. For a comprehensive study of this subject, see Mikio Higa, "The Japanese Bureaucracy."
40. Nishioka Takao, "ILO to Nihon no Rōshi Kankei," Nihon ILO Kyōkai Ōsakafu Shibu, ed., *ILO to Shakai Seigi*, pp. 261–64.

committee with markedly different drafts of a trade union bill. The draft of the former strongly emphasized regulation of labor unions rather than permissiveness (although it advocated, in principle, legal recognition of unions). The draft of the latter was far more progressive, providing a legal framework that afforded protection to unions. The Diet discussed the bills intermittently for the next decade. A modified version of the drafts passed the lower house of the Imperial Diet in 1930, but was killed by the non-representative House of Peers.

The issue of freedom of action for Japanese unions figured in the rivalry between the two major parties: the Rikken Seiyūkai (Friends of Constitutional Government Association) and the Kenseikai (Constitutional Association), later renamed the Rikken Minseitō (Constitutional Democratic party). The Kensei Kai, in opposition until 1924, used the issues of universal suffrage and liberal labor legislation in its bid to unseat the Seiyūkai. The Seiyūkai was constantly opposed to both measures. Its opposition to a liberal trade union bill was joined by employer associations led by the Japan Industrial Club; by government agencies other than the Home Ministry—primarily the recently formed Ministry of Commerce and Industry and the Ministry of Education (whose concern with the inculcation of traditional ethics put it in the front line against the spread of individualistic tendencies associated with Western-inspired trade unionism); and by the army and navy arsenals.[41]

The period 1924–1930 was the most democratic in prewar Japanese history. Unlike in the preceding years, cabinets were formed by parties that had won majorities in the lower house; the parties alternated in power. The best opportunity for the passage of a trade union bill was during the rule of the Kensei Kai (Minseitō) in 1924–1927 and 1929–1930. In addition to the support of the Kensei Kai and the Home Ministry, the bill had the backing of several organizations, including the International Labor Office.

The drive for a trade union law spurred the Right and Center streams of the labor movement to join hands. They formed the Japan Labor Club and set up the Committee for the Promotion of Labor Legislation (Rōdō Rippō Sokushin Iinkai). The com-

---

41. Kishimoto Eitarō, *Nihon Rōdō Seisaku Shoshi*, pp. 102–4; Morita, *Nihon Keieisha Dantai Hatten Shi*, pp. 124–31.

mittee met with Diet members, presented an outline of a progressive trade union bill, and recommended revision of the bill offered by the government. The official launching of the committee took place on December 5, 1928, the day Albert Thomas, ILO director general, arrived for an extended visit.

During his visit, Thomas attempted to achieve two objectives. His presence enlivened the movement for the trade union bill by stimulating declarations, articles, and demonstrations by Japanese unions. At the same time he labored to dissipate employers' misgivings about the ILO, by making it clear that he was able to "understand" the special conditions prevailing in Japan at the time.[42]

Another supporter of the bill was the Japan International Labor Association (Kokusai Rōdō Kyōkai), formed in 1927 to deal with questions of labor legislation. Its composition centered around persons who had been associated with the ILO in various capacities: the head of the Tokyo office of the ILO, workers' and employers' delegates and advisers, and university professors.[43] The few employers' delegates who joined the association had undergone a socialization process within the ILO system; this gave them a more flexible attitude toward labor legislation.

While some employers became more flexible, employer associations stiffened their opposition to the bill in 1930 when it appeared that it might be enacted. They solidified their position by forming, for the first time in Japanese history, a national organization representing all employers' associations in the country, the Zensanren.

The feedback of the issue into the ILO system was twofold. The newly formed national employers' association began sending its leaders as employers' delegates to the ILO, and increased the involvement of Japanese employers in ILO organs. The unions also intensified their own activities within the organization, repeatedly pressing for international instruments guaranteeing freedom of association and the right to organize.[44]

SOCIAL DUMPING. Various efforts, such as the London Economic Conference of 1933, failed to reach international agreements to eliminate the effects of economic nationalism in the 1930s.

42. Morita, ibid., pp. 138–41.
43. Hanami, *ILO to Nihon no Danketsuken*, pp. 75–78.
44. Ibid., pp. 80–83.

Japan was particularly disappointed in this failure, for she was highly dependent on foreign trade. Between 1932 and 1934, the competitiveness of Japanese goods in the world market had increased markedly as a result of two factors: (1) the improvement in methods of technical and commercial organization, and (2) the depreciation of Japanese currency (which fell 50 percent in relation to the pound sterling and the United States dollar between November 1931 and September 1933).[45] In retaliation, trade restrictions were imposed on Japanese goods, especially on exports of Japanese textiles and staple fiber fabrics to the colonies of European powers in Asia. While Japanese and British representatives attempted to find a solution,[46] the allegation that Japanese competitiveness was a result of "social dumping" was made in various forums; it became an issue of major importance during the International Labor Conference of 1934. Although there was little unanimity in definitions of the term, there was some agreement that it involved deliberate exploitation of Japanese workers. Since this violated the ILO principle of social justice, the organization took up the issue.

Within the ILO, this issue was treated differently from the earlier issue of the selection of the Japanese workers' delegate. In the delegate selection case the pressure came from the workers' group and was endorsed by the ILO office; in the case of "social dumping," it came from all three groups—labor, government, and employers [47]—with the office attempting to mitigate the pressure. Furthermore, in the issue of the workers' delegate Japanese policy was defended only by the government and the employers of Japan; whereas in the issue of "social dumping" even representatives of organized labor defended the government's position. In Geneva, the Japanese government, employers', *and* workers' delegates coordinated their activities to weather the concerted attack on Japan.[48]

The International Labor Office sent ILO's assistant director general F. Maurette to Japan for three weeks in April 1934. The report published following his return to Geneva [49] was very con-

45. ILO, "Report of the Director," 1934, pp. 16–20.
46. C. Yanaga, *Japan Since Perry*, p. 579.
47. See, for example, *International Labor Review*, January 1935, p. 5.
48. Morita, *Nihon Keieisha Dantai Hatten Shi*, pp. 242–43.
49. "Social Aspects of Industrial Development in Japan"; hereafter cited as the Maurette Report.

ciliatory toward Japan, and contributed to an improved atmosphere within the ILO. The positions of the Japanese unions and the office raise special questions. Why did Japanese unions, which had consistently been critical of the government for limiting their freedom of action, suddenly come out in support of the government? Similarly, why did the office, which had been critical of Japanese labor policies, make an effort to tone down the criticism leveled against Japan?

By 1934, many labor leaders (with the eminent exception of the communists, who were either abroad or in jail) were engulfed by the sense of crisis engendered by the Japanese militarists. The militarists stressed the diplomatic isolation of Japan that would follow its withdrawal from the League of Nations and the expiration of the Washington and London naval treaties. To the unions, as to others, the criticism of "social dumping" was a challenge to the national interest rather than an attack on the Japanese government. In a critical situation, they preferred national unity to the pursuit of sectarian interests.

Several factors were behind the militarists' success in stifling the democratic process that evolved in the 1920s and in terminating Japan's peaceful diplomacy. To many, the Japanese depression of 1927 signified the failure of Japanese capitalism and accentuated resentment of the widespread corruption associated with the close relationship between the Zaibatsu and party politicians. The political parties were barred from power by constitutional limitations; in addition, they made the constitutional limitations more effective by confirming the emperor's sovereignty, and by forming alliances against each other with extraparliamentary forces. This contributed to the parties' own authoritarianism and, since they lacked mass membership, to their unrepresentativeness.

Agrarian and small-enterprise nationalistic organizations, swiftly increasing in number and membership, expressed dissatisfaction with industrialization and urbanization, which threatened the traditional way of life, and with the peaceful diplomacy, which allegedly endangered Japanese security. The frustration of the military, which had been demoted in both prestige and budgetary allocations during the peaceful 1920s, was replicated by frustrations in other segments of Japanese society. These frustrations were aggravated by external developments. A possible unification of a Chinese nationalist movement could be accompanied by stepped-up intervention by Western powers that could jeopardize Japan's security and economic viability.[50] The military feared that the limitations put on the Japanese navy by the London Naval Conference of 1930 were forerunners of further limitations to be imposed by a disarmament conference that was expected to be held a few years later.

For a number of years following the Tsinan Affairs of May 1928 and the Manchurian Incident of September 1931, Japanese governments (and especially the Foreign Ministry) were favorably inclined toward the perpetuation of the League of Nations system. However, the unfavorable report of the Lytton Commission to the League, disapproving Japanese contentions regarding Manchukuo, created such a strong resentment in Japan that the government served notice to the League on March 27, 1933, of its intension to withdraw in two years. By that time, the Foreign Office could not initiate an independent foreign policy because of entrenched military control.[51]

The unions were not only intimidated by the sense of crisis. They were also encouraged by the stepped-up military production, the "military orders inflation" designed to ease the effects of the 1931 depression. Hence, they saw fit to discourage industrial unrest in favor of harmony.[52] Yet, while adamantly refuting the allegation that "social dumping" was practiced in Japan, a major union organization took advantage of the issue to advance the interests of the Japanese workers. The organization was the Japan Union Congress (Nihon Rōdō Kumiai Kaigi), comprising the Right and Center segments of Japanese labor. In a guarded statement it asserted that "the exceedingly inferior labor conditions in Japan, in comparison with those of European and American countries, are among the most important factors contributing to the rapid advance of Japanese trade."[53] It remained within the fold of national unity, but at the same time it attempted to wrest concessions from the government by way of labor legislation.

50. For an analysis emphasizing this aspect of prewar Japanese policy, see J. B. Crowley, *Japan's Quest for Autonomy.*

51. M. Kajima, *A Brief Diplomatic History of Modern Japan*, p. 80; Y. C. Maxon, *Control of Japanese Foreign Policy*, pp. 72–107; Crowley, pp. 123–86.

52. For a comprehensive account, see Totten, *The Social Democratic Movement*, especially chap. 4.

53. Maurette Report, pp. 46–47.

The International Labor Office acted on the basis of two considerations. First, although the ILO's emphasis on standardization of labor conditions had given way to emphasis on economic planning, the issue of "social dumping" was defined in terms of standardization. Second, the office had given high priority to the principle of universality of membership in the organization, and apparently was anxious to avoid Japan's withdrawal from the organization.

When some action was considered necessary by the office in view of mounting pressures, efforts were made to find the formula least offensive to the sensitivity of the Japanese. For this purpose the office consulted with the senior Japanese official on the staff of the ILO, the head of the permanent Japanese Imperial Delegation to Geneva, and the head of the ILO Tokyo branch. The office was also equipped with a first-rate report on Japanese labor conditions, based on the best sources of data and scholarship in Japan. Published in February 1933, it contained extensive background material on the country's history, demography, culture, social relations, and politics.[54]

To the critics of Japan, Maurette's visit was heralded as a fact-finding mission. To the Japanese, it was sold as a friendly extension of a mission to neighboring China. On his arrival, Maurette emphasized that although he came to obtain first-hand information, his fact-finding would be far from definitive because of the complexity of the problems and the time limitation. Of course, it was commonly held in Japan that he had indeed come to check on the allegations of "social dumping," but his unassuming air was appreciated.

Maurette's strategy was first to clear the air of the ambiguity surrounding the term "social dumping," and then to show that the allegations were unfounded. He distinguished between "commercial dumping" and "social dumping." To him, "commercial dumping" meant "an operation that consists in exporting goods at less than cost of production plus a fair profit, and at the same time, selling the same goods on the home market at a higher price than the cost of production plus a fair profit." He defined "social dumping" as "the operation of promoting the export of national products by decreasing their cost of production as the result of

54. ILO, "Industrial Labor in Japan."

depressing conditions of labor in the undertakings which produce them or keeping those conditions at a low level if they are already at such a level." [55] Having somewhat narrowed the scope of the term, he proceeded to assert that "social dumping" as a deliberate policy did not exist in Japan.

However, he had to acknowledge the known fact that labor conditions in Japan were far worse than in European countries. In explanation, he emphasized the problem of overpopulation and described the wide gap between nominal wages and real wages owing to differences in *standards* of living, the *cost* of living, and the *manner* of living between Japan and other countries. Maurette referred to the considerable share of the economy still held by agriculture; the frugality of the Japanese people; the improvement in the standard of living of the industrial workers in comparison with that of the agricultural workers; and the lingering significance of the family principle in structuring Japanese society, including industrial relations. He did not give any conclusions to be used as policy guide, and he candidly admitted that several conflicting points of view could be supported by his report.[56]

The policy of the International Labor Office was spelled out more clearly by the director. He emphasized the temporary nature of Japan's advantageous position in world trade, her limited share of world exports, and her enormous imports of raw materials for her industrial survival. The director also pointed out that while certain countries might have been unfavorably affected by Japanese competitiveness, the people of the poor, non-European countries benefited immensely from the cheap goods—the only ones they could afford. Promoting the principle of freedom of trade, he preached to all sides that the issue concerned a problem "to be worked out, rather than fought out" within the expanded framework of the ILO.[57]

In fact, the issue was both fought out and worked out prior to the war. Japan retaliated with a Trade Protection Law, but at the same time used government-promoted "export guilds" for exercising self-restraint in order to soften her critics.[58]

55. Maurette Report, p. 58.
56. ILO, "Minutes of the 65th Session of the Governing Body," p. 297.
57. ILO, "Report of the Director," 1934, pp. 76–77.
58. W. W. Lockwood, *The Economic Development of Japan*, pp. 531–32, 569–70.

The reaction to the reports of Maurette and the director, as reflected in the International Labor Conferences and the meetings of the Governing Body, indicate that the pressures on the Japanese government were motivated not by concern for the welfare of Japanese workers but by the competitiveness of Japanese goods. Only members of the labor group (Jouhaux of France, Kupers of the Netherlands, Kikukawa of Japan) persistently demanded the ratification of additional conventions by Japan.

The War Experience

With the outbreak of hostilities in the China Incident of July 7, 1937, and the subsequent war in the Pacific, the military carried more weight with the labor and socialist movements, either as a result of conviction, or in view of what were regarded as insurmountable pressures.[59] Gradually, after disagreements and soulsearching, the labor movement integrated into the war effort. Existing unions were dissolved, and the members formed the Industrial Patriotic Society (Sangyō Hōkokukai—short for Sampō) to facilitate labor-management cooperation. The socialist parties, which had experienced several splits and unifications on ideological and personal grounds since 1925, also dissolved; their leaders (with some exceptions) participated in the Imperial Rule Assistance Association (Taisei Yokusankai) founded in 1940.

Significant progress was made in the area of labor policy. A Ministry of Welfare was established in 1938, with progressive bureaucrats of the Social Affairs Bureau of the Home Ministry as its backbone. At first, enforcement of welfare regulations was difficult; and, as the war progressed and taxed the productive capacity of the country, restrictions on workers' freedom were tightened. However, when the exhaustion of the workers threatened to backfire and disrupt the war efforts, more effective measures were taken to alleviate such labor problems as long hours and malnutrition.[60] Furthermore, during this period several social security laws were enacted.[61]

59. C. A. Johnson, *An Instant of Treason;* a Ph.D. dissertation in sociology by P. Golden Steinhoff, Harvard, 1969; K. Tsurumi, *Social Change and the Individual,* pp. 36–79.
60. ILO "Survey of Economic and Social Conditions in Japan," pp. 10–12.
61. These were the National Health Insurance Act, 1938; the Workers Annuity Insurance Act, 1940; the Seamen's Insurance Act, 1941; and others. See Ayusawa,

Other wartime factors proved significant in determining the content as well as the process of postwar labor legislation. These were the severe police repressions and the unprecedented social and political mobilization of the Japanese workers into larger organizations.[62] It was not completely a "period of vacuum in labor legislation," as one renowned Japanese scholar suggested.[63] However, the foundation of contemporary Japanese systems of labor law was laid, and the issue-area of labor policy developed its major characteristics in the next period, the Allied occupation.

A History of Labor in Modern Japan, p. 231; Takeshi Takahashi, "Social Security in Japan," p. 283.

62. R. A. Scalapino, "Environmental and Foreign Contributions: Japan," p. 87.

63. Teruhisa Ishii, "The Changing Role of Labor Legislation in Japan," pp. 227.

4

The Allied Occupation

The occupation of Japan (September 1945 to April 1952) is one of the most outstanding examples of the penetration of one state into another. It was a "saturation-type operation" [1] in its intensity and comprehensiveness. The operation had a sense of urgency, generated by General Douglas MacArthur, the Supreme Commander of the Allied Powers; it aimed at transforming practically every aspect of Japanese society in order to create a viable democracy.[2]

In actual fact, though not officially, this was an American operation. Formal machinery for a joint operation by the Allies was formed, and representatives of other governments protested occasionally; but the direct and overwhelming impact on developments in Japan was from American policies.[3] The bureaucratic apparatus for governing Japan was known as the General Headquarters (GHQ) of the Supreme Command for the Allied Powers (SCAP). SCAP was also used as a reference to the supreme commander, General MacArthur of the United States.

For the first few years of the occupation, Japan was deliberately isolated from the rest of the world. Her foreign relations were limited to contacts with SCAP, and her foreign policy throughout the occupation (and for several years after) consisted mainly of reactions to American initiatives.

1. R. E. Ward, "The Legacy of the Occupation," in Passin, ed., *The United States and Japan*, p. 35.
2. The list of publications dealing with the occupation is long and varied. For a balanced account, see K. Kawai, *Japan's American Interlude;* also Oka Yoshitake, ed.; *Gendai Nihon no Seiji Katei.* The official report concerning the first period is SCAP, *Political Reorientation of Japan (PRJ).*
3. J. S. Sebald and R. Brines, *With MacArthur in Japan,* pp. 126–50; W. M. Ball, *Japan—Enemy or Ally?* p. 33. The WFTU tried to obtain representation in SCAP but failed. See L. Lorwin, *The International Labor Movement,* p. 218.

The general goals of the operation were set in the United States Initial Post-Surrender Policy for Japan of August 29, 1945.[4] However, there was no centrally and meticulously designed plan for the operational policies.[5] These policies originated and developed incrementally within SCAP and reflected the individual values of MacArthur and other SCAP officials, their perception of the Japanese domestic situation, and their anticipation of reactions in Washington. MacArthur injected a sense of urgency into the operation in order to avoid a prolonged occupation that would be self-defeating. This urgency resulted in the high premium attached by SCAP to reforms institutionalized through legislation. Nevertheless, MacArthur realized that long-lasting reforms depended on faithful application of such legislation conditioned by a thorough transformation of Japan's political culture.

Labor reforms, through legislation, were among the very first to be instituted; they were also among the first to be revised in response to unintended consequences and to changes in general SCAP policies. By the end of 1947, the foundation of Japanese labor law had been laid. It consisted of what are commonly known in Japan as the Three Basic Labor Laws; the Trade Union Law (Rōdō Kumiai Hō) of December 12, 1945; the Labor Relations Adjustment Law (Rōchō Hō) of September 27, 1946; and the Labor Standards Law (Rōki Hō) of October 21, 1947. These three laws were supplemented in October 21, 1947, by the National Public Service Law (Kōkkō Hō).

The fundamental changes in occupation policies in general and labor policies in particular were reflected by the following series of laws: the Revised National Public Service Law of December 3, 1948: the Public Corporations and National Enterprises Labor Relations Law (Kōrō Hō) of December 20, 1948; the Revised Labor Relations Adjustment Law of December 20, 1949; the Revised Trade Union Law of June 1, 1949; and the Local Public Service Law (Chihō Kōmuin Hō) of December 13, 1950.

These pieces of legislation differed from one another both in substance and in the processes leading to their enactment. Each reflected changes in the factors that led to the enactment of the

4. *PRJ*, vol. 2, p. 425.
5. Lengthy preparations had been made by the United States prior to surrender, but were not carried out. For a critical account, see H. W. Wildes, *Typhoon in Tokyo*, pp. 1–37.

preceding one—from the early lack of effective action by the Japanese ruling elite (because of the awesome weight of SCAP) to the later dynamic interplay of old and new actors in an extended Japanese political process. Still, however, it was SCAP which held ultimate authority and, despite internal policy disagreements, initiated most laws.

The outcome resembled a transplantation of American and west European labor laws, with several modifications, into a foreign culture. This transplantation, and the subsequent attempts to adjust the new system to its environment, fostered the growth of a fragmented, highly complex, and often very confusing system of labor legislation. Grievances nourished by this system formed the core of ILO Convention 87 controversy, and the system's complexity was a major reason for the issue's lengthy duration.

THE TRADE UNION LAW: SCAP IDEALISM AND JAPANESE TOTAL COMPLIANCE. The United States Initial Post-Surrender Policy for Japan included the following: "Encouragement shall be given and favor shown to the development of organizations in labor, industry, and agriculture, organized on a democratic basis. Policies shall be favored which permit a wide distribution of income and the ownership of means of production and trade." [6]

The emphasis on unionization as an essential lever for democratization was based on the assumption widely held among SCAP members that Japanese deterioration toward authoritarianism in the 1930s was facilitated by the strength of Japanese business interests and by the absence of labor as an effective countervailing force. This emphasis was also due to the presence of labor leaders and New Deal-type labor experts, both in the machinery set up during the war to prepare policies for defeated enemy territories, and in the Labor Division of SCAP.

SCAP did not interfere in the drafting and enactment of the Trade Union Law; it was not necessary. Prime Minister Shidehara, a liberal statesman strongly identified with prewar peaceful diplomacy, received general guidelines in the spirit of the Post-Surrender Initial Policy. Shidehara entrusted the initiation of procedures to Ashida Hitoshi, his liberal minister of welfare. Ashida appointed a Labor Legislation Council composed primarily, but not exclusively, of knowledgeable people who were

6. See n. 4.

known for their favorable disposition toward liberal trade union legislation.

The council's thirty-four members formed the most representative group ever assembled in Japan for the purpose of drafting legislation,[7] a fact still cherished by Japanese labor leaders.[8] Significantly, one of its members was Communist leader Tokuda Kyūichi, who, following the abolition of the Peace Preservation Law of 1925, had been released after eighteen years in prison. The important part of the drafting was carried out by a subcommittee headed by Ono Rojuichiro, formerly of the Home Ministry; it included Ayusawa Iwao, former staff member of the International Labor Office and director of the ILO office in Tokyo; Suehiro Izutarō, professor at Tokyo University and the first professor of Labor Law in a Japanese university; Fujibayashi Keizō, professor at Keio University; Matsuoka Komakichi, former president of the General Federation of Labor Unions (Sōdōmei); Nishio Suehiro, former labor leader of Sōdōmei; Takahashi Tsuneya of the Home Ministry; and Yasukawa Daigoro, industrialist. In preparing the draft, council members not only utilized their profound familiarity with Western labor legal systems; they also exercised their discretion as to what type of bill would be acceptable to American officials. The result was a bill which followed the pattern of the Wagner Act in 1935 in the United States, in providing the unions with extensive protection as well as freedom; various provisions followed the pattern of other American as well as European labor laws.

An outstanding characteristic of the process leading to the Trade Union Law was the continued insignificance of the Imperial Diet, and the dominance of the cabinet and the bureaucracy as conveyors of SCAP policies. The bill was approved unanimously by the Eighty-Ninth Imperial Diet—the second after surrender, and the first to legislate. Diet members were overwhelmingly conservative, having been elected under Tōjō in 1942. A Diet thus structured would not have passed all twenty-five cabinet bills,[9] particu-

7. The following discussion of the drafting of the Trade Union Law draws heavily on reminiscences of a number of the major participants in Nihon Rōdō Kyōkai, ed., *Sengo no Rōdō Rippō to Rōdō Undo.* For a shorter account, see Ayusawa, *A History of Labor in Modern Japan.*

8. See, for example, Sōhyō Stōken Dakkan Tokubetsu Iinkai, ed., *Kumiai Katsudō Hendobukku,* pp. 24–25.

9. Tsuji Kiyoaki, *Shiryō,* p. 202.

larly those instituting sweeping reforms, had it not considered them to be implementations of SCAP orders. This was the only Diet to pass all government-initiated bills. Starting with the next Diet, convened after the first elections under the new constitution of 1947, it has been impossible for any cabinet to have *all* of its bills enacted during the session in which they were introduced.[10]

Two of the three powerful groups that had influenced cabinet policies in the prewar era, the military and business, were muted: the former by demilitarization and purges, the latter by restrictions on joint actions. The third group, the civilian bureaucracy, was able to maintain its prewar and wartime strength, and even to increase it; this was due to its unique position as the institution through which the occupation, eschewing a direct rule, exercised its authority.[11] Initially, the bureaucracy was disposed to offer full compliance with the occupation's formal directives and informal prodding, as in the case of the Trade Union Law. Later, however, as the occupation became a better-known entity, the bureaucracy learned of the conflicting viewpoints within SCAP, and the occupation became less awesome. Consequently, the bureaucrats then offered an increasingly eclectic compliance, most conspicuously with SCAP's initiatives for reform of the bureaucracy itself (which had an impact on labor policy as well).

THE LABOR RELATIONS ADJUSTMENT LAW: FOR A SMOOTHER FUNC-TIONING OF THE NEW SYSTEM. In its initial labor policy, SCAP conceived of a law that would facilitate a smooth operation of the new system of labor relations to be created by the Trade Union Law. This was the purpose of the Labor Relations Adjustment Law of September 1946. Between the promulgation of the Trade Union Law and the Labor Relations Adjustment Law two significant developments took place. First, the Trade Union Law facilicated a spate of unionization. Second, the first freely held general elections, on April 10, 1946, gave rise to a multiparty system.

The number of Japanese unions and their memberships had increased tremendously, from 379,631 workers in 508 unions in December 1945 to 3,813,665 members in 12,923 unions in July

10. The two rare exceptions were the one-day session in 1952 and a special session lasting 21 days in 1958; both passed all four and five cabinet bills, respectively. Ibid.

11. GHQ was divided into sections that paralleled Japanese government ministries. Until 1948, communications were channeled through a Central Liaison Office.

1946.[12] The motivations for joining a union varied. Prominent was the aura of respectability conferred by the occupation, which was regarded as both a liberating force and a new source of authority. The trend toward unionization was enhanced not by party leadership or ideological motivation; [13] rather, it came from the misery of the war's devastation, and the shortages in essential goods. Not only the workers pinned their hopes on unionization; in many cases, so did the employers—in order to gain an effective lever for the resumption of production.[14] The rapid unionization encompassed not only workers but also employees in management ranks and, in some cases, even the employers themselves; this set the dominant pattern of postwar unionism as the "enterprise unions" became the basic unit of labor organization.

The labor movement followed the prewar pattern of Left, Center, and Right. On the left, the communists embarked on an organizational and recruitment drive under the leadership of Tokuda Kyūichi and Shiga Yoshio. They profited from the spread of labor disputes by propagating the democratization of management and the prevention of industrial sabotage (by employers who either saw no prospects for resumption of production or preferred to engage in black-market profiteering).

From October through December 1945 they initiated a new tactic of seizure and operation of plants by the employees known as "production control" (*seisan kanri*) during a labor dispute at the *Yomiuri Shimbun*.[15] Initially, this tactic won the sympathy of SCAP because it assured continuous production and because the United States Supreme Court did not consider sitdown strikes illegal; the tactic was used in subsequent disputes in other enterprises. However, as the Communist leadership overplayed this tactic, the Japanese government declared it illegal in June 1946.

When the Labor Legislation Council proposed a Labor Relations Adjustment Bill, SCAP's Labor Division interfered in order to simplify and make more effective the machinery proposed in the

12. Ayusawa, *History of Labor*, p. 258.
13. Sumiya Mikio, "Rōdō Undō niokeru Miyakuto Renraku." in Oka, ed., *Gendai Nihon no Seiji Katei*, p. 390.
14. R. A. Scalapino, "Japan," in W. Galenson, ed., *Labor and Economic Development*, pp. 116–25; S. Levine, *Industrial Relations in Postwar Japan*, pp. 48 ff.
15. Sumiya Mikio, "Rōdō Undō niokeru Miyakuto Renraku," in Oka, ed., *Genai Nihon no Seiji Katei*, p. 391; K. Ishikawa, "The Regulation of the Employer-Employee Relationship: Japanese Labor Relations Law," pp. 430–79.

council's draft. Despite the council's dissatisfaction,[16] SCAP rewrote the bill and insisted on the creation of a "conciliation" function (*assen*) and the imposition of penalties for noncompliance. Although the machinery was a novelty in Japan, the *assen* function has been well suited to Japanese society, which prefers the use of quiet intermediaries instead of direct confrontation.[17]

Another novelty was the series of public hearings that SCAP initiated prior to enactment of the law. It was for educational purposes only, because SCAP did not anticipate a need to change the draft in response to criticism.[18]

The reaction to the draft differed from that accorded the draft of the Trade Union Law. Rather than unanimous approval, there was hesitation on the part of industrial circles and opposition from the labor movement. The new draft imposed certain contraints on the freedom of union activities: (1) civil servants actually engaged in government administration were denied the right to strike; (2) provisions were made for a cooling-off period and advance notification of intention to engage in acts of dispute by employees engaged in public welfare works; (3) the labor relations commissions, created in conformity to the Trade Union Law, were given a central role in settling disputes.

Labor leaders' initial opposition was motivated by their belief that the bill was written by the government. Kato Kanju confided in Theodore Cohen, the head of SCAP's Labor Division, that May Day slogans criticizing the bill had been prepared prior to reading the bill's provisions; after reading the bill carefully, they realized that its provisions were not as restrictive as they imagined, but then they felt bound by the May Day slogans and kept criticizing the bill. Especially, they were doubtful about the degree of neutrality that could be expected of the commissions; union leaders still resented the prewar Act of Conciliation of Labor Disputes. Therefore, they insisted on a safety device in the form of a comprehensive labor standard law to be enacted before the proposed bill. Their suspicions were only partially justified, however, since the

16. This was partly because Theodore Cohen, the head of the Labor Division, GHQ, was still in his twenties and had little expertise in labor legislation. Cohen was a former graduate student at Columbia University. He studied the labor movement in Japan while at Columbia.

17. Nihon Rōdō Kyōkai, *Sengo no Rōdō Rippō*, pp. 108–9.

18. Interview with T. Cohen.

commissions included Communists among their members. Their
opposition to the bill reflected the growing radicalization of the
labor movement.

The emergence of the multiparty system, with the socialists as
serious prospects for partnership in a coalition government, could
have affected the attitude of the cabinet toward the draft of the
Labor Division; both major conservative parties were wooing the
Japan Socialist party (JSP). But the JSP refrained from joining
a coalition because of internal strain: its left wing favored a united
front with the Japan Communist party, while its right wing wanted
to join the coalition. The JSP's decision to stay out of the cabinet
formed by Yoshida Shigeru in June 1946 cleared the way for
Yoshida to promulgate the law, in the face of an imminent strike
by the Electrical Workers' Union (Densan).

THE LABOR STANDARDS LAW: CONSTITUTIONAL GUARANTEES AND
ATTEMPTS TO CO-OPT THE SOCIALISTS. The constitution of 1947 was
intended by SCAP to provide the legal bedrock guaranteeing the
effectiveness and permanency of the various reforms—social, economic, military, educational, political, and judicial—through the
principles of popular sovereignty, the renunciation of war, and
guarantees of human rights. The question whether the new constitution was an American creation became a problem of political
significance following the termination of the occupation. We shall
not settle this question here.[19] For our purposes, it is sufficient to
note that although SCAP played an important role in drafting the
constitution, the general public and liberal politicians were favorably disposed to its provisions and accepted it as their own. Union
leaders were particularly satisfied to find that minimum labor
standards, freedom of association, and the right to act collectively
were among the human rights to be guaranteed. Article 27 of the
constitution stipulated that labor standards were to be determined
by legislation.

The Labor Standards Law of April 1947 was primarily the product of the Labor Policy Bureau of the Ministry of Welfare.
Bureau officials surveyed labor standards legislation in industrial
countries and examined ILO conventions and recommendations.
The opinions of labor and of employers' organizations were solic-

19. See R. E. Ward, "The Commission on the Constitution and Prospects for
Constitutional Change in Japan."

ited,[20] but only for creating a semblance of a democratic process, since the opinions were basically ignored.[21]

The law showed some resemblance to the Fair Labor Standards Act in the United States. In the process of drafting the bureau had the assistance of a SCAP labor expert. The drafting, however, was primarily the work of bureau officials. The final product covered more ground than did the American law.

The early approval of the draft by the cabinet was apparently influenced by the imminence of the general elections. The popularity of the Yoshida cabinet had declined because of widespread resentment toward inadequate financial and food-distribution policies. An *Asahi* national public opinion poll conducted on January 15, 1947, indicated that support for the Japan Socialist party exceeded support for both of the government conservative parties.[22] Consequently, the government intensified its attempts to co-opt the Japan Socialist party, and its readiness to approve the draft in February 1947 should be considered in this context. According to Cohen there may have been another reason as well. The official of the Labor Policy Bureau of the Ministry of Welfare conveyed the impression to his minister that SCAP, rather than bureau officials, drafted the bill; SCAP had done nothing to change this impression.

THE NATIONAL PUBLIC SERVICE LAW: BUREAUCRATIC REFORM AND THE RELEVANCE OF DOMESTIC POLITICS. The nature of the party system, the organizational strength of the unions, and the weight of the articulate public opinion became clearly relevant for the first time in the process leading to the enactment of the first National Public Law in October 1947. While the Japan Socialist party fell far short of the rate of support indicated by the *Asahi* poll, it won the highest percentage of the vote and commanded 30.7 percent of the seats in the lower house of the Diet. Most significant was the advance made by the Democratic party to 20.6 percent of the vote. The Democratic party resulted from the merger of the Progressive and the Cooperative parties; by advocating "reformed capitalism," it became a center party, able to

---

20. Although prohibited by SCAP from organizing nationally, employers associations began mushrooming at the local level. Morita, *Nihon Keieisha Dantai Hatten Shi*, pp. 329–42.

21. *Sengo no Rōdō Rippō*, pp. 130–31.   22. *Asahi Shimbun*, February 3, 1947.

cooperate with the socialists and to function as a viable channel between the leftists on the one hand and the conservatives on the other. The postelection Socialist-Democratic coalition played an important role in minimizing the restrictions on the government employees, which SCAP initially had intended to incorporate into the National Public Service Law.

This law reflected some of the dissatisfaction of SCAP officials with the undemocratic character of the Japanese bureaucracy (specifically, the higher civil service), and their apprehension about revolutionary consequences of the radicalization of the labor movement. They felt that SCAP reforms of the bureaucracy did not go far enough, whereas those of the labor movement had gone too far.

The Japanese bureaucracy was considered indispensable to SCAP because of the latter's insistence on indirect rule. This attitude was reflected in the purge that removed from public life those individuals connected with the wartime military regime. While the purge was designed to achieve both *demilitarization* and *democratization,* its implementation emphasized demilitarization and barely scratched the surface of the bureaucracy.[23] SCAP knew that the various reforms would be fruitless unless they were implemented by a more democratic bureaucracy; it attempted to solve this problem in a roundabout way—by emphasizing the need for bureaucratic efficiency, to be achieved through a comprehensive reform of the Japanese civil service system.

The bureaucracy—especially the Cabinet Bureau of Legislation —offered various forms of resistance to SCAP's desire for reforms. In September 1945 the bureau even proposed a token reform in anticipation of harsher measures by SCAP. Although the proposal was rejected as insufficient, SCAP refrained from issuing a directive that would compel the bureaucracy to reform.

The opportunity for a thorough survey of the Japanese civil service was offered to SCAP when the Ministry of Finance (without consulting the Cabinet Bureau of Legislation) approached SCAP for expert American advice on how to cope with certain technical problems. SCAP was happy to oblige; a United States Personal Advisory Mission arrived in Tokyo in 1946, headed by

23. H. H. Baerwald, *The Purge of Japanese Leaders under the Occupation;* J. D. Montgomery, *Forced to Be Free.*

Blaine Hoover, the president of the Civil Service Assembly of the United States and Canada. The mission criticized the existing system and suggested several changes; prominent among these was the creation of a national personnel agency independent of the cabinet.[24] To its surprise, the mission discovered that, unlike in the United States, public employees were allowed to strike; the Trade Union Law applied to unions in both the private and the public sectors. The mission recommended that this right be restricted.

The mission's conviction that public employees should be treated differently was based on the American system. Japanese unions in the public service provided ample proof that the importation of this principle to Japan was desirable. These unions played a major role in a series of large-scale disputes, which culminated in a call for a general strike on February 1, 1947. These disputes reflected the strengthening of Communist leaders' control of the labor movement. Communist successes were derived from their leadership of aggressive labor disputes; in most cases, these disputes ended with the acceptance of union demands by demoralized and, because of SCAP policy, incapacitated managements.

Unions comprising 1,550,000 members, with an overwhelming number of Commuists in key leadership positions, formed the National Congress of Industrial Unions (Zenkoku Sangyō Betsu Rōso Kaigi—Sanbetsu for short) in August 1946. Sanbetsu prevented wide-scale discharges of railway workers and seamen, and won an offensive staged by several major unions in the private sector in October 1946. Emboldened by these successess, Sanbetsu embarked on a massive struggle for higher wages for government employees. This year-end wage struggle centered around the National Railway Workers' Union (Kokutetsu Sōren) and the Communication Ministry Workers' Union (Zentei), both led by Japan Communist party (JCP) members. The Japan Socialist party (JSP) joined the struggle; it organized a popular movement for the protection of people's livelihood and the overthrow of the Yoshida cabinet.

Unlike managements in private industries, the government was adamant in its refusal to increase wages. However, it also failed to

24. M. Higa, "The Japanese Bureaucracy." The following draws heavily on this dissertation.

arrest the inflationary spiral that justified the demands for a wage hike. A general strike was called for February 1, 1947, and an explosive atmosphere prevailed throughout the country. SCAP officials, on MacArthur's instructions, communicating with San-betsu leadership on an informal basis, attempted to dissuade them from carrying out the general strike, stating that it would not be tolerated by SCAP. However, the JCP held fast to its belief that SCAP, the liberating democratic force, would not stand in the way of a "peaceful revolution."

SCAP tried to avoid a showdown by exhorting the Yoshida cabinet to take a more conciliatory stand in the wage struggle. The government complied, and formed a Salaries Deliberation Committee, which failed to solve the problem. The Central Labor Relations Commission also stepped in and tried to mediate, but to no avail. The government tried to divide the ranks of the strike leadership by offering the JSP participation in a coalition; but the JSP could not cooperate, because of internal disagreements over the conditions for participating in the coalition.

On January 30, the unions reaffirmed their determination to carry out the general strike by an estimated 2,600,000 members. But they overestimated SCAP's tolerance of a "peaceful revolution." Nine hours before the strike was to begin, MacArthur *ordered* the unions to call it off. They complied with dismay, and promptly dissolved the joint-struggle organizations. Subsequently, negotiations with the government were renewed; a compromise on February 27 raised wages and concluded labor agreements for unions in the public sector.

The failure of the general strike to materialize prompted the Communist leadership to change its strategy. It shifted its emphasis from national to local struggles within the framework of the law, counting on a future cumulative effect. Yet these could not erase the strong impression which the threatened general strike had made on SCAP. This impression was reflected in the Hoover mission's proposal to restrict the rights of unions in public employment.

The proposals of the Hoover mission were opposed by various actors in Japan, each for its own reasons. The bureaucracy resented the challenge to its privileged status, especially the independent personnel authority proposed as its watchdog. Unions, scholars, and the press were also opposed to the personnel authority, but for the opposite reason. They felt that it would not function as a watchdog, but would perpetuate the power of the bureaucracy instead. Therefore, they called for the strengthening of *Diet* control of the bureaucracy.

The unions opposed the mission's recommendations to restrict union activities of government employees, and socialist members of the cabinet sided with them. Following the general elections of April 1947, in which government parties suffered a serious defeat that reflected public resentment of the prevailing social and economic malaise, the coalition cabinet was, for the first and only time in Japanese history, headed by a socialist, Katayama Tetsu. The socialist members of the cabinet told SCAP flatly that they could not approve the restrictions and still serve in the cabinet. SCAP officials themselves were not unanimously in favor of Hoover's proposals. In fact, the officials of the Labor Division and some members of the Government Section were still sympathetic with union demands, and opposed restricting their activities. Hoover himself was, at the time, back in the United States recruiting staff members for a newly formed Civil Service Division within the Government Section. This explains why SCAP acceded to the cabinet's request to remove the restrictions from the bill presented to the Diet.

REVISION OF THE NATIONAL PUBLIC SERVICE LAW: ASSERTION OF SCAP AUTHORITY. Following the abortive general strike, the Labor Division ushered in a period of strong emphasis on workers' education in democratic trade unionism. However, these efforts were not successful in decreasing the radicalization of the labor movement. The labor movement did not give solid support even to the coalition cabinets in which the socialists participated (Katayama cabinet: May 24, 1947, to February 10, 1948; Ashida cabinet: March 3 to October 7, 1948). Sanbetsu-led local struggles reached alarming proportions in their subtlety and effectiveness. The centrally controlled local "spontaneous" strikes would have amounted to a general strike had they not been forthrightly forbidden by SCAP. Consequently, Hoover's position within SCAP had been buttressed; when disagreement with the Labor Division came to a head, he solicited and won MacArthur's support.[25]

25. *Sengo no Rōdō Rippō* 1: 206.

SCAP's strategy of blunting the edge of the radical labor movement was twofold. (1) It began to tolerate the resuscitation of organizational efforts of Japanese employers, and (2) at the same time it set out to restrict union activities of public employees and to fragment the labor movement through legislation.

Previously, only local associations of employers had been tolerated, while national unionization had been encouraged. Then, in May 1947, SCAP approved the formation of the League of Employers' Associations (Keieirengō). In April 1948 SCAP gave its formal blessing to the new trend when the League expanded and was transformed into the current Japan Federation of Employers' Associations (Nikkeiren).

The socialist coalition government continued to resist Hoover's insistence on the enactment of his proposals. Their resistance necessitated strong measures on the part of SCAP. These took the form of a letter from MacArthur to Prime Minister Ashida dated July 22, 1948; [26] subsequently SCAP officials explained that those parts of the letter that could be interpreted as mere suggestions were expected to be complied with as orders.[27] The letter expounded the following themes:

(1) A democratic and efficient bureaucracy, free from the pressures of politics and privilege, is indispensable.

(2) A distinction must be made between labor relations in the private and public sectors.

(3) The people are sovereign through the National Diet and the preeminence of the "public interest," the latter being vaguely defined as the "general welfare." Orderliness and continuity of the services rendered by public employees are to be enforced, if necessary, by the application of the state police power.

(4) A labor union is a private entity, and does not possess the attributes of government.

(5) Resort to acts of dispute by public employees should be construed as a betrayal of the public trust. Moreover, public employees, by virtue of their being employed by all the people, cannot bargain with their employers; their terms of employment should be regulated by the Diet. Yet, the employees

26. *PRJ* 2: 581–83.   27. *Sengo no Rōdō Rippō* 1: 174.

should be allowed to express their interests, and should have methods to safeguard their welfare.

(6) Employees of railway, salt, camphor, and tobacco enterprises owned by the government "might well be excepted" from the regular civil service, and public corporations "should be established" to manage and operate these activities. In these corporations, and mediation and arbitration measures should be instituted, and at the same time public welfare should be safeguarded.

(7) A complete reorganization of the Ministry of Communications is desirable, by the separation of the postal services from its other functions, and the establishment of two separate cabinet agencies.

In short, the letter introduced three new concepts to the legal framework of Japanese labor relations: (1) the viewing of government employees as "public servants" working for the general welfare; (2) the exclusion of government workers from the general category of workers; and (3) the need for compensatory mechanism in lieu of their right to strike and to bargain collectively. These concepts became major themes in subsequent discussions of labor relations in the public service.[28]

The Ashida cabinet interpreted the letter as an order, and decided to comply. It issued Cabinet Order 201, implementing the provisions at once, pending a revision of the National Public Service Law. The socialist members of the cabinet considered resigning in protest; however, they decided to stay and try to salvage as many union rights as possible.[29] When the cabinet fell, it was in the wake of a scandal unrelated to the issue of labor legislation.

The radical segment of the labor movement strongly criticized the government and organized protests around the country. The moderates within the movement, thoug unhappy about the restrictions, expressed support for the government's position; they blamed the Communists for playing into the hands of SCAP by engaging in extremist activities. Appeals were made to the American Federation of Labor, the Congress of Industrial Organizations,

28. Yokoi Yoshihiro, "Gendai Nihon niokeru Rōdō Undō to Hō," in Ogawa Masaaki, et al., eds., *Gendai Hō to Rōdō*, pp. 109–10, 118.
29. See E. Colbert, *The Left Wing in Japanese Politics*, pp. 270–78.

and the Americans for Democratic Action.[30] However, the protests expressed by these organizations and those within Japan were unheeded by SCAP. The revised National Public Service Law was enacted on November 30, 1948, following the formation of the second Yoshida cabinet (October 19, 1948, to December 7, 1954).

Under the revised law, all government employees were removed from the purview of the Three Basic Labor Laws, and their rights to engage in acts of disputes and to bargain collectively were denied. The National Personnel Commission (Jinji Iinkai) was renamed the National Personnel Authority (Jinjiin); its independence was safeguarded through powers to issue executive orders, to establish rules without the prime minister's approval, and to make recommendations directly to the Diet.

THE PUBLIC CORPORATIONS AND NATIONAL ENTERPRISES LABOR RELATIONS LAW: LEGAL BASIS FOR THE FRAGMENTATION OF ORGANIZED LABOR. Items six and seven in MacArthur's letter to the Ashida cabinet "recommended" the creation of a new category of public employees, and the split of the Communciations Ministry into two separate agencies. The resulting law served to fragment the labor movement into three categories: workers in the private sector, under the jurisdiction of the Trade Union Law; workers in the national public service (i.e., employees of government ministries), under the National Public Service Law; and workers in the public corporations and national corporations and national enterprises (such as the Japan National Railways, the Postal Communications Ministries, the Tobacco Monopoly, etc.), under the Public Corporations and National Enterprises Labor Relations Law passed in December 1948. SCAP was so concerned with union militancy in the last category that it insisted upon the enactment of a law regulating labor relations in this category of public undertaking—even before the laws establishing these undertakings had been given thorough consideration. (These laws were enacted on June 1, 1949.) This was understandable in view of the fact that the Communication Ministry Workers' Union (Zentei) and the National Railway Workers' Union (Kokutetsu Sōren) had spearheaded the most serious and most defiant labor disputes.

The employees in this category were denied the right to strike; but unlike employees of the national public service, they were

30. R. B. Textor, *Failure in Japan*, pp. 132–39.

permitted to bargain collectively. However, the law excluded matters affecting the management of the undertaking. Moreover, agreements involving expenditures of funds not provided for in the budget had to be approved by the Diet before they could take effect. In other words, the bargaining was in fact potently restricted because the parties to the resulting agreement were not authorized to carry it out autonomously. In addition, the law provided that membership was limited to employees only—a provision that triggered the issue of ILO Convention 87 in 1957—and prohibited union shops. Finally, the law established a tripartite commission distinct from the Central Labor Relations Commission (set up by the Trade Union Law) and the National Personnel Authority (set up by the National Public Service Law).

The law fragmented the labor movement by creating, through the legal differentiation of types of employment, different *conditions* for union activities, hence different *targets* for union activities. Further fragmentation was achieved in December 1950 with the enactment of the Local Public Service Law; this created a new category of employees with different interests and, consequently, with different organizations to fulfill these interests.

Fragmentation was the sole reason for splitting the Communications Ministry into two separate government agencies, one for postal services, and one for communications. Since membership in a union was limited to members of a single undertaking, splitting the ministry meant splitting Zentei into two separate unions. Communications Ministry officials failed to see any economic sense in separating the functions of posts and communications, hitherto carried out through the use of the same facilities.[31] The haphazard formation of the two agencies attracted widespread criticism from Japanese scholars and agency officials for a number of years.[32]

Like the splitting of the ministry, the Public Corporations and National Enterprises Labor Relations Law was first and foremost a creation of SCAP. SCAP's first draft was presented to several interested government agencies. It underwent several revisions, involving competition between the Ministry of Transportation and the young Ministry of Labor (formed on America's Labor

31. *Sengo no Rōdō Rippō* 1: 231–32.
32. Amazawa Fujiro, "Denden Kōsha niokeru Rōmu Kanri no Mondaiten," pp. 15–25.

Day, 1948) over the authority to administer the proposed law. However, even after the cabinet reached a consensus on the bill following interministerial adjustments, SCAP did not hesitate to overrule the cabinet and insist that SCAP's original draft be presented to the Diet. The Japanese government complied, and the Labor Ministry steered the bill through the Diet.[33]

REVISION OF TRADE UNION LAW: TRIMMING ORGANIZED LABOR. The radicalization of the labor movement was not the only development considered unhealthy by SCAP's GHQ and members in the field. The phenomenon of enterprise unionism was considered to be just as unhealthy. In the eyes of SCAP, enterprise unionism amounted to management unions unable to genuinely represent workers in their relationship with management. Most outstanding among the features of enterprise unionism was the wide scope of union membership, including those employees of the enterprise who, by virtue of their position, were actually considered part of the management. To change this practice, SCAP initiated a program of union education; but, as progress seemed unsatisfactory, legal measures were initiated.[34]

The Yoshida cabinet did not require much pressure from SCAP to revise the Trade Union Law and the Labor Relations Adjustment Law. A draft put out by the Ministry of Labor emphasized the drafting of labor agreements and union constitutions. It specified such items as a restrictive registration system that would exclude unions with a wide category of supervisory personnel; a prohibition against management financing of the activities of union officers (which had become a common practice); regulation of the scope of the bargaining unit; and a requirement for specifying the term of labor agreements, ruling out automatic extension.

Vehement protests by Sanbetsu were ignored, and the public hearings were not taken seriously by the bureaucrats who conducted them. However, quiet lobbying did pay some dividends. The unions appealed to the United States undersecretary of labor, who arrived in Tokyo late in January 1949. At the undersecretary's suggestion, management was permitted to provide the union with some aid, such as office space. Although he felt that the

---

33. *Sengo no Rōdō Rippō* 1: 198–223.

34. Suehiro Izutarō, *Nihon Rōdō Kumiai Undō Shi*, p. 208. Professor Suehiro served as chairman of the Central Labor Relations Commission and maintained close contacts with SCAP officials.

Japanese government had gone too far in restricting the rights of unions in public employment, his views were ignored by both SCAP and the Japanese government.[35]

A serious challenge came from the bureaucracy itself, but it was brushed aside on a technicality. The Justice Department claimed that the draft was in violation of Article 28 of the constitution. When this was denied by the Ministry of Labor, the Justice Department did not push its claim vigorously. Its lack of enthusiasm was not because the case lacked merit, but because of internal departmental politics: the original claim had been made by only one bureau, which had not secured the approval of the whole department. Still, this interference by the Justice Department had some effect in eliminating the provision regulating the bargaining unit; the law left it up to the individual labor agreement in each undertaking. The final product was enacted on June 1, 1949. On the same day, the Labor Relations Adjustment Law was amended with some restrictions on acts of dispute in several circumstances.[36]

THE CARROT AND THE STICK: THE DEMOCRATIZATION MOVEMENT AND THE "RED PURGE." SCAP supplemented its legislative efforts to fragment the labor movement with policies designed to enhance the ideological division between the moderates and the radicals. The Japan Communist party controlled the labor movement and led it to the abortive general strike. However, other segments of the movement joined the preparations for the strike only half-heartedly. Even within the militant Kokutetsu and Zentei there were pockets of resistance to Communist control.[37] The unions of the National Federation of Trade Unions (Sōdōmei) were especially moderate. Following the general strike, the anti-Communist leadership began to reassert itself. In order to maintain its influence, the Communist-led Sanbetsu adopted conciliatory measures toward the moderates; it convinced Sōdōmei to join it in forming a loose organization based on the principle of unanimity in decision making.[38] This organization, the National Labor Union Liaison Council (Zenrōren), was inaugurated in March 1947; it comprised twenty-eight organizations with a total membership of 4,460,000, constituting 84 percent of organized labor. A strong

35. *Sengo no Rōdō Rippō* 2: 24. The source was the undersecretary's interpreter.
36. Ibid., pp. 89–150; Ōkōchi, *Shiryō*, pp. 134–39.
37. Kokurō, *Kokutetsu Rōdō Kumiai 20-nen Shi*, pp. 32 and 34.
38. Hosoya, *Nihon no Rōdō Undō*, pp. 95–96, 105–7.

impetus for this inconvenient marriage between the radicals and the moderates was provided by the arrival of a mission representing the World Federation of Trade Unions;[39] this was the first sign of international solidarity with Japanese labor since the surrender. However, the marriage did not last long. Sōdōmei seceded from Zenrōren in June 1948, and Zenrōren was left in the hands of the Communists.

Meanwhile a democratization movement (Mindō) had been gaining strength within Sanbetsu and Zenrōren; it ultimately led to the formation of the General Council of Japan's Trade Unions (Sōhyō). It started within Kokutetsu, and then was reinforced by a confrontation between the headquarters of the Japan Communist party and the executive committee of Sanbetsu; the issue was the interference of the JCP in union affairs, which had proved disastrous during the abortive general strike. Hosoya Matsuta, Sanbetsu's deputy secretary-general and a member of its Communist leadership faction, together with a number of prominent leaders of Sanbetsu's major unions, founded the Sanbetsu Democratization League (Sanbetsu Mindō).

The democratization movement within Kokutetsu had somewhat mitigated the union's militancy during the struggles that precipitated MacArthur's letter to the Ashida cabinet, whereas the movement's weakness within Zentei had left Zentei as the forerunner in the struggle. Zentei was, therefore, singled out by SCAP for special treatment. Not only was it driven to split, but its ministry's employees were left for awhile in the category of the national public service, whereas the national railway employees were transferred immediately to the more privileged category under the Public Corporations and National Enterprises Labor Relations Law.

SCAP helped the democratization movement both directly and indirectly. It assisted it directly by unofficially coaching non-Communist union leaders in organizational tactics, and by making statements (which obtained extensive coverage in the press) concerning the desirability of ridding unions of Communist influence. Indirectly, it assisted Mindō through the imposition of a new economic policy designed to achieve rapid recovery, which resulted in wide-scale discharges, including that of a great number of Communists.

39. Utada Tokuichi, *Kokusai Jiyū Rōren*, p. 229.

The Nine Points of Economic Stabilization [40] rigorously implemented in the Dodge plan, and SCAP's backing of the government's Three Wage Principles,[41] reflected a marked change in SCAP from a policy of *demilitarization* and *democratization* to one of *rehabilitation* and *stabilization*. Similarly, SCAP approved of the organizational efforts of Japanese employers in their bid to recapture the initiative in labor relations, and thus provided the needed muscle for the rationalization drive. The first to be discharged in these drives were Communist labor leaders. In turn, these leaders lost their union positions because of the custom that limited union membership to employees of a particular enterprise. This custom, which evolved with enterprise unionism in Japan, became mandatory by law for public employees.

It was estimated that 26,000 members of Zentei were affected by the drive.[42] Those who were discharged included members of Zentei's Central Struggle Committee, of whom sixteen were Communists, seven were non-Communist leftists, four were neutral, and only one was of the Mindō-oriented Reconstruction League (Saiken Dōmei).[43] Following a serious confrontation between the Communist segment of Kokutetsu and the Japan National Railways authorities over the issue of discharges (heightened by a series of incidents connected with the National Railways),[44] fourteen members of Kokutetsu's Central Struggle Committee were discharged. All fourteen (out of a total of thirty-five members) belonged to the Left Unity Faction (Tōitsu Saha), which consisted of the Communist Faction and the Revolutionary Comrades Association (Kakudō). In the cases of both Zentei and Kokutetsu, the discharges left control of the Central Struggle Committee in the hands of the remaining Mindō leaders.[45] In other words, the Mindō leaders who took over the control of the labor movement

40. These were as follows: (1) balancing the budget; (2) enforcing tax collections; (3) limiting extension of credit; (4) stabilizing wages; (5) strengthening price control; (6) improving foreign trade and foreign exchange controls; (7) improving the allocations and rationing systems; (8) increasing the production of raw materials and manufactured goods; and (9) improving the food collection program.

41. The principles prohibited the following: (1) extending bank loans for credit financing; (2) increasing prices as a result of wage increases; and (3) government subsidization of wage increases.

42. Watanabe Tōru, *Gendai Rōnō Undō Shi Nenpyō*, p. 175.

43. *Sengo no Rōdō Rippō* 2: 214–15.

44. For a study of the evolution of the court cases related to these incidents, see C. A. Johnson, *Conspiracy at Matsukawa*.

45. *Asahi Shimbun*, July 19, 1949. For the exchange of statements between Kokurō factions see Ōkōchi, *Shiryō*, pp. 131–33.

were benefiting from the restrictions on union rights. Then, when these restrictions were turned against them in 1957, they raised the issue in the ILO.

The strong impact of the Mindō-Communist struggle on the strength of Communist leadership in the unions is reflected in table 1.

TABLE 1

Membership in Sanbetsu, 1948–1950

Year	Number
1948	1,372,000
1949	1,020,000
1950	290,000

SOURCE: Ōkōchi Kazuo, *Shiryō*, p. 150.

A succession of events involving the Japan Communist party prompted SCAP to take direct, legal measures to remove the party's influence from the Japanese scene. First, the party was assumed to have been implicated in the three incidents in the National Railways. Next, the JCP was exposed to the Japanese public as a subservient arm of world communism when, in January 1950, its leader was openly criticized by the Cominform for assuming that a peaceful transition to socialism was feasible under the American occupation.[46] Then, after the dust had settled on that issue, it became known that on February 14 the Soviet Union and Communist China had signed an alliance directed at Japan and its allies. Next, in the People's Plaza Incident on May 30, demonstrators under the leadership of the JCP collided with American servicemen, thus provoking the first incident involving occupation forces.

In retaliation, SCAP ordered the purge of all twenty-four members of the JCP executive committee and seventeen of the editorial board of the party organ, *Red Flag (Akahata)*. The day after *Akahata* supported the North Koreans when the Korean War broke out on June 25, SCAP suspended the paper's publication for thirty days; on July 17, it made the suspension indefinite. The next

46. R. A. Scalapino, *The Japanese Communist Movement*, pp. 60 ff.

measure was directed at the labor movement—the disbanding of the Communist-dominated Zenrōren on August 30.

The Yoshida cabinet, emboldened by SCAP's measures, embarked on a "red purge" of its own in coordination with the business circles.[47] Starting with 704 press and broadcasting employees, dismissals in the private industrial sector came close to 11,000.[48] The government dismissed 1,196 of its employees; National Railways, Communications, and Post Office headed the list with 467, 217, and 218, respectively.[49] The impact of these measures can be gauged partly by the statistics in table 2.

TABLE 2

Union Membership in Major Federations
and in Government Employment

	Total Union Membership (x 1,000)	% of Labor Force	Sanbetsu (x 1,000)	Sōdōmei (x 1,000)	Govt. Emp. (x 1,000)	%
1948	6,534	53.0	1,372	873	616	—
1949	6,655	55.8	1,020	914	628	—
1950	5,777	46.2	290	835	550	—
1951	5,687	42.6	47	313	569	48.6

SOURCE: Ōkōchi Kazuo, *Shiryō,* pp. 546–547 and 550, tables 18 and 22.

The sharp decrease in Sanbetsu membership in 1949–1950 and 1950–1951 was due only partly to the dismissals. The primary cause was the secession of member unions and the formation of the National Federation of Industrial Organizations (Shinsanbetsu) by Hosoya Matsuta and his associates in the *Sanbetsu Mindō* group; it was created on December 10, 1949, with a membership of 55,000. Other former Sanbetsu affiliate organizations took part in the formation of the General Council of Japan's Trade Unions (Sōhyō) on July 12, 1950. The decline in Sōdōmei membership was due to its affiliates' participation, under the leadership of Takano Minoru, in the formation of Sōhyō.

47. For Nikkeiren's statement, see Ōkōchi, *Shiryō,* pp. 155–56.   48. Ibid., p. 157.
49. Ōkōchi, *Sengo Nihon no Rōdō Undō,* p. 176. According to Yoshida, there were 22,000 people affected; *The Yoshida Memoirs,* p. 241.

THE FORMATION OF SŌHYŌ: A LINKAGE GROUP FOUNDED ON A DUAL
COMPROMISE. The anti-Communist segment of organized labor
consisted of several organizations with only one thing in common:
anti-Communism. They varied in their attitude toward the political role of unions; some advocated a high posture of political
struggles for the protection of union rights, while others preferred
low-keyed lobbying. They also varied in their disposition toward
affiliation with the international trade union movement. Despite
these divisive factors, the various groups perceived a clear need
for unification to arrest the decline in Japanese unions and re-
vitalize the labor movement.

SCAP expounded affiliation with the newly formed International Confederation of Free Trade Unions, (ICFTU) as the major
theme in the unification of the Japanese non-Communist labor
movement. When steps toward unification were initiated early
in 1949, the breakup of the World Federation of Trade Unions
into the WFTU and the ICFTU had already taken place. SCAP
made it possible for five Japanese labor leaders (representing the
Council for Promoting the Affiliation with the ICFTU) to attend
the ICFTU founding conference in London late in 1949, accompanied by the head of SCAP's Labor Division.[50] Zenrōren, which
kept its affiliation with the Communist-controlled WFTU, was
denied permission to send delegates to the WFTU conference in
June and July 1949.[51]

While the unions identified with the ICFTU played a central
role in the creation of Sōhyō, they shared this task with a number
of organizations. These included the Private Railways Workers'
Union (Shitetsu Sōren), the Postal Workers' Union (Zentei), and
others which were either uncommitted on the question of international affiliation or opposed to affiliation with either the ICFTU
or the WFTU. Therefore, although the question of Sōhyō's collective affiliation in the ICFTU was considered, it was shelved in
deference to the uncommitted and to those opposing. For the sake
of unity, however, all agreed to express an intent to approve collective affiliation sometime in the near future.[52] Also for the sake
of unity, it was agreed that domestically the unifying theme would

50. Utada, *Kokusai Jiyū Rōren*, p. 131; Kokusai Jiyū Rōren Tōkyō Jimushō, ed.,
Kokusai Jiyū Rōren, p. 40; Hosoya, *Nihon no Rōdō Kumiai Undō*, p. 120.
51. Utada, ibid., p. 302.
52. Okazaki, *Sōhyō 15-nen*, pp. 93–94; Ōkōchi, *Shiryō*, pp. 158–60.

be "democratic unionism"—without specifying too strictly its operational meaning.

At the time of its inauguration, therefore, the main current of Sōhyō leadership was committed to the double-tiered, united-front banner of "ICFTU internationally, democratic unionism domestically." However, Sōhyō as a group has never affiliated with the ICFTU; and those unions that maintained their affiliation internationally and advocated democratic-socialist parliamentarianism have since lost their central position in the Japanese labor movement. As we shall see below, the type of relationship that Sōhyō developed with the ICFTU affected Sōhyō's effectiveness in attempting to enlist the support of the ILO in its conflicts with the Japanese government.

During the occupation, Sōhyō's estrangement from the ICFTU was accompanied by its disillusionment with some of SCAP's policies. These were connected with the imminent peace treaty with Japan, and the American role in the Korean War. Following the United Nations' crossing of the 38th parallel and the Chinese response, the possibility of further escalation threatened to involve Japan in the war.

The ICFTU antagonized Sōhyō's leadership, including some affiliated with the ICFTU, at its Second Conference in July 1951. It came out in support of a partial peace treaty with Japan (excluding the Soviet Union and Communist China); the rearmament of "freedom loving" countries like Japan, Austria, and Germany; and unlimited backing of the United Nations forces in Korea. Disagreement over these issues caused cracks in the house of Sōhyō as a national center, and plagued its constituent union organizations. After independence, this resulted in secessions and the formation of rival organizations.

REVIEW OF SCAP-INSTIGATED LEGISLATION: THE POLICY OF "RE-JAPANIZATION." SCAP's aim was to make Japan an economically viable and politically stable ally of the United States. Thus, it decided to allow the Japanese government a free hand in reviewing the various hastily planned reforms and making the necessary adjustments prior to the official termination of the occupation. In May 1951, Prime Minister Yoshida entrusted the review to a Government Ordinances Advisory Council (Seirei Shimon Iinkai). The council considered questions of labor policy, among other issues, and made a number of recommendations. Organized labor interpreted the recommendations as threats to its rights and mounted a strong campaign in opposition to them.

The government appointed a tripartite committee to review the major points of contention in the field of labor legislation. The committee was composed of workers, employers, and individuals of knowledge and experience representing the public interest. The atmosphere of the deliberations was tense; the workers and the employers expressed mutual suspicion, and held diametrically opposed positions. The employers insisted on turning the wheel back to the pre-occupation era. The workers agreed that the wheel should be turned back, but only as far as the first, liberal phase of the occupation, as institutionalized in the Three Basic Labor Laws. The major controversy was over the question of limits on the rights of workers (primarily in public employment) to engage in acts of dispute. Under these circumstances, the committee refrained from presenting a formal report. Instead, the "public interest" members reached a consensus among themselves and expressed their views "unofficially"; these were subsequently incorporated into a draft legislation prepared by the Ministry of Labor [53] and passed by the Diet in 1952 after the termination of the occupation.

The revisions concerned both the private and the public sectors. With regard to the private sector, major revisions were made in the Labor Relations Adjustment Law. These were (1) the requirement of a ten-day notice of strikes in the public utility industries, and (2) emergency adjustment of disputes when the national economy or the people's livelihood appeared to be jeopardized. The latter conferred upon the prime minister the authority to interrupt such disputes and refer them to the National Labor Relations Commission for settlement.

In the public sector, the category of public corporations and national enterprises was expanded to include—in addition to the Japan National Railways (Kokutetsu) and the Japan Monopoly Public Corporation (Sembai Kōsha)—the Nippon Telegraph and Telephone Public Corporation (Denden Kōsha) and five national enterprises: postal services (Yūsei), state-owned forests (Rinya), government printing (Insatsu), mintage (Zōhei), and the alcohol

53. *Sengo no Rōdō Rippō* 2: 153–86.

monopoly (Arukōru Sembai). The provisions of the Public Corporations and National Enterprises Labor Relations Law were made applicable, with minor changes in local jurisdictions. The labor representatives requested that teachers be included in this category of local employees, in order to enable the Japan Teachers' Union (Nikkyōso) to bargain collectively; the request was denied.[54] Nikkyōso's right of collective bargaining later became a major issue in the ILO Convention 87 controversy.

One serious attempt to improve the whole system of labor legislation was made by the Ministry of Labor. The ministry presented a detailed plan for consolidating, into one comprehensive labor relations law, the provisions regulating labor relations that were currently incorporated in various laws. Similarly, it advocated the consolidation, into one comprehensive agency, of various labor relations committees and administrative divisions scattered through several ministries. Had this plan been approved by the cabinet, the overly complicated system of labor law and labor administration would have become more intelligible to union members and to the general public, as well as to ILO committees that were later called upon to examine Japanese labor relations.

The consolidation plan was opposed by labor leaders, scholars, and bureaucrats of other ministries. The ministry was criticized for publishing the plan without paying due consideration to the views of knowledgeable people; its action was considered to be a manifestation of traditional Japanese bureaucratic arrogance. In addition the plan was seen as an unsubtle attempt by the ministry to strengthen its own authority in the field of labor legislation. Finally, it ran counter to the sectarian interests of the administrative agencies concerned; they were reluctant to change their positions in the bureaucratic structure that had already taken root.[55]

The most offensive measure from the point of view of the labor movement was the Subversive Activities Prevention Bill (Habō). Although the bill was aimed at subversive activities of any kind, from any source—either left or right—organized labor interpreted it as a frontal attack on its basic rights. The unions were supported in their opposition not only by the parties on the left, but also by newspaper editors, "men of culture" (bunkajin artists, writers, actors, etc.), and a number of conservative politicians. Organized

54. Ibid., p. 166.　　　　　　　　55. Ibid., pp. 177 ff.

labor, both Communist-controlled and anti-Communist unions, staged one of the most comprehensive protest movements Japan had seen up to that time, including three waves of strikes with extensive participation.[56] The bill was not passed prior to the termination of the occupation, and the strikes took place after Japan gained its independence.

The government responded to the massive protests with an amendment guarding against abuses of bona fide union and human rights. This clarified the government's intention to prevent the activities of subversive organizations only and provided machinery for redressing abuses if they occurred.[57] As in the past, the Japan Communist party helped to reinforce the government's hand by engaging in violence. Molotov cocktails were thrown during the May Day celebration in 1952, resulting in a flame of public indignation that drove the wind out of the sails of the opposition to the bill. The law was enacted in July 1952, and a Public Peace Investigative Agency (Kōan Chōsa Chō) was set up in order to put teeth into the law.

THE JUDICIAL SYSTEM: RELUCTANCE TO EXERCISE NEW AUTHORITY. One occupation reform that the conservative government could not change was the Japanese Constitution. As was indicated earlier, the constitution guarantees freedom of association. Furthermore, it explicitly provides for judicial review of the constitutionality of legislation (article 81). As the unions and the parties on the left became powerless to challenge government restrictions of union rights politically, they resorted to litigation in anticipation of constitutional protection. The issues of Cabinet Order 201 (which followed MacArthur's letter to Ashida) and the red purges were taken to the courts. However, the courts were reluctant to exercise their authority of judicial review (conferred upon lower courts in addition to the Supreme Court); they insisted that since these measures had been initiated by the occupation, the latter's sovereignty superseded any kind of domestic legislation, including the Japanese Constitution.[58]

JAPAN'S READMISSION TO THE ILO: ADMISSION TICKET TO INTERNA-

56. Okazaki, *Sōhyō 15-nen*, p. 201; 500,000 participated.
57. Ōkōchi, *Shiryō*, p. 192.
58. *Nōmura Heiji, Nihon Rōdō Hō no Kessei Katei to Riron*, p. 290; Kurt Steiner, *Local Government in Japan*, pp. 117–18; Ushiomi and Matsui, "Sengo no Nihon Shakai to Hōritsuka," in Ushiomi, ed., *Gendai no Hōritsuka*, p. 65.

TIONAL INVOLVEMENTS. In 1919, Japan had joined the ILO because it was an integral part of the international system in which she was an equal partner. During the occupation, Japan became eager to rejoin the ILO because it was a condition for Japanese rehabilitation and the recovery of her respectability abroad. Readmission was also considered an economic necessity; it was an admission ticket to far more coveted memberships in international organizations such as the International Monetary Fund and the United Nations Economic Commission for Asia and the Far East (ECAFE).

The initial steps to restore Japanese international involvements were originated not by Japan but by some of her Asian neighbors. These neighbors, especially India, were concerned with promoting trade relations in the region and in guarantees against the renewal of Japanese "social dumping." During the first years of the occupation, Japan's isolation was not only diplomatic and military but also economic. Whatever trade was allowed by SCAP was "blind," because Japanese tradesmen were not allowed to travel or to set up branch offices or agencies in other countries. India advocated the promotion of Japanese trade in order to alleviate the impact of the postwar dollar shortage in the region and to safeguard Asian autonomy.[59]

At first, India's initiative was rebuffed by SCAP and its allies, who were still apprehensive of Japanese competition. But with the change in the American attitude toward Japan's role in Asia —from that of a potential threat to that of an ally in the cold war —facilities for trade promotion were extended in 1949, despite British and French protests.[60]

As early as 1946, efforts had begun within the ILO to safeguard against potentially unfair competition from Japan by pressuring her to reconfirm her prewar international obligations. In 1947 the first meeting of the ILO Asian Regional Organization adopted two resolutions in reference to Japan. One, presented by the Chinese delegate, called for Japan to apply the conventions she had ratified, for the sake of protecting and improving labor conditions *in neighboring countries.* The other called for a survey of Japanese

59. L. P. Singh, *The Politics of Economic Cooperation in Asia,* pp. 118–20.
60. Japan entered ECAFE in 1952. For SCAP policies, see *Oriental Economist* 16, no. 343: 676; and 17, no. 402: 947.

social and economic conditions, and asked the Governing Body of the ILO to consider Japan's readmission to the organization.[61] Furthermore, the 1948 International Labor Conference in San Francisco urged SCAP to have Japanese representatives attend various ILO meetings; in the same year an ILO mission to Japan stressed the desirability of an early resumption of Japan's participation in international cooperation.

Promotional activities for Japan's return to the ILO were also initiated within Japan. The first to act was a small but dedicated group of Japanese whose prewar experience included association, in one capacity or another, with the ILO. Significantly, an ILO committee was established within the Japanese Association for the United Nations, reflecting Japanese interests in being admitted into the United Nations system.[62]

In May 1948, the Ministry of Labor (then still headed by a socialist member of the Ashida coalition government) discussed with union members the question of Japan's return to the ILO.[63] The unions' reaction varied in accordance with their respective ideologies. Communist-controlled Sanbetsu, following the pattern of the prewar Japanese Left's disdain for the ILO—and in line with postwar Soviet and WFTU denunciation of the organization [64] —opposed participation.[65] On the other hand, unions belonging to the democratization movement (Mindō) were eager to participate. Support also came from the Japan Employers' Association and from bureaucrats and scholars.[66]

The ministry supported private initiatives in promoting Japan's rejoining the ILO. The Japan ILO Association (Nihon ILO Kyōkai) was formed in 1949; from 1950, the association's chairmanship was held by Maeda Tamon, a prestigious personality with a broad background of public service both at home and abroad.[67] In 1950, various efforts were made by the Japanese to secure international support for Japan's readmission; they met with success in 1951. Japan's motivation for joining the ILO was made clear in a

61. *International Labor Review*, May 1948, p. 435.
62. Kihata Koichi, "Kokusai Rōdō Undō Monogatari," pp. 80–85.
63. Ōkōchi, *Shiryō*, p. 182.
64. Haas, *Beyond the Nation State*, pp. 199–200.
65. Ōkōchi, *Shiryō*, pp. 182–83.
66. Interview with Mr. Kudo Tomio, secretary of the Japan ILO Association, Tokyo, July 7, 1967.
67. See Tōkyō Shisei Chōsa Kai, ed., *Maeda Tamon*, pp. 36–41, 147–52, and 231–37.

suprapartisan resolution adopted in June 1952; it expressed Japan's readiness to examine her ability to ratify ILO conventions, as a reflection of her earnest wish to cooperate internationally.[68]

We pointed out earlier that the Japanese courts were reluctant to exercise their authority of judicial review over seemingly unconstitutional labor policies. Could the ILO step in and attempt to redress the grievances of the Japanese unions?

As far as the postwar ideology of the organization was concerned, the period paralleling the occupation seemed most opportune. The revised program of the ILO, expressed in the Philadelphia Declaration of 1944,[69] emphasized the principle of freedom of association. In 1948, the Convention Concerning Freedom of Association and Protection of the Right to Organize (87) was adopted, followed in 1949 by the Convention on the Right to Organize and Collective Bargaining (98). In 1950, a Fact-Finding and Conciliation Commission was set up for the purpose of settling disputes related to conventions 87 and 98. Moreover, a standing committee—the Committee on Freedom of Association—composed of workers', employers', and government delegates, was formed to deal with complaints of violations of these conventions.[70]

The advocacy of freedom of association (as well as other human rights) within the ILO system was a manifestation of the structure of the global international system during the cold war of 1948–1951. It was a tight, bipolar system of Western and Communist blocs, and one of the propaganda tactics used by the West was to expose the absence of human rights in the Commuist bloc.[71]

Japanese unions indeed resorted to the machinery of the ILO, but relied on the wrong sponsor. In 1951, the WFTU—then already split and comprising only Soviet-oriented union organizations— filed a Representation to the Economic and Social Council of the United Nations in liaison with its French and other affiliates. The representation criticized alleged violations of freedom of association by SCAP and the Japanese government, especially the purges of Communist union leaders and the dissolution of Communist-controlled Zenrōren. The represenation was transferred to the ILO Committee on Freedom of Association for review and

68. *Sekai no Rōdō*, July 1952, pp. 7 ff; Hanami, *ILO to Nihon no Danketsuken*, p. 95.
69. Haas, *Beyond the Nation State*, pp. 155–61.
70. Ibid., pp. 352–54, 381–83.
71. Haas, *Human Rights and International Action*, p. 138.

recommendations. The committee did not take any action, on the
ground that by the time it had examined the case, the occupation
was already over.

It is doubtful whether the organization would have found it
advisable to challenge SCAP even while the occupation was still
in force; it would have been different, however, if Japan had been
under Soviet occupation. It would also be safe to assume that
SCAP would have ignored any criticism from the ILO, just as it
had ignored appeals from the AFL, the CIO and the ADA in 1948
on the restriction of union rights of public employees. The case was
significant, however, in two respects. First, it established the principle within the ILO that allegations made in reference to a
political situation which ceased to exist would not require further
examination.[72] Second, it conveyed to Japanese unions an impression of ineffectiveness of the ILO.

72. C. W. Jenks, *The International Protection of Trade Union Freedom*, p. 473.

5
Incubation

The process of adjusting the labor law system, constructed under the auspices of the occupation, to the realities of Japanese society ended a year after independence. The occasion was the enactment of the Law Concerning the Regulation of Methods of Acts of Dispute in the Electric and Coal Mining Industry. This law, commonly and misleadingly referred to in Japan as the Strike Regulation Law (Stō Kisei Hō), imposed selective restrictions on acts of dispute in the coal mining and electric power industries. It followed lengthy disputes in these industries, in the course of which safety facilities had been neglected and the power-consuming public had been widely inconvenienced.[1] Under strong pressures from the two industries and the Japan Federation of Economic Organizations,[2] and with widespread approval of public opinion,[3] the law was passed—despite the Left's accusation of unjustified and systematic repression.[4]

The question of labor law revision did not become a major domestic issue before 1957, and it did not reach international significance before 1958. In view of the strong manifestation of union and socialist dissatisfaction with the existing labor legislation, why did the question of revision not assume major proportions before then? To answer this question, we shall describe the events leading

1. For details concerning union demands and the evolution of the disputes, see Ōkōchi, *Shiryō*, pp. 200–211.
2. Nōmura Heiji, *Nihon Rōdō Hō no Kessei Katei to Riron*, pp. 119 ff.; Takeshi Ishida, "The Development of Interest Groups and the Pattern of Modernization in Japan," p. 12.
3. D. Mendel, "Revisionist Opinion in Post Treaty Japan," pp. 769–70; *Mainichi Shimbun*, December 27, 1952.
4. For a fuller account, see Harari, "Politics of Labor Legislation in Japan," pp. 163–67.

to the surfacing of the issue in 1957; then, tracing the evolution of the system of labor politics and its domestic and international environment, we shall identify the combination of factors that determined the timing of the issue.

The Escalation of a Labor Dispute

In 1956, Sōhyō began to stage its annual "Spring Offensive" (Shuntō)—the coordinated wage struggles by its unions in both private and public employment. In 1957, Sōhyō designated the National Railways Workers' Union (Kokurō) as the spearhead of the Spring Offensive by the unions in the public corporations and national enterprises. While the offensive in the private sector was settled with a compromise, Kokurō's struggle turned into a major battle when the government suspended action on a conciliation proposal that Kokurō had accepted.[5] In retaliation, the Public Corporations and National Enterprises Workers' Unions' Council (Kōrōkyō) held union meetings during working hours and engaged in other activities in violation of the Public Corporations and National Enterprises Labor Relations Law—the most effective of which were the disruptions of train schedules on major passenger and freight lines.

Further escalation was temporarily averted during a midnight meeting between Premier Kishi Nobusuke and Suzuki Mosaburō, chairman of the Japan Socialist party (JSP), the major opposition party. They agreed that the government would respect a new effort at conciliation, and would exercise discretion in regard to penalties that might be imposed for legal violations during the disputes. When the railway authorities, in response to pressures from the ministries of Finance and Transporation, failed to make good on a promise to pay (fiscal) year-end bonuses, Kokurō launched a new wave of disruptions; these were subsequently discontinued when a settlement securing the bonuses was reached.

Developments took a sharp turn on May 5 and 6 when the authorities of the several public corporations and national enterprises (PCNE) penalized 888 of their employees for participation

5. Ōkōchi, *Shiryō*, p. 337. For an explanation of the conciliation procedure in Japan, see Kichiemon Ishikawa, "The Role of Government in Labor Relations in Japan."

in the Spring Offensive. Ranging in severity from warnings to dismissals, the penalties included nineteen dismissals in Kokurō and four in the Union of Locomotive Engineers (Kirō); the latter was another union of employees of the Japan National Railways (JNR), and participated in the Spring Offensive even though it was not affiliated with Sōhyō. Among those dismissed were the top officials of both organizations. The penalties provoked more acts of dispute, which led, in turn, to more penalties.

Sensing a critical situation in view of pressures from the authories and mounting public resentment of union tactics, Sōhyō convened the first Special Convention in its history on May 30. After heated deliberations, it adopted a long-range program aimed at revocation of the penalties, restoration of the right of public employees to strike, and ratification of ILO Convention 87.[6]

In June 1957, Haraguchi Yukitaka presented two draft resolutions to the International Labor Conference. These urged the early ratification of two conventions related to prominent problems in Japan: Convention 87, on freedom of association, and Convention 26, on a minimum wage system. His resolutions were rejected by the Resolutions Committee on the ground that they were not concrete. Haraguchi approached the Workers' Group—in effect, the ICFTU—for help; the latter led him through the maze of ILO committees and exerted pressures to have the case of Japan taken up for serious consideration.

Haraguchi's appeal traveled from the Resolutions Committee to the Steering Committee, with the recommendation that the case be referred to the tripartite Conference Committee on the Applications of Conventions.[7] The Conference Committee invited the Japanese government delegate to participate and requested an explanation as to why Japan had failed to ratify the two conventions. Under prodding from representatives of the Workers' Group, the Japanese government delegate expressed his government's intention of examining, in consultation with employers' and workers' associations, the possibility of ratifying these con-

6. Okazaki, *Sōhyō 15-nen*, p. 209.
7. The Conference Committee relies on reports from the Governing Body's Committee of Experts, on summaries of reports presented by the director general, and on additional information provided by the governments. See E. A. Landy, *The Effectiveness of International Supervision*, pp. 36–49.

ventions, as well as others adopted by the organization during Japan's absence from 1937 to 1951.[8] Consequently, Labor Minister Ishida Hirohide requested a tripartite Labor Problems Deliberation Council (Rōdō Mondai Kondankai) to examine the implications of the ratification by Japan of Convention 87.

The reactions of various sections of Kokurō to the dismissals increased the union's internal strains. On the one hand, branches (or segments thereof) in several cities refused to carry out the orders from headquarters and criticized the latter for preoccupation with political struggles.[9] On the other hand, a few branches engaged in acts of dispute exceeding the limits prescribed by Kokurō headquarters. In view of its internal conflicts and the public's resentment, Kokurō's June 1957 convention adopted a resolution for milder tactics. However, it also reelected the dismissed officials to their top union leadership posts, in violation of section 4(3) of the Public Corporations and National Enterprises Labor Relations Law (PCNELRL), which limited union membership (and leadership) to employees of a particular undertaking. Kirō, at its convention, also reelected its dismissed leaders.

The authorities retaliated with the application of a provision of the PCNELRL. They refused to engage in collective bargaining and suspended all existing labor agreements so long as the unions retained the dismissed officials. A wildcat strike by Kokurō's branch in Niigata, in the face of scathing criticism by the press [10] and of information intimating that more restrictive legislation was being contemplated by the ruling party,[11] placed the union in an untenable position. The Niigata struggle exacerbated internal dissension within the union; this resulted in the formation of a second union in several cities, weakening Kokurō's numerical strength and lowering its members' morale.[12] This state of affairs prompted Ōta Kaoru, Sōhyō's president, to "sound the trumpet"

8. Zentei, ed., *Shiryō: ILO Jōyaku Hijun Tōsō Shi* 1: 18–19.

9. Ōkōchi, *Shiryō*, p. 340.

10. Editorials in the *Asahi Shimbun, Mainichi Shimbun,* and *Yomiuri Shimbun,* all of July 16, 1957.

11. Saito Kunikichi, "Kōrōhō Kaiseijō no Mondaiten," in Zentei, *Shiryō* 1: 372, 376. Kunikichi, an LDP Diet member, had been a central figure in the evolution of the issue.

12. Minshushugi Kenkyūkai, ed., *Nihon no Rōdō Kumiai no Seiji Katsudō*, pp. 285–86; Kokurō, ed., *Kokutetsu Rōdō Kumiai 20-nen Shi*, pp. 115–17.

of retreat for the sake of reorganization and renewed offensive at a more propitious time.[13]

Both Kokurō and Kirō took their cases to the courts. They petitioned for a "provisional disposition" on the authorities' refusal to bargain collectively and, later, filed a suit to determine the authorities' obligation to negotiate.

While the case was pending in court, Professor Fujibayashi Keizō, chairman of the Public Corporations and National Enterprises Labor Relations Commission, took the initiative. He stepped in with a conciliation proposal whose gist was as follows: (1) The union should, at a special convention, appoint temporary representatives from among officials who were not dismissed employees; (2) bargaining should thereupon be resumed; (3) at the next regular convention, the union should elect officers from the union members who were employees; and (4) all lawsuits instituted by the unions to test the legality of existing labor legislation should be withdrawn.[14] Late in October, it was accepted by Kokurō and the National Railways authorities; Kokurō withdrew its lawsuits, and bargaining was resumed. Kirō, however, refused to accept the proposal, on the ground that it would not eliminate the basic factor of management's interference in union affairs; it therefore continued its litigation. Kirō suffered a setback on November 11, 1957, when the court rejected its petition on the ground that PCNELRL, having been enacted in defense of the public welfare, did not violate article 28 of the constitution.[15] However, Kirō decided to persist in its legal struggle and entered an appeal to a higher court; concomitantly, it sought remedies from the PCNELR Commission against alleged unfair labor practices by the railway authorities.

The struggle reached the Diet on November 6, 1957, when the Japan Socialist party introduced a bill calling for the amendment of the PCNELRL. Deliberations continued during the next Diet (January 25, 1958, to April 25, 1958) but were suspended—together with a draft resolution the party introduced on March 3,

---

13. Ōta Kaoru, *Waga Tatakai no Kiroku*, pp. 67–71.
14. Rōdōshō, ed., *Shiryō: Kokusai Rōdō Jōyaku Dai-87-go Hijun Shi*, pp. 18–19. This collection of primary sources will be cited hereafter as *Rōdōshō 87*.
15. For the court's opinion, see ibid., pp. 21–23.

1958, calling for the ratification of Convention 87—when the Diet
was dissolved.

In September 1957, Iwai Akira, Sōhyō's secretary-general and a
former Kokurō leader, solicited the assistance of the ICFTU and
the International Transport Workers Federation (ITWF). The
two organizations sent a mission of inquiry to Japan in November.
The mission published a report in January 1958, which appealed
to the authorities to rescind the various punishments and supported the unions' demand for the restoration of the right to
strike, for freedom of association, and for the institution of more
adequate machinery to settle labor disputes.[16] At the same time,
the mission urged Japanese unions to coordinate their activities.
Consequently, Sōhyō and other national union centers formed the
Liaison Council for the Promotion of the Ratification of ILO
Convention 87. The council promptly presented a statement to the
cabinet and the ruling Liberal Democratic party (LDP); it emphasized the dire consequences to Japan's foreign trade that could
occur through a loss of international trust due to Japan's failure to
ratify.

With Kokurō on the defensive and licking its wounds, the 1958
Spring Offensive against the restriction of the Public Corporations
and National Enterprises Labor Relations Law (PCNELRL) was
spearheaded by the Postal Workers' Union (Zentei). Zentei under-
took the task with determination and vigor. Its activities were
brought to a climax in an incident on March 20, in which union
members clashed with the police near Tokyo's Central Post Office.
Five days later, an inquiry mission of the Postal, Telegraph, and
Telephone International (PTTI) arrived in Japan. In April the
mission published a report on the low wages of the Japanese in
comparison with postal workers in other industrialized countries;
the slow, unfair, and unauthoritative conciliation and mediation
machinery caused by budgetary restrictions; and the absence of the
fundamental human right to strike. While admitting that an
absolute right to strike without adequate machinery to protect the
general welfare was undesirable, the mission asserted that once
such machinery had been established, the rights of workers to engage in acts of dispute should be respected. Furthermore, in anticipation of probable dismissal of Zentei's leaders, the mission urged

16. *Rōdōshō 87*, pp. 24–30; Utada, *Kokusai Jiyū Rōren*, p. 206.

the railway authorities to revoke the penalties against railway employees and to respect the collective bargaining rights of Kokurō and Kirō.[17]

On April 30, 1958, Kirō and Sōhyō filed a complaint with the ILO, largely patterned on the reports of the two missions of inquiry. The complaint was followed by a supporting letter from the ICFTU and the ITWF. On May 22, 1958, the PTTI filed its own complaint concerning police interference in Zentei's labor dispute. Zentei's complaint was filed following the sequence of dismissals, reelection, and refusal to bargain with a legally unqualified union. The complaints (especially regarding collective bargaining) were precise and carefully substantiated, although some charges, such as the one concerning the right to strike, were not relevant to the convention on freedom of association. The Committee on Freedom of Association accepted the complaints for consideration, thus internationalizing the issue and pressing for recognition of its legitimacy in Japan.

Let us now examine the factors that delayed or facilitated the internationalization of the issue.

Evolution of the Party System

The multiparty system that had developed during the occupation was transformed into a two-party system in 1955, following the unification of the socialist parties, on the one hand, and the conservative parties, on the other hand. A center party might have evolved through the unification of the Democratic party (which advocated "reformed capitalism") and the right wing of the Socialist party. However, when the Democrats realized that their power aspirations could be better fulfilled within the fold of the conservative camp—which could count on steady contributions from the financial community—the Democratic and Socialist parties drifted far apart.

The Socialist party split in 1951 over the issue of the Peace Treaty and the Security Treaty with the United States. The two segments—the Left Socialist party and the Right Socialist party—had gradually increased their support at the polls; the Left had gained at a faster rate than the Right. Voting trends, especially the voting behavior of youth, indicated that the two socialist parties

17. Zentei, *Shiryō* 1: 25–54.

could capture the reins of government within ten years.[18] This possibility spurred the leadership of the two parties to attempt to reunite the parties on a compromise formula.

Sōhyō and its affiliates played an outstanding role in the increase of the Left's effectiveness at election time. They provided financial and organizational support to their leaders (who ran as socialists), and to nonunion candidates endorsed by the party. In the lower house elections of 1953, Sōhyō organizations supported 114 candidates: 106 of the 108 Left Socialist party candidates, 6 Labor-Farmer party candidates, and 2 independents. Of the 114, 77 were elected.[19] Since the total number of Left Socialists elected was 72, and the total number of Labor-Farmerite winners was 4, the percentage of Sōhyō-supported successful candidates was obviously overwhelming. Similarly, in the 1953 upper house elections, Sōhyō supported 29 of the 50 Left Socialist candidates, and 20 of them were elected. In 1956, Sōhyō supported 43 of the 68 candidates of the reunited Japan Socialist party (JSP), and 32 were elected.

Despite the increasing election support of the socialists, the conservative governments still commanded safe Diet majorities. Consequently, the socialists were unable to prevent the conservatives from carrying out the program of revision of occupation reforms, with the exception of the revision of the new constitution. The issue of labor legislation was raised occasionally, but with no response.

The conservatives, despite factional and personal rivalries, were spurred into unification by the reunification of the socialists. The financial community's mounting resentment of the constant bickering within the conservative camp, which resulted in frequent elections necessitating overwhelming expenditures, was another source of pressure toward solidarity. Following the crystallization of the new party system, the rate of socialist growth approached a plateau, which further reduced the chances of organized labor to improve labor policy through legislation.

The Bureaucracy

During the first phase of the occupation, the bureaucracy tolerated the recruitment of a small number of liberal officials. How-

18. N. Ike, *Japanese Politics*, pp. 180–81. K. Hirasawa, "Politics in Review," *Japan Times*, December 2, 1960.
19. Okazaki, *Sōhyō 15-nen*, p. 65.

ever, with the entrenchment of the conservative parties in power, the conservative character of the bureaucracy was strongly reinforced, and a close alliance developed between the bureaucracy and the conservative parties. The quotient of ex-bureaucrats among conservative Diet members increased, as did the number of prime ministers who came from the bureaucracy. Moreover, the bureaucracy played an important role in providing party organs with the necessary expertise and data required for policy making. The bureaucracy—especially such departments as the Finance Ministry and the Ministry of International Trade and Industry—emphasized industrialization and political stability, and was apprehensive of the advances of organized labor. The Ministry of Education and the agencies in charge of internal security kept a wary eye on the politicization of organized labor.

In comparison with officials in other ministries, the officials of the Ministry of Labor included a substantial number of ex-Welfare Ministry liberals, in addition to other liberals recruited from outside the bureaucracy. Through constant research, plus formal and informal contacts with union leaders, ministry officials tried to improve the system of labor law and administration with minimal friction.

Although relationships with the ILO were officially maintained through the channel of the Foreign Ministry, the Ministry of Labor was in fact the ministry in charge of ILO affairs. The ministry sent its delegates to the International Labor Conference and prepared the annual reports on Japanese labor policies and administration for the ILO committees.

In 1953, the Ministry of Labor recommended that the Japanese government ratify conventions 98 (Right to Organize and Collective Bargaining) and 96 (Labor Exchanges). In our discussion, Convention 98 is directly relevant. But the Ministry of Labor, when recommending its ratification, did not see its relevance to the issue, because of a misunderstanding in the translation. Article 6 of the convention specified that the convention did not apply to "public servants engaged in the administration of the state." In the version presented to the Diet for ratification, this phrase was translated as *kōmuin,* "public employees." *Kōmuin,* however, applies to a broader category than "public servants engaged in the administration of the state" (i.e., employees of national, prefecture, and local government offices); it also includes employees of the national and local public corporations and enterprises. Therefore, the ministry assumed that Convention 98 was inapplicable not only to the public service but also to employees of the public corporations and enterprises. Moreover, ministry officials felt that because these employees were provided with a machinery for dealing with unfair labor practices, there was actually no conflict between the Japanese law and Convention 98.[20]

Since Convention 87 (Freedom of Association and Protection of the Right to Organize) applies to *all* workers, the Ministry of Labor harbored grave doubts about ratifying it at that time. Gradually, however, the ministry (especially its "international faction") realized that section 4 (3) of the Public Corporations and National Enterprises Labor Relations Law, which limited union membership to employees of the undertaking, was way out of step with common international practice. Therefore, the ministry favored the abolition of section 4 (3) at a propitious moment. This fact was known to the Zentei leadership before it embarked on its vigorous struggle in 1957.[21]

The role of the Ministry of Labor should be put into proper perspective. Despite its relatively progressive character, it did not operate in a political vacuum. In fact, it was one of the weakest ministries, and the post of Minister of Labor was the least coveted among conservative politicians.[22] The relatively low status of the ministry was correlated to the conservative's traditional indifference to labor policy, and to the fact that the ministry was one of the youngest. Moreover, its expertise and authority had neither political significance nor economic value in comparison with other ministries.

For example, high officials of the strong ministries, after retiring (customarily at the age of fifty-five), would either enter politics (after cultivating the necessary connection while still in the bureaucracy) or join a prestigious firm from among the ministry's

20. I am indebted to Dr. Hanami for this explanation. The applicability of Convention 98 to the public corporations and national enterprises was pointed out, for the first time, by the ILO Committee of Experts in 1959; Hanami, *ILO to Nihon no Danketsuken*, pp. 51–52. Since then, the unions were careful to use the new interpretation in their publications whereas the government continued to use *kōmuin* in its publications. Cf. Zentei, *Shiryō*, 1: 661, and *Rōdōshō 87*, p. 956.

21. Interview with Takaragi Fumihiko, vice-president (subsequently president) of Zentei and the driving force behind the ILO controversy, Tokyo, August 25, 1967.

22. See M. Leiserson, "Factions and Coalitions in One-Party Japan."

clientele. In the case of labor relations, however, the financial and industrial circles preferred to rely on their own labor experts, and required little in terms of favors from the Labor Ministry. As a result of this situation, ministry officials usually found an outlet in the ministry's own auxiliary organs. By 1957, only one of its officials had been elected to the Diet (as a conservative, to the upper house), and only one had joined the management of a major private firm.[23] Consequently, although the union could count on some sympathy and possibly some support from the Ministry of Labor, they needed stronger and more effective support in order to succeed.

The Judiciary

Despite early occupation reforms freeing the judicial system from the hold of the bureaucracy, there was a high degree of continuity in the system. Judges of high rank were overwhelmingly of the prewar vintage in terms of both experience and education.[24] Although Japanese judges had traditionally labored to maintain their independence from the Ministry of Justice in criminal cases, in both the prewar and the postwar eras,[25] the Japanese courts were reluctant to exercise their right of judicial review. They did not declare any law unconstitutional, because they strictly interpreted the principle of legislative supremacy included in the Japanese Constitution. On the other hand, they interpreted only very broadly the clauses of the constitution emphasizing the supremacy of the "public welfare." [26] Since the government justified all labor laws as necessary measures for the public welfare, and the courts' attitude toward judicial review was negative, the courts held very little promise for a change in the government's labor policy. Indeed, the unions tried to obtain judicial remedies on a number of occasions, but failed.

Major Issues in the Conservative-"Progressive" Confrontation

Labor legislation was related to several issues that figured prominently in the confrontation between the conservatives and the leftists. The latter were commonly known as the "progressives"

23. Interview with two officials of the Ministry of Labor.
24. Ushiomi and Matsui, "Sengo Nihon no Shakai to Hōritsuka," in Ushiomi, ed., *Gendai no Hōritsuka*, pp. 63–105.
25. For a discussion of this question, see C. A. Johnson, *Conspiracy at Matsukawa.*
26. Articles 12, 13, 22, and 29. See J. Maki, *Court and Constitution in Japan*, pp. xl–xliv.

and included the socialists and the Communists. Generally speaking, the confrontation involved the conservatives' efforts to eliminate what they considered to be the harmful effects of the occupation's reforms. However, the progressives interpreted this as an attempt to completely eliminate the reforms and take a reverse course toward the restoration of a police state.

This general confrontation was symbolized by the issue of constitutional revision. The progressives opposed *any* revision, including revision of parts of the constitution they themselves considered unsuitable to Japanese conditions. They were able to mobilize public opinion against all attempts at revision, which then faltered. All the government could accomplish in this regard was the passage of legislation setting up the Constitutional Investigation Committee (Kempō Chōsa Kai). Its purpose was to review the constitution and to ascertain its origins, in order to see whether they were American or Japanese.

To the progressives, the issue of recentralization was an omen of the restrictions that a revision of the constitution could inflict on human rights. Most aggravating in this respect was a series of laws in the areas of police and education.[27] Both institutions had been decentralized under the close supervision of SCAP because, as in the American model, decentralization was identical with democratization. These reforms, like labor reforms, were the first to be considered for revision during the last days of the occupation.

Education policy was considered not only on its merits but also, to a considerable extent, as a matter of internal security. This suggested to the progressive opposition an inherently ominous connection between two of the government's goals: recentralizing control over the police, on the one hand, and recentralizing state control of education (and restricting the rights of teachers to engage in political activities), on the other. The first two occasions on which the socialists felt the need to adopt obstructionist tactics in the Diet (nowadays these are standard procedures in the legislative struggle over major issues) was the forceful passage of a revised

27. Shuichi Sugai, "The Japanese Police System," in R. E. Ward, ed., *Five Studies in Japanese Politics*, pp. 1–14; K. Kawai, *Japan's American Interlude*, pp. 183–200; K. Steiner, *Local Government in Japan*; R. S. Anderson, "Japan," in Reller and Morphet, eds., *Comparative Educational Administration*, pp. 250–74; M. B. Jansen, "Education, Values, and Politics in Japan," pp. 666–78; L. Olson, *Dimensions of Japan*, chap. 10.

police law in 1954, and the passage of the new board of education law (described below) in 1956.

Conservative attempts to revise occupation reforms in education were aimed at both the *content* of education and the *structure* of the educational system. Under the Education Basic Law of March 1947, popularly elected local boards of education had been entrusted with educational policy, including hiring and dismissing personnel, determining the curriculum, and selecting textbooks. The Ministry of Education had only an advisory function. A substantial number of conservative politicians aimed at the restoration of state control over education. State control was considered desirable for the purpose of reintroducing traditional values into the the curriculum, on the one hand, and uprooting the growing influence of the radicalized Japan Teachers' Union (Nikkyōso), on the other.

Nikkyōso had become anathema to the conservatives for a variety of reasons. It utilized its organizational rights guaranteed by the constitution and engaged in ordinary trade union activities to improve teachers' working conditions, thus tarnishing the halo of Japanese teachers, who had been traditionally cast in the role of members of a sacred profession. Moreover, after setting up a study group for the purpose, Nikkyōso began to formulate policies on education. It also made leftist political ideology a frequent subject for instruction, and the participation of teachers in political movements a common phenomenon. Finally, the teachers were able to compound their influence on students and parents by seizing positions on numerous boards of education. This was the institution which, since the Meiji period, had performed an integrative function in perpetuating a value system stressing loyalty to family and state; now it appeared to conservative politicians and bureaucrats to be the very institution that might lead to the disintegration of Japanese society and its falling prey to communism.[28]

Restrictions on teachers' political activities were imposed in 1954 with the passage of the Two Education Laws. One stipulated the political neutrality of teachers at the high school (*kōtōgakkō*) and lower levels; the other made them employees of the local governments, thereby subjecting them to all restrictions in this

28. See H. Passin, *Society and Education in Japan*, pp. 149–60.

category. In 1956 the cabinet determined to force through the
Diet a law making boards of education appointive rather than
elective—despite protests from the press, from the socialist opposition (which used obstructive tactics), and from educators, who
included ten presidents of major Japanese universities. Another
bill, which provided central review of textbooks, was rejected because some conservatives who thought it was too reactionary joined
the progressives in opposing it.

In the fall of 1956 a new storm was building up in the relations
between Nikkyōso and the ultraconservative-dominated Ministry
of Education (and a large number of boards of education under
the ministry's influence); the issue was the application of an "efficiency rating system," which was common in industry, to teachers.
Nikkyōso considered its application to be a not too subtle device
for fastening controls on teachers' activities. In 1957–1958 the issue
surfaced in Aichi-ken, spread throughout Japan, and became an
integral element in the conservative-progressive confrontation.

The most controversial item in the fight over revision of the
constitution was that of defense. The matters of rearmament and
the alliance with (and reliance on) the United States were divisive
issues, since the occupation intimated that Japan should shoulder
its own defense. The conservative government considered the
special relationship with the United States to be a marriage of
convenience, if not an absolute necessity for Japan's welfare; for
the progressives it was a device to strengthen monopoly capitalism
in Japan and suppress the labor movement. The dominant foreign
policy theme advanced by the majority of socialists was one of
neutralism buttressed by multilateral collective security arrange-
ments.[29] Article 9 of the constitution stipulates that "the Japanese
people forever renounce war as a sovereign right of the nation and
the threat and use of force as a means of settling international disputes. In order to accomplish the aim of the preceding paragraph,
land, sea, and air forces, as well as other war potential, will never
be maintained. The right of belligerency of the state will not be
recognized." However, the Japanese government embarked on a

29. G. R. Packard, III, *Protest in Tokyo;* D. H. Mendel, Jr., *The Japanese Peo-
ple and Foreign Policy;* R. A. Scalapino and J. Masumi, *Parties and Politics in
Contemporary Japan;* J. W. Morley, *Japan and Korea: American Allies in the
Pacific;* Cole, Totten, and Uyehara, *Socialist Parties in Postwar Japan;* J. A. A.
Stockwin, *The Japanese Socialist Party and Neutralism.*

program of gradual rearmament, justifying it on the ground that it provided only for defense capability rather than for the advent of militarism and aggression.

Postwar Japanese independent foreign policy was limited because of Japan's dependence on the United States for defense, economic assistance, trade, and "sponsorship" [30] in regaining international trust and cooperation. Most activities were confined to setting the conditions for the expansion of Japanese trade. In 1952 Japan affiliated with the International Monetary Fund (IMF) and the World Bank. In 1954 she joined the Economic Commission for Asia and the Far East (ECAFE) and the Colombo Plan. Most important were Japan's admission to the General Agreement on Tariff and Trade (GATT) and the seventeen trade agreements that followed. Moreover, in order to dissipate resentment toward Japan on the part of her neighbors, the government signed (though only after long and hard bargaining) reparations agreements, first with Burma in 1954, and then with the Philippines in 1956.[31] By 1957 Japan had joined several international organizations concerned with the performance of specific tasks, not necessarily related directly to trade.

The intensification of Japan's international involvements was signified by the elevation in 1957 of the Japanese Consulate General, which had been posted in Geneva in 1952, to the status of a Permanent Delegation of the Japanese Government to International Organizations. Yet, despite the resurgence of Japanese self-confidence accompanying her economic recovery and the beginning of her postwar boom, sensitivity to foreign criticism and anxiety concerning her image abroad was still strong among the public, the press, scholars, and politicians. A lingering reminder of the consequences of foreign suspicions regarding Japan's economic and social policies was the decision of fourteen members of GATT to invoke article 35 against Japan. This article allows protective discriminatory practices under certain conditions, and its invocation caused great concern in Japanese industrial and diplomatic circles.

The progressives were in favor of international involvements

30. J. B. Cohen, "International Aspects of Japan's Economic Situation," in H. Borton et al., eds., *Japan between East and West*, pp. 144–45; R. E. Ward, "The Legacy of the Occupation," in H. Passin, ed., *The United States and Japan*, p. 34.

31. Olson, *Japan in Postwar Asia*, pp. 13–73.

that would lessen Japan's dependence on the United States. They advocated cooperation within the United Nations system, and at the same time they insisted that involvement should not be limited to Western-dominated organizations. Prospects for progress in this respect became brighter in December 1956, when Prime Minister Hatoyama, who had succeeded in normalizing relations with the Soviet Union, was replaced by Ishibashi Tanzan, who was known to favor improving relations with Communist China. Ishibashi's accession to power stimulated intensive public debate involving politicians, commentators, scholars, and other public figures concerning the implications of the new circumstances for the relations between Japan and the United States. The progressives were bitterly disappointed when, early in 1957, Ishibashi had to resign because of illness. He was replaced by Kishi Nobusuke, whose wartime experience and archconservative reputation portended a change in policy toward the "reverse course" both domestically and in foreign relations. The progressive politicians and organized labor prepared themselves for a possible showdown.

Evolution of Unions and the Union Movement

THE THREE LEVELS OF ORGANIZATION. Japan's union movement evolved in three levels of organizations. At the lower level were the various *enterprise unions*. Only permanent employees with a lifelong commitment to a particular enterprise could belong to an enterprise union. The practice of lifelong commitment had originated in government service during the early days of Japanese industrialization and spread in somewhat modified forms to private industry.[32] The employers came to consider it as an extension of paternalism and a means of guaranteeing a stable supply of skilled labor. The workers came to appreciate the security and predictability which the permanent employment provided, and developed a sense of pride in belonging to the enterprise. Enterprise unionism reflected the allegiance of union members (and of many leaders [33]) to the enterprise as much as to the union itself.

32. Masumi Tsuda, *The Basic Structure of Japanese Labor Relations*. For a discussion of the three levels, see Alice H. Cook, *Japanese Trade Unions*.

33. See the report of a study conducted in 1958, in Ōkōchi, et al., *Nihon no Union Rīda*. Few of the union leaders among Sōhyō affiliates had given up their employee status (p. 190). Leadership positions in the unions corresponded to their holders' length of service in the undertaking (pp. 59–77). A marked difference in

The enterprise union was the basic unit, which engaged in collective bargaining and, in some cases, in consultation with management. As such, it encouraged the decentralization of authoritative decision making in the union movement, and localized the social and economic impact of labor disputes.[34]

At the middle level were the *national unions*. In the private sector they were composed of unions in one industry, such as the mining, the automobile, or the chemical industry. In the public sector they were composed of unions of employees of the same ministry or of a particular public corporation or national enterprise. The national unions represented the common interests of enterprise unions in relations with the leaders of a particular industry or the top officials of a particular government organization. Gradually, national unions played an increasingly larger role in collective bargaining on an industry-wide basis; but the final decision on labor agreements still rested with the enterprise union, especially in the private sector.

At the highest and most comprehensive level were the *national centers*. These organizations, such as Sōhyō, Zenrō, and others, were confederations of national federations and national unions in both the private and the public sectors. The national centers played a lesser role in collective bargaining because of the enterprise unions' lack of response to central authority; consequently, they filled a primarily political role as critics of the government, raisers of issues, supporters of leftist (and sometimes nonleftist) candidates, and recruiters of candidates from among their own leaders.

MUTUAL ADJUSTMENTS TO THE NEW LEGAL FRAMEWORK. Despite the vociferous claims of repression leveled by the unions against the government, and the lingering protests made by employers about the overpermissiveness of the new legal framework, both sides were able to make several mutually beneficial adjustments. This was especially so in the case of the enterprise unions and, to a lesser extent, in the national unions connected with the public

status was found between union officials who were employees and those who were not, in favor of the former (pp. 129–32).

34. For a thorough analysis of labor disputes in Japan from 1951 to 1961, see Fujibayashi Keizo, "Waga Kuni no Rōdō Sōgi no Tokushitsu," pp. 4–11. For an excellent analysis of two enterprise unions based on participant-observation, see R. E. Cole. *Blue Collar,* espec. pp. 225–70.

corporations and national enterprises, the local public enterprises, and the local public service (with the exception of the teachers).

In the private sector, unions and management both understood, in principle, the rationale behind occupation-instigated restrictions on management financing of union officers and union facilities; however, the realities of enterprise unionism made it expedient for both to circumvent the restrictions. Both management and unions at the lower level recognized that Japanese *rōdō kumiai* were different from American "trade unions" in their composition and practices. Labor disputes in Japan, while frequent, were ordinarily of short duration in order to avoid damage to the enterprise (which operated under very competitive conditions). Even the emergency measures imposed by law during labor disputes were often advantageous not only to management and the public—they also offered a graceful way out of the situation to union leaders, who were eager to avoid prolonged disputes but could not surrender voluntarily without losing face.[35]

An outstanding example of mutual adjustment in the public sector was the establishment of the "full-time union officer system" (*zaiseki senjū seido*). The system enabled employees engaged in union work, even on a full-time basis, to retain their highly coveted employee status, without pay, thus making it easier for the unions to recruit qualified officers. It was also instrumental in blunting the sting of the legal provision requiring that union leaders in the public sector be employees of the particular governmental organization.[36]

In the public service, where the sense of identification with the enterprise had been as strong as in the private sector, unions engaged in acts of dispute to test the managements' scale of tolerance and to determine the degree to which managements could accommodate union demands without the interference of higher authorities. Despite the restrictions and punishments for violations of work rules and legal provisions, some community of interest developed. Because the service depended on budgetary allocations

35. Kichiemon Ishikawa, "The Role of Government in Labor Relations in Japan," in Japan Institute of Labor, *Labor Relations in the Asian Countries*, pp. 140–41.

36. Dreyer Report, par. 920 and pars. 1112–34; for a balanced discussion of this system and its historical background, see Shirai Taishiro, *Rōdō Kumiai no Zaisei*, pp. 173–82.

from the national government, unions and managements both were interested in increasing their particular governmental organization's share of the national financial pie. Diet members hailing from unions in the public sector could be counted on to represent a wide range of interests in Diet committees, not only those of organized labor or their own particular unions, but also those of management when the welfare of a specific enterprise was at stake (if a strictly partisan confrontation was not involved). Similarly, it was widely believed by reliable informants that unions, especially in the Japan National Railways, had the sympathy of the managements when they staged disruptive struggles; because of budgetary restrictions imposed by the ministries of Finance and Transportation, the managements could not accommodate union demands even when, through collective bargaining, they deemed them justifiable.[37] The government's frequent reluctance to carry out conciliation proposals was another reason why the managements sympathized with the unions.

Serious labor disputes did take place in the Japan National Railways (JNR) even before 1957. However, as they involved only the JNR authorities and the union (Kokurō), they ended in compromise. In 1953 the cycle (union legal violations, the JNR's dismissal of top union officials, the officials' reelection by their union, and management's refusal to bargain with the legally disqualified union) was triggered by the government's failure to respect a mediation award by the Public Corporations and National Enterprises Labor Relations Commission (PCNELRC).[38] The issue was settled when Kokurō's president was elected to the upper house of the Diet in April 1953, and the union elected new officers from among leaders with employee status.

The vote-getting ability of Sōhyō's national unions, which enabled their top leaders to be "kicked upstairs" to the Diet, functioned as a safety valve in union-management relations during this period. It was also a convenient outlet for the graceful withdrawal of these leaders in response to various pressures, such as that from the promotion-seeking second echelon of union leadership, or from opposition factions. There were many internal

37. See, for example, Ariga Sokichi "Kokutetsu niokeru Rōshi Kankei no Jissai," pp. 26–31.
38. *Kokutetsu Rōdō Kumiai 20-nen Shi*, p. 92; Nōmura, *Nihon Rōdō Hō*, p. 282.

changes resulting from ideological and power struggles within the unions.

In 1954, when the cycle repeated itself, there were no national elections. Hence, union and management accepted a different compromise. Following Kokurō's appeals to both the PCNELRC and the courts, both sides accepted the PCNELRC's proposal, under which the JNR authorities agreed to negotiate with union officials with employee status, and the dismissed union leaders retained their union positions. The subsequent replacement of the latter by union leaders *with* employee status was unrelated to the dispute. Having succeeded in settling these disputes, the union did not even consider taking the matters to the ILO.

By 1957–1958, however, the direction of the struggles had changed substantially. The unions' demands increased; their participation in the struggles became greater and more diversified; and the labor movement's decision-making process became more centralized. The key to these changes was the evolution of Sōhyō's composition, ideology, and leadership. We shall, therefore, trace these from Sōhyō's formation in 1950 through 1957.

sōhyō's composition. The composition of Sōhyō underwent significant changes in three respects: the number of national federations and national unions among its affiliates; the ratio of affiliates from the private sector to those from the public sector; and its total membership.

In July 1950 Sōhyō was the only comprehensive union organization in Japan. A compromise led to its formation and brought under its wing most of the existing organizations in the country. It comprised two federations—Sōdōmei and Nichirō—and fifteen national unions.[39] In 1951 it comprised two federations—Sōdōmei and Shinsanbetsu [40]—and twenty-seven national unions; in 1952 the right-wing Sōdōmei canceled its affiliation, and Shinsanbetsu remained, with twenty-eight national unions. In 1953 the compromise suffered a severe setback. In the wake of the prolonged strikes in the electric power and mining industries, which softened the opposition to the "Strike Regulation Law," four affiliates of

39. The following discussion of Sōhyō's structure draws heavily on Okazaki, *Sōhyō 15-nen*, especially pp. 38–43.
40. Nichirō was dissolved; Shinsanbetsu joined Sōhyō as a unit but withdrew late in 1952; some of Sōdōmei affiliates seceded from Sōdōmei and affiliated with Sōhyō directly.

Sōhyō formed the National Democratic Labor Movement Liaison Council (Minrōren). In 1954 three of the four, together with Sōdōmei, founded the Japan Trade Union Congress (Zenrō Kaigi), which became Sōhyō's rival within the union movement. Zenrō was soon joined by splinters of several Sōhyō affiliates, and in 1955 by the Japan Automobile Workers' Union (Jidōsha Rōren), a major affiliate of Sōhyō.

By its convention of July 1955, Sōhyō consisted of thirty-nine national unions. No major changes have occurred in their number since then, although some of the national unions changed their composition, membership strength, and leadership. A number of national unions joined Sōhyō after 1955, but they were small and of little influence.

The ratio between national unions of public employees and those of the private sector shifted markedly. In 1952 Sōhyō's membership of about 3,101,000 was divided evenly between workers in the two sectors. Of the twenty-eight national unions, sixteen belonged to the private sector and twelve to the public sector. By 1955, however, there were 1,620,000 members in twenty-three national unions in the public sector and only 830,000 in sixteen national unions in the private sector, out of a total due-paying membership of 2,450,000.[41] Moreover, of the six largest organizations, four were in the public sector in 1952, and five were in the public sector in 1955.[42]

Sōhyō membership, as well as its percentage of the country's organized labor, rose steadily, save for the temporary upset in 1954 caused by the withdrawal of three co-founders of Zenrō, Sōhyō's rival. An especially marked increase took place between 1956 and 1957, as table 3 indicates.

41. Okazaki, *Sōhyō 15-nen;* The total figure of 2,450,000 that the two membership figures add up to is far below the figure of 3,090,500 published by the Ministry of Labor. The gap is due to the fact that Sōhyō's own figures, as presented by Okazaki, include only members eligible for representation at the national convention by virtue of payment of dues. For the ministry's figures, see Japan Institute of Labor, *Japan Labor Statistics,* p. 156.

42. They were as follows (pu = public; pr = private): In 1952, Nikkyōso (Japan Teachers' Union), pu; Kokurō (National Railways Workers' Union), pu; Tanrō (Japan Coalminers' Union), pr; Zensen Dōmei (Textile Workers' Union), pr; Zentei (Postal Workers' Union), pu; and Jichirōkyō (Prefectural and Municipal Workers' Union), pu. In 1955, Nikkyōso; Kokurō; Jichirō (descendant of Jichirō-kyō); Tanrō; Zentei; and Zendentsū (Telecommunications Workers' Union), pu. Zensen Domei seceded from Sōhyō to form Zenrō Kaigi.

TABLE 3
Sōhyō Membership and Its Percentage of
Organized Labor, 1952–1957

Year	Total Organized Labor	Sōhyō Membership	Percentage
1952	5,719,560	3,101,829	54.0
1953	5,842,678	3,272,672	56.0
1954	6,075,746	3,003,127	49.0
1955	6,285,878	3,093,513ᵃ	49.5
1956	6,463,118	3,137,551	50.0
1957	6,762,601	3,410,228	51.0

SOURCE: Japan Institute of Labor, *Japan Labor Statistics,*
p. 156.
ᵃ See note 39.

SŌHYŌ'S LEADERSHIP: FROM THE TAKANO LINE TO THE OTA-IWAI
LINE. Until 1955 the dominant figure within Sōhyō was its secre-
tary-general, Takano Minoru. His policies were known as the
Takano line. In 1955 Takano was replaced by Iwai Akira of the
Ota-Iwai group; in 1957 Ota Kaoru became president of Sōhyō,
and the Ota-Iwai line dominated Sōhyō for the next decade.

The Takano line symbolized the transformation of Sōhyō from
a SCAP-supported, anti-Communist group to a pro-Communist
organization—in Takano's own words, "from a SCAP-hatched
chicken to an ugly duckling." Domestically, the Takano line emphasized political agitation and popular struggles at the national
and local levels. Moreover, it reflected the rise of the Left Socialist
party within the socialist camp and, by 1955, the rise of the extreme
left within the reunified Japan Socialist party. The extremists identified American imperialism rather than Japanese monopoly capitalism as the prime target of the revolution in Japan. Hence,
Takano's foreign policy preference was with the "third force"
theory, supporting those forces in Europe and Asia (gradually more
in Asia than in Europe) that were active in preventing World
War III. By 1953 Takano had shifted his emphasis from the
"third force" to the "peace forces" theory, which amounted to

support for the Soviet Union and Communist China, and opposition to the United States.[43]

The Ota-Iwai line, on the other hand, supported the main current of the Left Socialist party on the identification of the Japanese working class's major enemy. The line emphasized that Japanese monopoly capitalism, having reached an advanced stage of development, was expected to be the prime target of the Japanese proletarian revolution. However, having paid tribute to Marxist dogma, the Ota-Iwai line rejected Takano's strategy (which had led to a series of defeats in labor disputes, and to fragmentation through the creation of splinter unions and the formation of Minrōren and, later, Zenrō). Rather, the Ota-Iwai group preferred unified action within each industry for the purpose of realizing union members' rudimentary demands. The action was to be in proportion to each union's organizational capacity to carry out an effective action instead of making a blind rush into certain defeat. This emphasis took concrete form in the evolution of the Spring Offensive.

THE SPRING OFFENSIVE. In essence the Ota-Iwai line was both a reflection of a bargaining pattern and an attempt to provide national leadership within that pattern. The pattern had emerged spontaneously during the wage struggle of government employees in 1953. When they realized that action on an enterprise basis was insufficient, the unions of the public corporations and national enterprises coordinated their struggle by forming the Public Corporations and National Enterprises Workers' Unions' Council (Kōrōkyō), which included both affiliates and nonaffiliates of Sōhyō. In 1955 Ota Kaoru, in his capacity as chairman of Gōka Rōren (Synthetic Chemical Workers' Union), organized a joint wage struggle of eight national unions in private industry, of which seven were Sōhyō affiliates and one was an independent. All eight participants won wage increases, and the pattern gained wide notoriety and acclaim among hitherto hesitant unions.

The Spring Offensive amounted to a joint wage struggle of the various national unions (in both the private and the public sectors). Political themes were included in the slogans of the offensives, but the primary target was a wage increase. Thus, Sōhyō took advantage of the trend to centralized authority in preference to the

43. Stockwin, *The Japanese Socialist Party and Neutralism*, chap. 4, pp. 39–48.

enterprise union as the focus of effective decision making. It was also hoped that the offensives would stimulate unionization in small and middle-sized enterprises; in these, unlike in the large-scale enterprises, the rate of unionization was either very low or nonexistent.[44]

In 1956 Sōhyō staged its first Spring Offensive. In that offensive, Sōhyō leaders attached political demands to the demands for wage increases, hoping that the struggle for higher wages would result in a spontaneous political spillover. They advanced, for example, a slogan opposing the Japan Productivity Movement; they conceived it as an American plot to facilitate Japanese remilitarization and to oppress Japanese workers through personnel adjustments, widespread dismissals, and harder work.[45]

The 1956 wage struggle was a success, but the political spillover did not occur; as soon as the respective wage agreements were concluded, the offensive was over. Therefore, the preparations for the Spring Offensive of 1957 (which triggered the ILO Convention 87 controversy) were more comprehensive and the political posture was more aggressive than in the year before. Sōhyō was encouraged by its success (which turned out to be temporary) in its struggle with the police at Sunakawa; the incident concerned the American presence at (and expansion of) the Tachikawa Air Base at the outskirts of Tokyo.[46] It was also influenced by the sharp turn in the conservative-progressive confrontation with the replacement of the ailing Premier Ishibashi by Kishi early in 1957.

FOREIGN POLICY AND INTERNATIONAL CONTACTS. The Ota-Iwai line's identification with the position of the Left Socialists' main current included matters of foreign policy—particularly its support for the "third force theory" in opposition to Takano's "peace forces theory." However, this fine theoretical distinction had little practical implication for Sōhyō's international contacts.

Under the Takano leadership, Sōhyō had failed to affiliate collectively with the ICFTU, despite Sōhyō's declared intention to do so "as soon as possible." The Ota-Iwai leadership did not change

44. See Cole and Nakanishi, *Political Tendencies of Japanese in Small Enterprises;* Ujihara and Nōmura, *Chūshō Kigyō no Rōdō Kumiai;* and L. Olson, *Dimensions of Japan,* chap. 2.

45. Concerning the movement, see Nihon Seisansei Honbu, ed., *Seisansei Undō 10-nen no Ayumi; Ōkōchi, Shiryō,* pp. 306–8; Sōhyō had modified its stand in 1962.

46. Ōta, *Waga Tatakai no Kiroku,* p. 60.

that. Moreover, the fraternizing with the Communist countries and the Communist-dominated World Federation of Trade Unions (WFTU), which had existed under Takano, continued after the election of Iwai as secretary in 1955. The first contacts with the WFTU were made during the WFTU director's visit to the ILO Asia Regional Conference in Tokyo in September 1953. His visit was followed by an official Sōhyō delegation's visit to the Third WFTU Conference in Finland in 1954. There were also other exchanges of visits and information with all international labor movements and with labor movements not affiliated with any international organization, especially in Asian countries.[47] In 1953, Sōhyō issued a call for the formation of an All Asian Union Conference, to be composed of members of the ICFTU and the WFTU as well as nonaffiliates. The ICFTU was opposed to the formation of such an organization because of the danger of Communist domination. Nevertheless, the Ota-Iwai group went even further; it made efforts to launch an Afro-Asian Labor Council, an idea even more offensive to the ICFTU than that of the All Asian Union Conference.

Sōhyō's attitude toward the ICFTU was continuously correct, though cool. The latter was unsuccessful in its attempts to win over new affiliates from among Sōhyō organizations. Furthermore, it failed to maintain unity among its affiliates in Japan following the withdrawal from Sōhyō of the Japan Seamen's Union (Kaiin), the Japan Textile Workers' Union (Zensen), and the Motion Picture and Theater Workers' Union (Eien). At Sōhyō conventions and conventions of ICFTU affiliates, the anti-main-current factions presented resolutions for withdrawal from the ICFTU, but these were rejected.

How did the ICFTU react to the mounting hostility? First, it scolded Sōhyō's leadership for resenting ICFTU's support of the separate peace treaty with Japan, the security treaty with the United States, the United Nations forces in Korea, and the rearmament of Japan and Germany. In 1952 an ICFTU representative lectured Sōhyō, criticizing its failure to see the need for defending the "free world" from the menace of communism. He also refuted the allegation that the ICFTU was West European-centered, and warned against the reemergence of Japanese totalitarianism on the

47. Okazaki, *Sōhyō 15-nen*, pp. 102–3.

wave of either extreme rightism or extreme leftism. Second, ICFTU offered Sōhyō some support in 1952 during the struggle against the "Strike Regulation Law"; it pressured Japan's government delegate in Geneva and sent cables to the Japanese government in Tokyo.[48] The ICFTU protests were ignored by the government. Third, in 1953, as Sōhyō's drift to the left intensified, the ICFTU opened a branch office in Tokyo in order to maintain closer ties with its affiliates in Japan and to promote unity among them. In fact, this move added another divisive element to the picture: disagreement over the choice of the head of the branch office.

Nevertheless, these efforts were significant in cultivating the loyalty and international involvement of a small group of top leaders within the Ota-Iwai group. Prominant among these were Haraguchi Yukitaka, president of the Japan Metal Mines Labor Unions (Zenkō) and former head of the ICFTU Tokyo office; and Takaragi Fumihiko, then vice-president of the Japan Postal Workers' Union (Zentei) and active participant in the Post, Telegraph, and Telephone International (PTTI) and the joint committee of the four International Trade Secretariats of public employees.

ICFTU's most serious mistake, prior to 1957, was its failure to support Sōhyō's attempt to enlist the help of the ILO in its drive to eliminate government restrictions of union rights.

SŌHYŌ AND THE ILO. Within the ILO, ICFTU's assistance was essential for two related purposes, one technical and one political. In order to present its case effectively to the ILO, Sōhyō needed expert knowledge of the details of the program and the ideology of the organization. In order to have the case acted upon seriously, it needed backing from a powerful group within the organization.

Sōhyō lacked the required expertise for several reasons. In contrast to the prewar days—when Japanese unions had played an increasingly active role within the ILO (especially in the area of freedom of association) [49] while playing a rather passive role within the international labor movement—in the postwar era, Sōhyō had played a passive role in the ILO, having been preoccupied with

48. Utada, *Kokusai Jiyū Rōren*, pp. 135–37.
49. T. Landelius, *Workers, Employers, and Governments*, pp. 176–81. All persons interviewed agreed that prior to 1957 Japanese labor representatives had played a markedly passive role within the Workers' Group in Geneva.

domestic affairs and those of the international labor movements. Conventions 87 and 98 were adopted in 1948 and 1949, respectively, when Japanese labor leaders were practically isolated from international contacts by SCAP orders. Moreover, Sōhyō shared with others in Japan its ignorance of the ILO system and ILO's relevance to Japanese domestic labor policy.[50] The failure of the Ministry of Labor to grasp the applicability of Convention 98, which Japan had ratified, to the legal restrictions imposed on employees in the public corporations and national enterprises, has already been mentioned. A committee of scholars and others interested in the ILO was appointed by the Japan ILO Association to examine the possible implications of conventions 87 and 98 to Japanese domestic legislation. They concluded that there was no discrepancy between the conventions and the constitution, the Trade Union Law, the Labor Relations Adjustment Law, the National Public Service Law, or the Public Corporations and National Enterprises Labor Relations Law and their local counterparts.[51]

Politically, since the split in the international labor movement in 1949, it had been the ICFTU that had held the dominant position in the ILO Workers' Group, and had articulated the workers' interests and communicated them to the International Labor Office. No complaint could be effective without its cooperation.[52] The WFTU, on the other hand, was much less influential because of its antagonistic attitude toward the ILO and its emphasis on cold war propaganda rather than on the merit of each case.

But it was the WFTU, not the ICFTU, that took the initiative in 1953; it presented the case of Japanese unions to the ILO in the form of a complaint to the Committee on Freedom of Association. It is no wonder, therefore, that the complaint, to which Sōhyō added its allegations, was dismissed by the committee.

The allegations concerned with occupation policies were dismissed outright because the occupation had already terminated; this followed the precedent set in the previous WFTU complaint (Case 48). More significantly, Sōhyō's attack was focused primarily

50. Interviews with Mr. Kaite Shingo, formerly of the Ministry of Labor; Mr. Toda and Mr. Utada, Ministry of Labor; Dr. Takahashi, chief of research, ILO Tokyo branch office; and Mr. Kubo, secretary of the Japan ILO Association.
51. Hanami Tadashi, *ILO to Nihon no Danketsuken*, p. 95.
52. E. B. Haas, *Beyond the Nation State*, pp. 4–5.

on the denial of the right of public employees to strike, and on the restrictions of the "Law Regulating the Right to Strike." Sōhyō claimed that the right to strike was a basic human right which the ILO had been committed to protect. However, while the organization was increasingly committing itself to human rights, there was widespread reluctance within the organization to consider that this right was a basic human right; had Sōhyō defined the issue in terms of freedom of association rather than the right to strike, its complaint could have been more successful. The committee indicated broadly that unions whose right of dispute was denied should be afforded adequate guarantees to safeguard their interests, but it declined to examine the matter further. Other allegations were found to be either overly exaggerated—since government policies were not out of step with those commonly accepted in other countries—or ill substantiated. Sōhyō, it appeared, had beaten the wrong tune on the wrong drum.

The dismissal of the case was a big disappointment to Japanese labor leaders, and diminished their propensity to try to use the ILO machinery again.[53] It did not, however, encourage even the leftists among them to boycott the organization. Even those among Japanese labor scholars who were closely identified with Sōhyō, and who served as its legal advisers, chose to become more indifferent toward the organization, rather than try to enhance their effectiveness by mastering the intricacies of the ILO system. For example, the leader of this group, Professor Nōmura Heiji of Waseda University, published a famous book in 1957: *The Theory and Process of Japanese Labor Law (Nihon Rōdō Hō no Keisei Katei to Riron)*. In this comparative study of Japanese and other labor law systems, the ILO was not mentioned even once. Similarly, the quarterly *Labor Law (Rōdō Hō)*, the scholarly publication of the Labor Law Institute (Rōdō Hōgaku Kenkyūjo) that over the years carried numerous articles by Nōmura and his associates and disciples, did not publish a single article on the ILO from its first issue in 1951 until its twenty-ninth issue in 1958 (after the decision to appeal to the ILO had already been made).[54]

53. Interviews with Mr. Takaragi, president of Zentei, and Dr. Takahashi, chief of research, ILO Tokyo branch office.
54. The 1958 article was by Sato Susumu, "Kokusai Rōdō Hō niokeru Rōdō Kihon Ken no Ichi Kōsatsu."

Had the ICFTU been more alert to the concrete problems of Japanese labor relations in 1955, and had Japanese labor scholars not turned a cold shoulder to the ILO, the issue could have been internationalized two years earlier. In 1955 the ILO Governing Body appointed the McNair Committee to study the question of freedom of association in ILO members countries. The committee was to rely on three sources: official information already in the possession of the ILO office; governments' reports; and "such opinions as might be offered by the most representative organizations of employers and workers." [55] Japanese unions did not avail themselves of the opportunity to publicize their opinion. The committee grew essentially from the efforts of the Workers' Group (i.e., the ICFTU) to disqualify representatives from Communist countries; in the context of the cold war, the ICFTU did not sensitize Japanese unions to this opportunity.

The McNair Committee was under pressure to present its report swiftly and, therefore, was unable to undertake either on-the-spot inquiries or full-scale examinations. It relied mostly on government responses to the committee's requests for clarifications of particular legislation.[56] Significantly, among the legal provisions singled out for clarification were section 4(3) of the Public Corporations and National Enterprises Labor Relations Law, and section 5(3) of the Local Public Enterprises Labor Relations Law, which in 1957 became the initial focus of the ILO Convention 87 controversy. In 1955 the government did not consider these provisions to be a problem, and the unions did not press the matter.

Sōhyō's renewed interest in the ILO as a possible lever for advancing Sōhyō's interests domestically was propelled by the election of its chairman, Haraguchi (concomitantly Zenkō's president and former head of ICFTU's Tokyo office), to the post of deputy member of the ILO Governing Body; he was the first postwar Japanese workers' delegate to be elected to this prestigious post. His election, with the concurrence of the ICFTU, stimulated Sōhyō's International Department to reexamine ILO conventions and their applicability to Japanese labor legislation and practice.[57]

55. ILO, "Report of the Committee on Freedom of Employers' and Workers' Organizations," p. 485; hereafter cited as the McNair Report.
56. Ibid., Appendix II, pp. 924–54.
57. Takaragi Fumihiko in "Zadankai," in Zentei, ed., *Shiryō*, 1:366.

In the course of the reexamination, the department discovered the connection of sections 4(3) and 5(3) to Convention 87. Therefore, Haraguchi's appeal to the ILO focused on that convention. Then, searching for an issue that would arrest Sōhyō's drift to the left and reunify the Japanese labor movement under its own banner, the ICFTU responded favorably to Sōhyō's request for assistance in the ILO.

6

The Expansion of a Unidimensional Issue: The Zentei Dispute

The recognition of the legitimacy of the issue took two forms. First, at the June 1958 International Labor Conference, Labor Minister Kuraishi Tadao indicated that, basically, the Japanese government was in favor of ratifying Convention 87 on the Freedom of Association and the Right to Organize. Second, in Japan, the Labor Problems Deliberation Council (Rōdō Mondai Kondankai) examined the various aspects of the prospective ratification. While the council deliberated, two other processes affected the issue. One was the Zentei–Postal Ministry dispute; the other was the inquiry by the ILO Committee of Experts concerning Japan's compliance with the ILO conventions that she had ratified.

The Labor Problems Deliberation Council (LPDC)

The LPDC was one of several dozen advisory bodies the Japanese government was utilizing for the examination of policy-oriented problems. The Ministry of Labor was one of the few ministries that included labor representatives in their councils. This was done not only to obtain the gamut of opinions and positions, but also to attempt to conciliate the conflicting positions of labor and management in a calm atmosphere. In the case of the LPDC, its primary function was conciliation, since the positions of both sides were clear from the start. The role of conciliation was performed by the thirteen members representing the "public interest," of whom the most active was the council chairman.

The thirteen "public interest" members included four university professors, three newspapermen (of *Asahi, Mainichi,* and *Yomiuri*), a social critic, a member of the National Safety Committee, a former chairman of the Japan Lawyers' League, the chairman of the Japan Committee for UNESCO (who was also chairman of the LPDC), and a former chairman of the Mediation Commission of the Public Corporations and National Enterprises. Representatives of labor and employers numbered eight each. Labor representatives included four leaders from Sōhyō, two from Zenrō, one from Sōdōmei, and one from Shinsanbetsu. The employers included a managing director of the Japan Federation of Employers' Associations (Nikkeiren), a managing director of the National Railways, a banker, and the presidents of five manufacturing firms.[1]

The chief of the Labor Legislation Section of the Labor Policy Bureau of the Ministry of Labor appeared before the council. He indicated that the controversial section 4(3) of the Public Corporations and National Enterprises Labor Relations Law (and section 5(3) of its local counterpart), which limited union memberships to employees, should be eliminated upon ratification of Convention 87. The unions, however, went farther; they insisted that the restrictions incorporated in the National and Local Public Service Laws should also be eliminated at the same time. This demand was refuted by a representative of the National Personnel Authority, who produced evidence that Japanese treatment of public servants was not out of step with practices abroad.

Following a process of conciliation, Tokyo University Professor Ishii Teruhisa, a leading authority on labor law and a public interest member of the council, presented a report to the council. This report incorporated the positions of the workers, the employers, the bureaucracy, and the ruling Liberal Democratic party (LDP). In the report, Ishii proposed the elimination of sections 4(3) and 5(3), together with ratification. As this elimination would have made it possible for nonemployees to hold union positions, he also proposed that the basis for disciplinary action for legal violations be broadened to include nonemployees. In anticipation of certain imbalances in labor-management power relationships, as a result of the elimination of the two sections, he further proposed

1. For the minutes of the council's meetings, see Zentei, *Shiryō,* 1: 193–202.

an examination of whether other legal measures would be necessary to maintain proper functioning of the public undertakings. Finally, he called for a reexamination of the total framework of Japanese labor legislation—in order to advance its congruity with the convention's principles of the autonomy of labor and employers' associations, and mutual noninterference in each other's affairs.

The report, which subsequently constituted the lion's share of the council's final report, broadened the scope of the issue considerably, since it could be interpreted as advocating that all of the proposed measures were of the same priority, and that each was conditioned by the performance of the others. The government indeed used the report to justify its postponement of the ratification and the relevant legislative adjustments. On February 20, 1959, the cabinet announced the following: (1) Ratification of the convention constituted a basic principle of the government's labor policy; and (2) before steps to ratify the convention could be initiated, two conditions had to be met: the revision of the related legislation (especially the current National Railways Law) in order to safeguard the proper functioning of public undertaking, and the normalization of the illegal state of Zentei.

The Zentei Dispute

Why was the Zentei dispute of such significance to the government in this context? In reelecting its dismissed leaders, Zentei showed its defiance of the postal authorities and the conservative force behind them. Zentei's adamant position was based on its faith in ICFTU and ILO support and the unity of its own ranks. The imminent convention ratification and revision of domestic legislation, according to Zentei, would automatically eliminate the legal justification for the government's refusal to recognize the union and bargain with its leaders. Therefore, it hardened its position and increased the severity of its tactics; the postal system was threatened with paralysis, which would prevent the delivery of Japanese New Year greeting cards and presents (which were very important to the Japanese people).

The cabinet, at the suggestion of the Ministry of Labor, was inclined to recognize the legitimacy of the ILO's concern with the freedom of association of Japanese unions. However, it could not

afford to give the impression that the ratification and revised legislation resulted directly from Zentei's defiance and the ILO's interference with Japanese internal affairs. While respecting the spirit
and resolutions of the ILO, the Ministry of Labor had no intention of submitting to the organization's control.[2] The Postal Ministry, on the other hand, was more concerned with the anticipated
public inconvenience. Consequently, it negotiated with the union
(including Zentei's dismissed officials), and agreed to pay year-end
bonuses at the same rate granted to employees of other public
enterprises and national corporations. The ministry's rationalization for doing so was that since the matter of year-end bonuses was
not a subject for basic labor agreements, the negotiations did not
amount to collective bargaining.

The Zentei dispute intensified against the background of further
escalation of the conservative-progressive confrontation. The progressives saw that their initial misgivings about Kishi's rise to
power had been well founded, in the wake of his trip to the United
States in June 1957 to start negotiations over the revision of the
security treaty. These misgivings were compounded by Kishi's
statement that the time had come for the elimination of article 9
of the constitution.[3] Moreover, on October 8, 1958, the government suddenly introduced the highly controversial Police Duties
Performance Bill. The bill had to be withdrawn because of stiff
resistance from the progressives and the public, and because of
disagreement within the LDP.[4] While the bill aggravated Sōhyō's
resentment toward Kishi, Sōhyō's success in mobilizing support for
withdrawal of the bill boosted its confidence in its capability to
resist the government. Meanwhile, the confrontation between the
Japan Teachers' Union (Nikkyōso) and the Ministry of Education
over the efficiency rating system had increased in intensity and
spread throughout the country. The controversy gave rise to
numerous disruptions, which led to various forms of punishment.[5]

As the ratification of the convention and the legal adjustments
became a commonly acknowledged possibility, several groups con-

2. *Rōdōshō 87*, p. 39.
3. G. R. Packard, *Protest in Tokyo*, pp. 81–173.
4. For an account of the controversy, see L. Olson, *Dimensions of Japan*, chap.
15. For party statement, newspaper editorials and reports, statements by union
organizations and others, see Tsuji, *Shiryō*, pp. 126–39.
5. Mochizuki Muneaki, *Nikkyōso 20-nen no Tatakai*, pp. 179–94.

sidered special measures (including stiffer penalties for legal violations) to keep unions from engaging in acts of dispute. Among them were the Labor Problems Special Investigation Committee (Rōdō Mondai Tokubetsu Chōsakai) of the LDP; the authorities of the various public undertakings, particularly the National Railways; and the Postal Ministry, the Ministry of Education, and several other government agencies in cooperation with the Ministry of Labor. Gradually, a wide range of safety valves were put forward and adjusted in meetings of a deliberative council of bureaucrats concerned with labor legislation (Rōdō Kankei Kakuryō Kondankai).[6] Sōhyō, apprehensive of these moves, mobilized the support of the Japan Socialist party (JSP), other national centers (Zenrō, Chūritsu Rōren, and Shinsanbetsu), as well as labor law groups in various prefectures;[7] these tried to goad the government into speeding up the work of the Deliberative Council and carrying out its recommendations without procrastination. Sōhyō's confidence was further boosted by the activities of the ILO.

ILO FORMAL PRESSURES: THE COMMITTEE OF EXPERTS. In March 1959 the Committee of Experts examined sections 4(3) and 5(3) and concluded that "in order to ensure fuller application of Article 2 of the Convention (98), which provides that, in particular, workers' organizations shall enjoy adequate protection against any act of interference, it would be desirable for the provisions in question to be repealed or amended." The committee also requested the government to indicate, in its next report, the measures it intended to take in this connection.[8]

Zentei interpreted the statement as an affirmation that section 4 (3) was *in violation* of Convention 98. But the government, while reiterating its intention to ratify Convention 87, insisted that Japanese laws did not violate Convention 98. In fact, claimed the government, even the Committee of Experts did not find the Japanese legislation to be in violation of the convention, since it merely called for a "fuller application." The head of the Labor Policy Bureau of the Ministry of Labor said that the importance of the committee's conclusions should not be overestimated, because the short duration of its deliberations and the great number

6. *Yomiuri Shimbun*, July 7, 1958.
7. Zentei, *Shiryō*, 1: 308–11.
8. ILO, "Report of the Committee of Experts," 43rd Session, 1959, p. 261.

of its cases (256 in 1959) made a thorough understanding of Japanese conditions unlikely.[9]

The government's tenacity on the matter of Convention 98 (which persisted until 1965) stemmed from its attempt to save face; the conclusions of the Committee of Experts meant that the government had failed in the past to report fully on the state of Japan's labor legislation. This was a serious affront, because the Japanese government had always been among the most faithful reporters to the Committee of Experts on the Application of Conventions and Recommendations. Therefore, the government ascribed the variance of its position from that of the committee to differences in interpretation rather than to a lack of good faith on its part.

ILO INFORMAL PRESSURES: THE CHAIRMANSHIP OF THE GOVERNING BODY. Zentei and its supporters obtained additional encouragement from the government's dilemma over the candidacy of the Japanese government delegate for the post of chairman of the Governing Body. Japan, as one of the ten major industrial countries, was a permanent member of the Governing Body. In 1959, for the first time in the postwar era, the Japanese government expected its delegate to be elected to the prestigious post of chairman and nominated its permanent representative in Geneva. However, the Workers' Group in Geneva refused to support his candidacy so long as the Japanese government failed to designate a date for ratification. The government reluctantly bowed to the long-established practice of unanimity in the election of the chairman, and on June 23 the cabinet decided to withdraw its representative's candidacy.[10] (Seven years later, one week after Convention 87 took effect in Japan, the Japanese minister to Geneva, Aoki Morio, was elected chairman.) [11]

ZENTEI AND THE CONSERVATIVE-"PROGRESSIVE" CONFRONTATION. Buoyed by developments in the ILO, Zentei interlocked its strug-

9. In another context, an official of the bureau made a sober appraisal of ILO conventions. He pointed out that by the 42nd session of the ILO held in 1958, 111 conventions had been adopted. As of January 1959, the eighty members of the organization had ratified a total of 1,863, or an average of 23 per member. As for Convention 87, only 36 (less than 50 percent) had ratified. Therefore, at that point he still had had no sense of urgency about ratifying. Zentei, *Shiryō*, 1: 381.

10. "Kokkai Gijiroku," in Zentei, *Shiryō*, 1: 563; Utada, *Kokusai Jiyū Rōren*, p. 219.

11. *Japan Report*, vol. 12, no. 15 (August 15, 1966).

gle and the drive against ratification of the Japan–United States Security Treaty. Zentei leaders resented the decision of Sōhyō, one of the drive's prime movers, to "share the mantle of Mindō's principle" of noncooperation with the Communists in internal politics. However, they found it advantageous to incorporate Sōhyō's opposition to the treaty into their own struggle with the Postal Ministry.[12]

Sōhyō supported Zentei in the streets and through informal talks with some members of the LDP, while the JSP supported Zentei's cause in the Diet. The JSP set up the Special Committee for the Promotion of the Ratification of ILO Conventions (ILO-Jōyaku Hijun Sokushin Tokubetsu Iinkai) to coordinate activities in the Diet and to negotiate with the leadership of the LDP.

Despite the fact that Diet deliberations during 1959 and the first half of 1960 were dominated by the Security Treaty issue, the question of Zentei's rights in the context of ILO conventions 87 and 98 was given intensive consideration. The deliberations reflected the multiplicity of points of contention, legal and otherwise, and the strategies employed inside and outside the Diet, including the use of unofficial contacts when they were deemed strategically advantageous.[18] In these minutely detailed and repetitive interpellations, the socialists (in constant coordination with Zentei and Sōhyō) attempted not only to win public opinion, but also to put on the record—for future use within the ILO—policy statements extracted from cabinet members and top-echelon bureaucrats.

For the JSP the ratification and the related revision were not of major concern. Party attention was focused on the Security Treaty; on the rationalization of Japanese industries (especially the coal industry) made necessary by foreign pressures on the Japanese economy through GATT and others;[14] on constitutional revision; on the efficiency rating system for teachers; on the cutting off of trade between Japan and Communist China following an incident

12. Nakamura Kenji, *Warera ni Sōhyō wa Hitsuyō Ka*, p. 85; Ōta, *Waga Tatakai no Kiroku*, p. 24; Zentei, *Shiryō*, 1: 328.
13. The following discussion of Diet activities relies heavily on Kokkai Gijiroku, in Zentei, *Shiryō*, 1: 423–642. For more selective excerpts, see *Rōdōshō 87*, pp. 47–50.
14. For studies of Japan's coal policy, see *Sōhyō News*, no. 167 (February 10, 1960); Nihon Shakaitō, ed., *Nihon Shakaitō Nijūnen no Kiroku*, pp. 306–17; Alice Cook, "Political Actions and Trade Unions: A Case Study of the Coal Miners of Japan"; Olson, *Dimensions of Japan*, chap. 17.

in Nagasaki in May 1958; and on the internal ideological and factional struggle in the JSP.[15] The JSP was not involved in the decision to raise the issue in the ILO, and it was only at Sōhyō's request that the party decided to carry it into the Diet.[16] It was a minor issue for the JSP, although it was ideologically interwoven with the major issues of the time. In fact, in the party's official history published in 1965 the issue was not mentioned at all.[17]

What made the JSP willing and able to engage the government in a substantial debate in the Diet was a group of former union leaders; some of them comprised the JSP's Special Committee for the Promotion of the Ratification of ILO Conventions, and a number of others also participated in the deliberations during 1959. The Special Committee was headed by Kōno Mitsu, a veteran leader of the prewar union and socialist movements and a central figure in the Kawakami faction of the JSP.[18] He had long been favorably disposed toward active participation in the international arena through the ILO, having himself served as Japan's workers' delegate to the organization. Kōno appointed the members of the Special Committee, all of whom were former union leaders active in the postwar labor movement. Among them was the dismissed president of Zentei.

THE PRESS. The evolution of the issue and the deliberations in the Diet were followed by the press. The editorial tone of the three major dailies (*Asahi, Mainichi,* and *Yomiuri*) and the conservatively oriented *Nihon Keizai Shimbun* was balanced. The big three urged the government to ratify the convention and make the relevant revisions in domestic legislation without delay. At the same time, they castigated Zentei for utilizing the ILO in its dispute with the government. They sided with the government on separation of the ratification from the normalization of the legal state of Zentei. The *Nihon Keizai* basically concurred with others, and put a stronger emphasis on the illegality of acts of disputes in public undertakings. It also lamented the failure of the Deliberative Council to specify the problems that would remain following rati-

15. See R. A. Scalapino, "Japanese Socialism in Crisis"; D. C. S. Sissons, "Recent Developments in Japan's Socialist Movement."
16. Interview with Kono Mitsu, chairman of the JSP Special Committee, Tokyo, July 10, 1967.
17. *Nihon Shakaitō Nijūnen no Kiroku.*
18. Ibid., pp. 539–50; Nihon Minsei Kenkyūkai ed., *Kokkai Giin Sōran*, p. 99; Cole, Totten, and Uyehara, *Socialist Parties in Postwar Japan.*

fication, and the concrete adjustments that should be made—thus passing the burden on to the government.

THE FUJIBAYASHI COMPROMISE. Toward the end of 1959 the Zentei dispute waxed to alarming proportions. Zentei allies in the international labor movement supplemented their original complaints to the ILO with new evidence related to the dispute. Zentei expected the Committee on Freedom of Association to act in its favor, in accordance with a recently adopted preference for thorough inquiry procedures over hasty inquiry and the imposition of sanctions.[19] The committee postponed its treatment of the case to the next session, hoping that by then the Zentei dispute would be over. Disappointed, Zentei intensified the severity of its actions (refusal to work overtime, absenteeism), again threatening a serious year-end bottleneck in mail deliveries. The Postal Ministry resorted to "divide and rule" tactics. It offered to negotiate with and pay year-end bonuses to every unit (a local branch of Zentei or a federation thereof), provided that it became distinctly separate from Zentei—thus posing a serious threat to Zentei's internal unity.[20] The ministry also sought to meet the emergency by training temporary workers to supplement Zentei's members; it soon realized, however, that public inconvenience could not be avoided, because of the insufficient training of the temporary employees and the large number of branches that still remained loyal to the national union.

Both sides realized that a total victory was impossible, and were ready to compromise; but neither could say so openly and thus lose face after such a lengthy confrontation. Consequently, public verbal exchanges, rather than diminishing in tone, became increasingly more hostile. An attempt was made by Haraguchi of Sōhyō and ex-Labor Minister Kuraishi of the LDP to reach an agreement in which the question of Zentei's dismissed officials would be avoided, but the agreement failed to materialize, because of strong opposition within the LDP.

The Zentei dispute was finally settled through the good offices of Fujibayashi Keizō, the chairman of the Public Enterprises and National Corporations Labor Relations Commission. As in the

19. E. B. Haas, *Human Rights and International Action*, p. 76.
20. Interview with Takaragi Fumihiko, Zentei's vice-president (subsequently president), Tokyo, August 25, 1967.

case of the National Railways, the preference of parties in labor disputes for conciliation rather than direct negotiations had manifested itself.

The minutes of the meeting between Fujibayashi and Zentei leaders pinpoint the crucial factor in Zentei's acceptance of Fujibayashi's offer to conciliate. It was Fujibayashi's report that (1) the government conceded Sōhyō's assertion that conditions of the Zentei confrontation differed from those prevailing in the National Railways two years earlier, and (2) the government was earnestly interested in an early settlement, including the resumption of collective bargaining between the Postal Ministry and Zentei.[21]

Fujibayashi's conciliation proposal, presented on December 21, 1959, succinctly stated that the union would elect temporary representatives from among Executive Committee members who were not dismissed; that these would perform the representational functions, such as collective bargaining and the conclusion of labor agreements; and that the authorities would accept these temporary representatives as a party to collective bargaining, labor agreements, and the like.[22] Consonant with the proposal, Zentei was to adopt a set of regulations that reaffirmed the control of the dismissed leaders over union affairs. The temporary representatives were to be appointed by Zentei's dismissed president. Their duties would entail the proposing of and engagement in collective bargaining, and the signing of labor agreements; the making of representations concerning conciliation, mediation, and unfair labor practices; and the exchanging of official documents with the Postal and Labor ministries. The remaining union functions would stay in the hands of the union president, including organizational control, contacts with other organizations, union finances, legal entity, and so forth. With the exception of the subsequent replacement of Nogami by Takaragi (both dismissed officials) as president, this is the arrangement that was in effect until the convention was ratified and section 4(3) was abrogated in 1965.

Conclusions

The terms of the settlement appeared to be short of what Zentei had hoped for. However, it was recognized in labor circles as a

---

21. Zentei, *Shiryō*, 1: 331. The minutes were unofficial.
22. Ibid., p. 337.

victory just the same; it deprived the authorities of a major device for weakening union leadership—the denial of collective bargaining, which was directly related to the economic, and primary, concern of union members. This sense of victory had several repercussions. It suggested to hitherto skeptical Japanese labor unions the possibility that the ILO, even though it comprised governments and employers in addition to workers, could be responsive to their appeals and could exert effective pressure to promote their interests.[23] On the other hand, it spurred segments of the bureaucracy and the LDP to impose a wide variety of restrictions and to attempt to legally prohibit the continuation of the labor practices that the unions had been anxious to preserve. Thus, a unidimensional issue, centered on sections 4(3) and 5(3), had expanded to incorporate other dimensions or subissues as well. The expansion was caused not only by the conservatives' apprehensions but also by Sōhyō's confidence in its ability to mount political campaigns (as demonstrated during the treaty struggle). This confidence prompted Sōhyō to renew its efforts to restore the right to strike, which, for awhile, was held in abeyance.

The expansion of the issue was reflected in the legislative package the government presented to the Diet, and in the proliferation of unions' complaints to the ILO.

23. Interviews with Haraguchi Yukitaka, August 29, 1967; Jichirō central executive committee member Kasai Homei, April 4, 1967; Makieda Motofumi, Nikkyōso's secretary-general, September 1, 1967; in the case of Kokurō, the impact had been vicarious through the persuasion of labor scholars, particularly Professors Nōmura Heiji and Nakayama Kazuhisa of Waseda University, whose interest in the ILO was stimulated by the Zentei dispute. Interview with Ishikawa Toshihiko, head of Kokurō's legal department, August 16, 1967.

7

The Legislative Package

At the Thirty-fourth Ordinary Diet session on April 28, 1960, the government presented the bills for ratification of ILO Convention 87 and revision of domestic legislation. Domestic legislation submitted for revision included not only the Public Enterprises and National Corporations Labor Relations Law and its local counterpart, which were the focus of the Kokurō and Zentei disputes and the target of the first complaints to the ILO, but also the National and Local Public Service Laws and the National Railways Operations Law. While the elimination of sections 4(3) and 5(3) was favorable to the unions, the rest of the revisions applied more restrictions to union activities in all categories of public employment, thus multiplying the number of unions affected. The bills triggered a long and complex process of conflict and bargaining between various actors in the government and the opposition, and were subsequently modified somewhat before the issue was settled. Throughout the process, the bills were referred to as the "original government bills."

The major provisions of the original government bills were as follows: [1]

(1) Despite certain changes, employees in managerial, supervisory, or confidential categories (*kanrishokuin*)—which would be determined in the case of national enterprises by the Public Enterprises and National Corporations Labor Relations Commission—would not be able to join the unions formed by general employees.

1. For details, see *Rōdōshō 87*, pp. 66–82; see also the Dreyer Report, pars. 621–754. The latter referred to them as "amendments proposed in 1963," but they were essentially the same as the original bills.

(2) Full-time union officers (*zaiseki senjū*) would be limited to three-year terms of office, during which time they would have temporary employees' status without remuneration. This provision would be applicable under the four different laws concerned with the public sector.

(3) Employees would be prohibited from following illegal union instructions.

(4) A Bureau of Personnel in the office of the prime minister would take over major functions from the purview of the National Personnel Authority (and consequently tighten the control of the premier and the bureaucracy over the civil service).

(5) Existing regulations of the National Personnel Authority setting registration as a prerequisite for union recognition would become law.

(6) Penalties for violation of work-rules in the National Railways would be stiffened.[2]

"PACKAGE DELIBERATION". The government insisted that all the provisions—both favorable and unfavorable to the unions—be deliberated together, as a package. The socialist opposition objected.

By then, the socialist camp in Japan had been divided again. The Nishio group (including part of the Kawakami faction) withdrew from the Japan Socialist party at the end of 1959 and formed the Democratic Socialist party (DSP) early in 1960. The JSP (with the support of Sōhyō) and the DSP (with the support of Zenrō) differed on matters of ideology, organization, and policy. They also differed on the strategy to be employed on the original government bills.

Once sections 4(3) and 5(3) had become practically a dead letter, the JSP, echoing Sōhyō's position, was no longer eager to settle, because a settlement of the issue now would only mean further restrictions of union rights without further compensations. The party and Sōhyō expected that the longer the issue remained unsettled, the more severe ILO sanctions would become—thus forcing the government to make more concessions to the unions. The DSP and Zenrō, on the other hand, were concerned about Japan's prestige abroad, and sought a prompt end to the internationaliza-

2. The latter was added in June 1960.

tion of the issue. Consequently, the JSP demanded that each of the various subissues be deliberated in the Diet committee directly concerned.[3] The DSP, in contrast, demanded that the convention be ratified without delay; that only sections 4(3) and 5(3) be abrogated; and that other matters, not directly related to the convention, be examined by a special tripartite commission *after* the ratification.

Formally, the only way for the government to hasten deliberations was by forming a special Diet committee to deal with the issue in all its ramifications. In accordance with article 46 of the Diet Law, such a committee would have required the concurrence of the other major parties in the Diet—the JSP and the DSP. The two socialist parties, having been opposed to package deliberation, rejected the plan.

On May 31, 1961, Kiyose Ichiro, speaker of the lower house, offered a compromise. He proposed that bills for ratification and the amendment of sections 4(3) and 5(3) be deliberated in a Special Committee; that bills related to the National Public Service Law and the Local Public Service Law be referred to the Cabinet Committee; and that the bills to amend the National Railways Operations Law be referred to the Transportation Committee.[4] The DSP accepted the proposal, since it was congruent with its own demand that ratification and revision of sections 4(3) and 5(3) be separated from the rest of the subissues. The JSP rejected the proposal.

Had the issue been a major and a pressing one for the government, it would have forced its will on the opposition, as it did in the ratification of the Security Treaty in 1960. However, as the ruling LDP itself was not in agreement over all of the provisions of the bills, and the cabinet did not consider the issue pressing at the time, Diet action on the issue was postponed and a showdown was averted.

PROLIFERATION OF UNIONS' COMPLAINTS. Encouraged by the mass movement against the Security Treaty, the JSP anticipated spec-

3. The following committees would have been involved: social and labor, foreign relations, education, cabinet, transportation, communications, commerce and industry, local administration, finance, and agriculture, forestry, and fisheries. Rōdōshō, ed., *Shiryō: Rōdō Undō Shi*, 1960, p. 689. This publication, hereafter cited as *RS Uundō Shi*, is an *annual* survey, not to be confused with the special collection on the ILO issue cited in this volume as *Rōdōshō 87*.
4. *Mainichi Shimbun*, June 1, 1961.

tacular gains in the general elections to the lower house on November 20, 1960, and the resurgence of mass movements under its leadership in the future. In this context, Sōhyō planned to consolidate and intensify the struggle of unions in the public sector. For that purpose, it formed the Special Committee for the Recovery of the Right to Strike (Stōken Dakkan Tokubetsu Iinkai), composed primarily of national unions in the public sector, on October 25, 1960.[5] The right to strike was not their immediate target, but its recovery symbolized to them the ultimate aim of their drive to recover *all* union rights.

The elections did not change the conservative-progressive ratio in the Diet; the JSP's strength increased at the expense of the DSP. Yet Sōhyō's Strike Committee did not diminish its efforts; it assisted several of its national unions in filing complaints with the ILO.

First to file was the National Employees' Joint Struggle Committee (Kokkō Kyōtō), comprising unions in the national public service. Its complaint was followed by the complaints of the Japan Teachers' Union (Nikkyōso), the National Railways Workers' Union (Kokurō), and the Prefectural and Municipal Workers' Union (Jichirō). Since the last three had played an important role in the evolution of the issue of Convention 87 and sections 4(3) and 5(3), we shall examine briefly the circumstances that led to their joining Zentei in its ILO struggle.

Nikkyōso, with 603,307 members in 1961, first raised the subject of ratification and related legislation at its June 1958 convention; however, the leadership was doubtful of the ILO's effectiveness.[6] Moreover, the convention was marred by confrontations over union leadership and the strategy to be employed against the efficiency rating system. The incumbent leadership, associated with Sōhyō's extreme leftist Takano group, was challenged by the Ota-Iwai line. The Ota-Iwai line subsequently prevailed,[7] but one of the concessions it made to the Takano group was the union's withdrawal from the ICFTU and the International Federation of Free

5. Major unions involved were the following: Jichirō, Nikkyōso, Zentei, Zendentsū, Kokurō, Dōryokusha (formerly Kirō), Zensembai, Tōshikōtsu, Nōrin, and Shihō.
6. Interview with Makieda Motofumi, Nikkyōso's secretary-general, Tokyo, September 1, 1967.
7. Mochizuki, *Nikkyōso 20-nen no Tatakai*, pp. 174–78; Nikkyōso, ed., *Nikkyōso 20-nen Shi*, pp. 449–51.

Teachers Unions (IFFTU). At the time, this move made any involvement in the ILO unlikely, since ICFTU-IFFTU support was indispensable within the organization.

Nikkyōso was spurred to file the complaint by two related developments: the introduction of the bills in the Diet, and the appointment of Araki Masuo, an inflexible right-winger, to the post of education minister. In August 1960 Araki intensified the Nikkyōso-ministry confrontation by refusing to continue his predecessors' practice of meeting with the union to discuss matters of mutual concern. Araki argued that since Japanese educational administration had ostensibly been decentralized, the proper authority for dealing with teachers' unions rested with the prefectural governments and not with the Ministry of Education. Araki also asserted that educational policy was not a proper subject for discussions with a teachers' union at any level.[8]

In fact, educational administration had been recentralized to a great extent by then, and ministry policy affected teachers' labor conditions, making their involvement in politics inevitable. Pushed into a corner by the new developments, Nikkyōso appealed to the ICFTU and the IFFTU for help in filing the complaint. The two organizations obliged, hoping that their renewed contacts with Nikkyōso and their support would be instrumental in bringing Nikkyōso back into the fold.

Kokurō, with 214,738 members in 1961, refrained from filing a complaint with Zentei in 1958—not only because it held the ILO in low esteem, but also because Kokurō's weakness drove it into accepting the Fujibayashi compromise. With the introduction of the government bills, the union faced a "clear and present danger" of stiffer penalties for violations of the National Railways Operations Law. It therefore availed itself of the services of the newly established Special Strike Committee and played an active role in it.

Jichirō, with 609,921 members in 1961, had been a latecomer on the national labor scene. It was formed in 1954 by two separate federations and numerous local units in response to the centralizing policies of the Yoshida cabinet.[9] In its organizational structure, Jichirō resembled a federation of unions in private industry,

---

8. *RS Undō Shi*, 1960, p. 707.
9. For a comprehensive account of these policies, see K. Steiner, *Local Government in Japan*, part 2.

with the local unit (as in the case of the enterprise union) being the authoritative source of decision making. But Jichirō lacked the unity of national unions in private industry, which had gradually shared concrete, economic interests across enterprise lines, during the Spring Offensive, or of Nikkyōso, which had been unified both by resentment to "reverse course" policies in education and by the growing national government interference in the determination of teachers' labor conditions. Instead, Jichirō affiliates constituted a diverse and loosely connected confederation of local units and prefectural federations, differing in local customs and traditions, in local political structures, and in propensity to cooperate with local authorities.[10]

Although the union's leadership had had a strong element of Japanese Communist party members,[11] the Ministry of Local Autonomy (unlike the Ministry of Education in the case of Nikkyōso) did not refuse to discuss matters regularly with Jichirō. The continuous communication between the union and the ministry was due to the considerable attention paid by the union to bread-and-butter issues, along with its leaders' bent for leftist ideology. Moreover, the union and the ministry had a wide area of common interest vis-à-vis the national government in view of the latter's preemption of a large share of local governments' finances. In one sense, the ministry was a representative of the national government and, as such, an instrument of control. It also functioned as a channel for demands made by local governments on those national agencies that were in a position to allocate resources. Jichirō, through its contacts with socialist members of the Diet's Budget and Local Administration committees, performed a similar function. And, in dealing with the Ministry of Local Autonomy, Jichirō served as a conveyor of local demands as well as of union demands. Ministry officials, especially those aspiring for a political career after their retirement at the relatively young age of fifty-five, could ill afford to neglect demands by groups holding the key to their future constituent support.[12]

Jichirō's position was threatened by the government bills, espe-

10. Jichirō, *Jichirō no Hata*, pp. 141–48; interview with staff members of Jichirō headquarters, April 4, 1967.

11. R. A. Scalapino. *The Japanese Communist Movement*, pp. 131–32; For an exposition of the areas of conflict between the two, see Kōan Chōsa Chō, *Nihon Kyōsantō no Rōdō Shintō Kōsaku*, pp. 219–22.

12. Interview with a staff member of Jichirō headquarters.

cially by a proposed prohibition of the full-time union officer system. The threat was made when Jichirō's confidence in its ability to mount a defensive campaign was at its highest. During the anti-treaty struggle, Jichirō had succeeded, for the first time in its history, in mobilizing its various affiliates for a nationwide joint action. The union was ripe for joining Sōhyō's Special Strike Committee and filing a complaint with the ILO.

THE COMPLAINTS. By 1963, the number of complaints and the volume of evidence had reached immense proportions. Here it should suffice to outline the allegations in a pattern adopted by the Committee on Freedom of Association and the Dreyer Commission.

(1) Restrictions on trade union membership and election of officers (Public Corporations and National Enterprises Labor Relations Law, and Local Public Enterprises Labor Relations Law)

(2) Denial of the right to strike, and defects in the mediation and arbitration system (PCNELRL and LPELRL)

(3) Denial of the right of association to supervisory employees (PCNELRL and LPELRL)

(4) Denial of collective bargaining (LPELRL)

(5) Denial of the right of association to the personnel of certain services, such as policemen, prison wardens, etc. (National Public Service Law)

(6) Elimination of the full-time union officer system in the national and local services

(7) Collective bargaining (NPSL and Local Public Service Law):
   (a) Denial of the right to conclude collective agreements (NPSL and LPSL)
   (b) Legislative interference with collective negotiations concerning the checkoff of union dues (LPSL)
   (c) Limitation of the matters covered by the negotiating rights of organizations of civil servants (LPSL)

(8) Registration and scope of organizations under LPSL

(9) Denial of the right to strike, and lack of compensatory guarantees (LPSL)

(10) Proposed amendments to the NPSL

(11) Allegations in relation to the Police Duties Law

(12) Acts of interference with Kokurō, and the adhesion of workers to the union
(13) Acts of antiunion discrimination affecting Nikkyōso, and nonrecognition of the union
(14) Acts of interference with, and nonrecognition of, certain organizations of government employees
(15) Acts of interference with regard to unions affiliated with Jichirō

The Committee on Freedom of Association, with the assistance of the International Labor Office, examined the evidence associated with the complaints. The committee also followed developments in Japan connected with the issue and periodically took note of the government's declared intention to settle the issue as soon as possible. As long as there was some semblance of progress toward a solution within the Japanese political system, the committee refrained from invoking sanctions. For three years the only international factor exerting persistent pressure on the Japanese government was the ICFTU, either directly or through the Workers' Group at the ILO.

Until 1963, officials of the Labor Ministry and the Ministry of Foreign Affairs who maintained contacts with the ILO had not found these pressures sufficiently authoritative to necessitate a swift and decisive action on the part of the government. Rather, they had been under the impression that the deputy director general of the International Labor Office, in charge of the Japanese case, was "sympathetic" to the difficulties the government faced in its attempt to close the issue.[13]

The cabinet succeeded in creating the impression of progress by faithfully introducing the bills in the Diet even when there were no prospects for their passage. Moreover, the Ministry of Labor promptly prepared (and the Ministry for Foreign Affairs promptly submitted) every report requested by the ILO committee involved, defending the government's position meticulously.

What were the obstacles to rapid settlement? We have already mentioned the opposition of the unions and the parties on the left. This opposition could have been mitigated through both formal and informal talks had there not been internal dissension

13. Jiyūminshutō Kōhō Iinkai, ed., *ILO Dai-87-go Jōyaku Hijun to Kankei Kokunai Hō Kaisei Mondai*, pp. 43–45.

on the issue within the ruling party and the bureaucracy. We shall, therefore, turn now to the factors determining government's policy in the issue-area of labor.

THE PRIME MINISTER'S "POSTURE". Prime Minister Kishi Nobusuke pursued an uncompromising line toward the leftist opposition. It gave rise to the large-scale conflict over the Police Duties Law in 1958, and the antitreaty crisis of 1960. Kishi was forced to resign because of these disturbances and concomitant pressures from rival factions within his own party, the Liberal Democratic party (LDP).[14] Kishi's successor, Ikeda Hayato, was committed to a "low posture" (*teishisei*) in his relations with the opposition—in order to secure their cooperation in his economic program, which was designed to double the national income in ten years. The "low posture" was typified by the avoidance of showdowns with the opposition.[15] In the context of the ILO issue, that partially explains why the government, during the incumbency of Ikeda from July 1960 to December 1964, resisted demands for either more restrictions or immediate passage of the original bills.

While the general posture was determined by the premier, the particular policies were formulated by the various divisions of the Policy Affairs Research Council (Seichōkai) of the LDP.

THE POLICY AFFAIRS RESEARCH COUNCIL. This council was the LDP organ formally entrusted with the study, research, and planning of policy.[16] It was composed of functional divisions which paralleled each of the ministries, other agencies of the national government, and the standing committees of the two houses of the Diet.[17] In addition, the council included commissions and special investigation committees consonant with the interests of the party members and the emergence of issues requiring special attention. Membership in the various units of the council was voluntary; however, each LDP member in the Diet required to participate in at least one division, but in no more than two divisions.

14. Scalapino and Masumi, *Parties and Politics in Contemporary Japan.*
15. C. A. Johnson, " 'Low Posture' Politics in Japan."
16. For a more detailed discussion of the role of the council in the formulation of policy, see N. B. Thayer, *How the Conservatives Rule Japan*, pp. 207–36; and H. Fukui, *Party in Power*, pp. 83–89.
17. These divisions were cabinet, regional administration, defense, justice, foreign affairs, finance, education, social welfare, labor, forestry and agriculture, marine products, commerce and industry, transportation, communications, and construction. Thayer, ibid., p. 210, n. 9.

The state bureaucracy had maintained a strong influence on the council. This was because of the high quotient of ex-bureaucrats among LDP Diet members, and the close interaction of high government officials with the members of the council units. The bureaucrats were an indispensable source of information and expertise, since the council's staff was undermanned. Often they also belonged to the same bureaucratic clique as the ex-bureaucrat council members.[18]

As the ILO issue was complex, involving a multiplicity of sub-issues and government organizations, a number of council units participated in the formulation of policy regarding its solution. Most active among them were the Labor Division, the Special Labor Problems Research Committee, the Cabinet Committee, the Administrative Research Committee, the Education Division, the Special Education Investigation Committee, the Special Safety Countermeasures Committee, the Foreign Affairs Division, and the Agriculture and Forestry Division. In order to sound out the views of the various council units and find a consensus, Fukuda Takeo (council chairman during the first Ikeda cabinet) appointed an informal committee known as the ILO Sewaninkai, headed by ex-Labor Minister Kuraishi Tadao. The Sewaninkai included two council vice-chairmen, the heads of the Labor and Cabinet divisions and of the Administrative Research Committee.[19]

The strongest opponents of a compromise solution with the unions were members of the so-called education–public peace (*bunkyō-chian*) group, composed largely of former Education Ministry bureaucrats, former Home Ministry bureaucrats (but not of the liberal segment of that ministry), and former officials in police administration. They monopolized the Education Division, the Special Education Investigation Committee, and the Special Safety Countermeasures Committee. This group's members identified union political activities with subversion, and they particularly resented Nikkyōso's leftist inclinations. Their attitude on the issue was brought into sharp relief in a statement made at a press conference on January 20, 1961, by their most notorious member,

18. J. Masumi, "A Profile of the Japanese Conservative Party"; For a popular study, see Matsumoto Seichō, *Gendai Kanryō Ron;* see also Fujiwara Hirotatsu, *Kanryō: Nihon no Seiji o Ugokasu Mono.*
19. *RS Undō Shi*, 1961, p. 617. Sewaninkai members were Kuraishi Tadao, Shirai Isamu, Nikaido Susumu, Saito Kunikichi, Ogasa Kōshō, and Noda Uichi.

Education Minister Araki. In effect, he said that Japan should leave the ILO if the Committee on Freedom of Association criticized the Japanese government in a manner consonant with the complaint filed by Nikkyōso.

In 1961, prior to the reintroduction of the government bills in the Diet, the "education–public peace" group pressured the Sewaninkai to add legal restrictions on the political activities of public employees (which hitherto were subject only to the regulations of the National Personnel Authority). They were joined by the Agriculture and Forestry Division, whose members insisted on retaining the right to deprive dismissed national public servants of union membership even after the ratification of Convention 87.[20] Their position was dictated by the fact that the union in the Ministry of Agriculture and Forestry (*Nōrin*) was controlled by Japan Communist party members aligned with the Takano group within Sōhyō.

Kuraishi's Sewaninkai rejected the proposal of the Agriculture and Forestry Division, but supported the reintroduction of the original government bills plus the prohibition of political activities of public employees. These recommendations were transmitted by the council's chairman to the chairman of the LDP's Executive Council (Sōmukai). Except for certain technical difficulties, the recommendations of the Sewaninkai were agreed upon in joint sessions that they—and later members of the Executive Council—conducted separately with representatives of the respective ministries.[21] However, as Premier Ikeda had been bent on early ratification, he is said to have instructed LDP Secretary-General Masutani and Research Council Chairman Fukuda to avoid the question of political activities.[22] At that point, the Policy Affairs Deliberation Committee (Seichō Shingikai), a body of the Policy Affairs Research Council consisting of the council's chairman and vice-chairmen, plus chairmen of related divisions, met with the Sewaninkai and hammered out a consensus that placated all concerned. The original bills were to be introduced; the question of political activities was to be shelved for further study by an Extraordinary Research Committee on the System of Public Employees,

20. *Tōkyō Shimbun*, February 25, 1961; later confirmed by official party sources. See Jiyūminshutō Kōhō Iinkai, *ILO 87 Hijun*, pp. 31–35.
21. *Asahi Shimbun*, March 17, 1961.　　　22. *Mainichi Shimbun*, March 23, 1961.

to be set up for that purpose. The plan was approved by the Executive Council and subsequently by the assembly of LDP members of both houses of the Diet. The cabinet introduced the bills to the Diet on March 25, 1961.[23]

MOVES TOWARD ACCOMMODATION. While the government and the opposition disagreed both on the substance of the bills and on procedural matters, serious efforts to reach some accommodation were made by the LDP Sewaninkai, headed by Kuraishi Tadao, and the JSP Special Committee for the Promotion of the Ratification of ILO Conventions (ILO Jōyaku Hijun Sokushin Tokubetsu Iinkai), headed by Kono Mitsu. Kuraishi and Kono conducted a series of semiformal negotiations (*madoguchi sesshō*) in some of which Sōhyō leaders, notably Secretary-General Iwai and Zentei's president, Takaragi, participated.

Kuraishi, who was usually identified with the right wing of the LDP, took an independent, more liberal position on the question of the party's relations with organized labor. An ex-minister of labor, he reached the conclusion that communication channels with Sōhyō leaders had to be kept open, despite the gap in ideology, in order to avoid constant confrontation. This view was shared by another labor minister, Ishida Hirohide (Bakuei), of the party's small "new right." Ishida published in *Chūō Kōron* his "vision," [24] advocating the reorganization of the party's ideological foundation to make it more appealing to the rapidly growing population. For that purpose he proposed a "labor charter" that included provisions for the establishment of a forty-hour working week and the realization of European wage levels. Kuraishi and Ishida maintained their own channels with different labor leaders—Kuraishi with Iwai, and Ishida with Ota. As Kuraishi and Ishida were rivals for a leading position with the party in labor policy making, Ishida remained on the sideline while Kuraishi conducted the negotiations with Kono and Iwai.

By January 1963 it appeared that the unions were ready to accept the abolition of the checkoff system on the condition that the "full-time union officer system" would be retained. The unions were also inclined to accept the establishment of a Bureau of Per-

23. *RS Undō Shi*, 1961, p. 618.
24. "Hoshuseitō No Bijon"; for excerpts in English translation, see *Journal of Social and Political Ideas in Japan* 2, no. 2 (August 1964): 55–58.

sonnel in the Office of the Prime Minister provided that public servants would be allowed to bargain collectively.[25]

In June 1963 progress reached a new stage. In a meeting between Maeo Shigesaburō, LDP secretary-general, and Narita Tomomi, JSP secretary-general, in the presence of Kuraishi, Kono, and others, agreement was achieved on two points: (1) a special committee would be formed in the Diet to deliberate on the provisions relating to the ratification of the convention; and (2) in the deliberations of this committee, both parties would endeavor to amend the government's original bills on the basis of semiformal negotiations.[26] Consequently, two special committees were set up in the houses of the Diet, headed by Kuraishi Tadao and by Kennoki Toshihiro.[27]

It was also agreed to placate the DSP, which, in addition to opposing package deliberations, resented having been left out of the semiformal negotiations.[28] Hence, the first stage of the special committees' deliberations was to be limited to the question of ratification and the amendments of sections 4(3) and 5(3); the questions of the formation of the Bureau of Personnel and the restoration of the right of collective bargaining would be examined in a separate Advisory Council on the Public Personnel System (Kōmuin Seido Shingikai).

The understanding between the parties was heartily welcomed by the daily press, although the secrecy of the talks was deplored.[29] The "main current" leadership of both Sōhyō and the JSP was optimistic about the prospect for an early settlement.[30] Haraguchi Yukitaka, the workers' delegate to the ILO, related this optimism to the organization.[31]

The issue took another turn at Sōhyō's convention late in July. Iwai outlined the results of the Kuraishi-Kono talks, which became

---

25. *Asahi Shimbun*, January 5, 1963.   26. *Asahi Shimbun*, June 14, 1963.

27. The latter was a former administrative vice-minister and currently vice-chairman of the LDP Education Special Investigation Committee.

28. The JCP opposed the talks, arguing that rights should have been struggled for by the masses rather than bargained out by union officials. *Akahata*, May 30, 1963.

29. *Asahi Shimbun*, *Mainichi Shimbun*, and *Yomiuri Shimbun*, June 15, 1963; *Sankei Shimbun*, June 18, 1963.

30. Interviews with Kono Mitsu, Takaragi Fumihiko, and Haraguchi Yukitaka; Tokyo, July 10, 1967; August 25, 1967, and August 27, 1967, respectively; *Sōhyō*, June 21, 1963.

31. *RS Undō Shi*, 1963, p. 516.

commonly known as the Kuraishi Plan (Kuraishi Mondaiten). Though all the daily papers had reported accurately the major points under discussion and the general shape of the compromise, neither side had previously made any authoritative announcement on the agreements.

The plan's major points in regard to the "full-time union officer system" were these: (1) the existing "full-time union officer system" would be prohibited; (2) those serving as full-time union officers would be able to retain their employee status for only three years, during which time they would neither receive a salary nor be entitled to pensions and other allowances; (3) the application of this regulation would be postponed for two years after promulgation.

The major points in regard to national and local public servants were as follows: (1) the improvement of conditions of work was defined as the *chief* purpose rather than *the* purpose of employees associations; (2) supervisory employees would not be allowed to form organizations with employees in other categories; (3) the scope of the category of supervisory employees would be determined by the National Personnel Authority in the case of the national employees, and by the local Personnel and Equity Committees in the case of local employees; [32] (4) union registration would cease to be a prerequisite for collective bargaining; (5) unions in the local public service would be allowed to combine with unions from other undertakings in order to lodge grievances and conduct talks with the authorities of the national government, the public corporations, and the national enterprises; (6) regulations of political activities of national servants would remain unchanged, rather than be determined by law; (7) an Advisory Council on the Public Personnel System, composed of Diet members, bureaucrats, corporation managers, persons of scholarship and experience, and employees' representatives, would be set up in the Office of the Prime Minister; (8) a Bureau of Personnel would also be set up in the Office of the Prime Minister.

The LDP's version of the plan did not include provisions regarding the checkoff system. The version produced by Iwai, however, suggested that unions would be allowed, by agreement with the

---

32. From the union's standpoint, this was preferable to centralized control through cabinet orders.

management, to check off funds for savings and welfare programs.[33]

The agreement would have cushioned the impact of the elimination of the "full-time union officer system" by allowing sufficient time for adjustments and by enabling union officials to maintain their strongly coveted employee status. It would have mitigated the centralizing trends in personnel control while facilitating the coordination (and possible centralization) of union demands beyond the confines of the divisive enterprise-wide (or agency-wide) organization.[34]

Because of the strong opposition of the "education–public peace" group within the LDP, the cabinet refrained from revising the original bills immediately. The JSP agreed to meet with the special committees on the understanding that the deliberations would adhere to the spirit of the plan.

We have seen that some progress was made toward the solution of the ILO issue during the period of the Ikeda cabinets (1961–1964). But it was not achieved smoothly, and by the time Ikeda was replaced by Sato, the issue had not yet been settled. Despite the efforts of Kuraishi and his associates, opposition to accommodation of the union demands persisted within the LDP. The opposition's hand was fortified by two factors: other issues, and the election of the LDP president.

OTHER ISSUES IN THE CONSERVATIVE-"PROGRESSIVE" CONFRONTATION. Prospects for an accommodation diminished periodically as the focus in the Diet shifted to confrontations over other issues, submerging whatever mutual trust had accumulated through negotiations. The other issues during 1961 included the Basic Agriculture Law, two defense laws providing for reorganization of the Japanese defense forces, and the Political Violence Prevention Bill. Issues of 1962 were the repayment of debts to the United States incurred during the occupation (the so-called GARIOA and EROA payments), the Thai Special Yen Agreement, the national coal policy, and two employment bills. The issues during 1963 included the coal policy, revision of wages of public servants, negotiations for the normalization of Japan–Republic of Korea relations, and the two employment bills.

33. For details, see Stöken Iinkai, "Sōhyō niyoru Kaiseiten no Yōkō," in *RS Undō Shi*, pp. 520–30.
34. For favorable mass coverage and opinion, see *Yomiuri*, September 16, *Mainichi*, September 17; *Sankei*, September 18; *Asahi*, September 18; and *Nihon Keizai*, September 20, 1963.

Of all these issues, only the two employment bills reached the legislative stage connected with the ILO issue, although the Political Violence Prevention Bill was related to union activities. The two employment bills were designed to phase out an archaic category of the "officially unemployed" workers (who were actually employed in public works, but with no prospects for advancement and with little productivity). Their careful preparation, with the assistance of an advisory committee of experts, was independent of the ILO issue.[35] However, their introduction in the Diet, at the instigation of the "high posture" members of the LDP, was timed for a point when LDP-JSP negotiations over the ILO issue had approached a mutually satisfactory conclusion.

The JSP, Sōhyō, and the JCP responded vehemently to the employment bills—thus jeopardizing a solution of the ILO issue—because the bills threatened the Japan Day Workers' Union (Zennichijirō), Sōhyō's third largest national union. Zennichijirō was controlled by JCP members aligned with the Takano group of Sōhyō. Sōhyō and the JSP did not want to alienate the union even further by remaining indifferent to the bills.[36]

Progress was also delayed periodically by election campaigns. Yet, the ILO issue did not figure prominently in either the upper house elections in 1962 or the lower house elections in 1963. Slogans related to the issue were adopted both by the JSP and by Sōhyō during the election campaigns, but all the parties focused their attention elsewhere. The platforms were built on more dramatic issues, such as defense and foreign policy, or on those directly related to the people's livelihood, such as the prices of consumer goods and taxes. The ILO issue did figure prominently in a different kind of election, however—that of the president of the Liberal Democratic party.

FACTIONAL RIVALRY AND THE ELECTION OF THE LDP PRESIDENT. The shadow of the July 1964 LDP presidential election significantly affected Ikeda's legislative strategy. Because of the party's Diet strength, the election of the ruling party's president amounted to the election of the prime minister; it was held every two years.

35. Interview with a member of the advisory committee, who preferred to remain anonymous.
36. H. H. Baerwald, "Parliament and Parliamentarism in Japan"; on Zennichijirō see Kōan Chōsa Chō, *Nihon Kyōsantō no Rōdō Shintō Kōsaku*, pp. 277–85. *RS Undō Shi*, 1963, pp. 1136–37. For a different interpretation, see A. Cook, "The International Labor Organization and Japanese Politics," p. 49.

In 1962, after less than two years in office, Ikeda ran unopposed. In 1964, however, he was challenged by other faction leaders. In order to win reelection to a third term, he had to preserve the allegiance of a coalition of factions.

Japanese party factions, the basic units of Japanese politics, had their roots in the prewar era. They emerged as an extension into politics of the leader-follower group, the traditional Japanese paternalistic type of relationship. Within the parties, the factions kept their own identities, organizations, and sources of finance. Since 1956 the procedure for electing the LDP president had changed from that of informal talks (*hanashiai*) among a few strong party leaders to that of a secret vote taken mostly by LDP Diet members. Consequently, a major function of the factions became the mobilization of as many votes as possible for the election of the faction leader (or his temporary ally) to the presidency. This development contributed to the institutionalization of the factions, with headquarters, internal hierarchies, and administrative and research staff. Since no faction had enough members to elect the president single-handedly, it was indispensable for every aspiring faction leader to win the support of other factions in addition to his own.[37]

In 1964 it became clear that Ikeda faced the challenge of the Sato or Kōno factions and possibly the Fujiyama faction. The race was expected to be very close. In order to win, Ikeda not only had to secure the allegiance of a sufficient number of faction leaders, but also had to refrain from antagonizing elements within the factions of his own coalition. The latter, because of their commitment to their prime objective over a particular current issue, could possibly violate factional discipline and vote against him in the secret ballot. He also had to beware of providing the opposing coalition with ammunition that could be used against him.

At the end of 1963 and during the first half of 1964, the Sato, Kishi-Fukuda, Kawashima, and Kōno factions were vehemently opposed to a compromise solution to the ILO issue.[38] Of the four,

37. For two intensive studies of LDP factions during this period, see H. H. Baerwald, "Japan: the Politics of Transition," and M. Leiserson, "Factions and Coalitions in One-Party Japan." A more recent study is N. B. Thayer, *How the Conservatives Rule Japan.*

38. Information obtained from staff workers of the Policy Affairs Research Council. Also *Yomiuri Shimbun,* August 22, 1963; *Asahi Shimbun,* September 14 and 27, 1963; February 4 and March 10 and 15, 1964.

the first two were clearly in opposition to Ikeda's reelection; the support of the last two was indispensable to the success of his coalition.[39] The chairmen of the Policy Affairs Research Council's divisions who were strongly opposed to any compromise with the unions belonged to the Kōno, Sato, and Kishi-Fukuda factions. These were Inaba Isamu, chairman of the Education Division (Kōno); Saigo Kichinosuke, chairman of the Special Public Peace Countermeasures Committee (Sato); Masuda Kaneschichi, chairman of the Education Research Committee (Sato); and Kogane Yoshiteru, chairman of the Special Labor Problems Research Committee (Kishi-Fukuda).

An inkling of this group's numerical strength within the party was demonstrated on March 25, 1964, when 126 LDP Diet members of both houses, the majority of whom belonged to the "high posture" factions led by members of the Fukuda faction, met at the Akasaka Prince Hotel in Tokyo and formed the Conference of the Concerned with the ILO Problems (ILO Mondai Yūshi Kondankai). In the meeting it was resolved to present a petition to the party leadership against any kind of compromise with the JSP over the issue, and in favor of passage of the original bills presented in April 1960; and similarly, to insist that the composition of special committees should reflect all shades of opinions in the party.[40]

As for those cabinet members and party executive officers who promoted early ratification and advocated maximum respect for a compromise solution, all were members of the Ikeda faction. They included Secretary-General Maeo Shigesaburo, Chief Cabinet Secretary Kurogane Yasumi, Labor Minister Ōhashi Takeo, and Foreign Minister Ōhira Masayoshi.

However, the confrontation within the LDP over the issue was not strictly a factional affair; the "education–public peace" group also included Diet members who belonged to factions other than those mentioned above. Araki Masuo, for example, was a member of the Ikeda faction, while Nadao Hirokichi, his successor as min-

39. To win, he needed the support of Kōno, Miki, Kawashima, and Funada factions. Factional distribution among LDP Diet members of both houses was as follows: Ikeda, 59; Kōno, 65; Ōno-Funada, 41; Miki, 49; Sato, 94; Fujiyama, 33; Kawashima, 18; Fukuda, 17; Ishii, 34; and minor factions and unaffiliated, 31. Watanabe Tsuneo, *Habatsu*, pp. 181–91, reproduced in Baerwald, "Japan: The Politics of Transition," p. 35.

40. *Asahi Shimbun*, March 25, 1964, evening; *Mainichi Shimbun*, March 25, 1963.

ister of education, was a ranking member of the Ishii faction. On the other hand, Kuraishi Tadao, who insisted on reaching an agreement with the JSP and Sōhyō, was a member of the Kishi-Fukuda faction, which had been in opposition ever since the Kishi broke up into the Fukuda, Fujiyama, and Kawashima factions. As was indicated earlier, his was a personal role relating to his concern and experience with labor problems.

Ikeda opted for the most logical strategy under the circumstances. Despite his willingness to accommodate some of the unions' demands and revise the original government bills, he decided to postpone action on the divisive issue of ratification and to concentrate on the issue of Japan–Republic of Korea (ROK) relations, on which there was unity within the party.[41] Only when internal factors in the ROK made the prospects for a satisfactory solution of the ROK issue remote, did the ILO issue shift back to the center of the stage.[42] Then Ikeda found it imperative to accommodate not the demands of the unions but those of the opposition within his own party. His lieutenant, Secretary-General Maeo Shigesaburo, produced a new version of his year-old agreement with JSP Secretary-General Narita Tomomi to respect the results of the semiformal negotiations. While Narita's version read, in part, "both parties shall sincerely carry it out" (*ryōtō wa seii o motte okonou mono to suru*), Maeo's version read, "shall sincerely make efforts to carry it out" (*okonou yō dōryoku suru*).[43]

As the LDP presidential elections drew nearer, the party's Policy Affairs Research Council reached an agreement on an emasculated version of the Kuraishi Plan.[44] Interparty negotiations at the level of the respective Diet policy committees broke down; the JSP requested a vote of no-confidence in the Ikeda cabinet, but to no avail.[45]

On July 17, 1964, Ikeda won reelection to the party presidency by the slim margin of four votes.[46]

DISUNITED UNIONS. Progress in solving the ILO issue was also delayed by disagreements among the progressives. A semblance of unity, based on the agreement on principles, was reflected in the 1961 reconvening of the Deliberative Council for the Promotion

41. *Asahi Shimbun*, March 10, 1964.
42. Ibid., March 13, 1964.
43. *Asahi*, April 7, 1964.

44. Rōdōshō, *Shiryō 87*, pp. 546–49.
45. Ibid., pp. 549–52.
46. Baerwald, "Japan," pp. 35–36.

of Ratification of ILO Conventions (ILO Jōyaku Hijun Sokushin Kondankai). This council was formed jointly by the four national federations: Sōhyō, Zenrō, Shinsambetsu, and Chūritsu Rōren. However, disagreements over strategies and tactics soon became evident. As was indicated earlier, the JSP and Sōhyō disagreed with the DSP and Zenrō on the position concerning the Kiyose compromise. Disagreements also surfaced within Sōhyō's Special Committee for the Recovery of the Right to Strike, whose members were involved (together with the JSP's Kōno and his associates) in the negotiations with Kuraishi of the LDP.

At an early stage in the interparty negotiations, Sōhyō's unions were divided into two distinct groups. The unions of the Public Corporations and National Enterprises Workers' Unions' Council (Kōrōkyō) were in favor of mitigating their opposition to some of the new restrictions for the sake of early ratification. The Joint Struggle Conference of National and Local Government Employees (Kōmuin Kyōtō), on the other hand, called for stiff opposition to unfavorable revision even if it meant delaying the ratification.[47]

Furthermore, even the Kōmuin Kyōtō, formed in 1960 to coordinate wage and political struggles, was internally divided. One of its two components, the Joint Struggle Conference of Unions of Local Public Employees (Chikōrō), was controlled by Sōhyō's "main current" leaders in the Japan Teachers' Union (Nikkyōso), the Prefectural and Municipal Workers' Union (Jichirō), the Municipal Traffic Workers' Union (Tōshi Kōtsu), and the Water Supply Workers' Union (Zensuido). The other component, the Joint Struggle Conference of National Government Employees (Kokkō Kyōtō), was controlled by Sōhyō's "anti-main-current" leaders in such unions as the Construction Ministry Workers' Union (Zenkenrō), the Ministry of Labor Workers' Union (Zenrōdō), the Ministry of Transportation Workers' Union (Zenunyu), and others.[48] In 1962, while the Kuraishi-Kōno talks were in progress, Kokkō Kyōtō unilaterally informed the government that there could be no compromise on the issues of political activities and the proposed Bureau of Personnel, and that the ratification of Convention 87 would be unthinkable unless the right of collective

47. *Tokyo Shimbun*, June 8, 1961; *RS Undō Shi*, 1962, p. 615.
48. Kōan Chōsa Chō, pp. 209–14.

bargaining was granted to their unions.[49] At that time, an uncompromising attitude that hampered negotiations was also displayed by officials in Kōrōkyō affiliates.[50] Whatever bargaining leverage the unions were able to gain was thus diminished, and the hand of the right wing of the LDP was strengthened.

UNION VICTORY IN THE COURT. One moral-boosting victory was clearly scored by the unions despite their political ineffectiveness. It may be recalled that in Kirō's 1957 suit connected with the National Railways dispute, the Tokyo District Court did not consider section 4(3), which limited union membership to employees only, to be unconstitutional. However, on October 22, 1962, the District Court of Morioka, in a criminal case involving Zentei's district organization, pronounced section 4(3) in violation of article 28 of the constitution.[51] But the new ruling had little practical effect within the legislative process, because sections 4(3) and 5(3) had had "lame duck" status since February 1959, when the Kishi cabinet had decided to abrogate them upon the ratification of Convention 87.

INCREASE OF INTERNATIONAL PRESSURES. As the Japanese government was unable to settle the issue swiftly, its arguments at the ILO in defense of its policies became less and less convincing. Criticism of the Japanese government had gradually mounted. In 1960 and 1961, the ILO Committee of Experts and the Conference Committee had limited themselves to asserting that Japanese legislation violated article 2 of Convention 98 (which Japan had already ratified), and to calling upon the government to carry out its pledge to ratify Convention 87 and amend the respective laws.[52] In May 1963, however, there was a change of attitude. The Committee on Freedom of Association requested that the Japanese government report what measures it intended to take in order to settle the issue in the current Diet session. Minister Aoki in Geneva was reported to have advised the Japanese government that in ILO terminology this was equivalent to an ultimatum.[53] Labor

49. *RS Undō Shi*, 1962, p. 532.
50. See, for example, Ishikawa Toshihiko (of Kokurō's legal department), "ILO No Hannō to Kongo no Tatakai."
51. *Japan Labor Bulletin*, n.s., vol. 1, no. 9 (December 1962), p. 6.
52. "Report of the Committee of Experts," 1960, pp. xxix and 52; 1961, pp. xxix–xxxi and 98.
53. *Asahi*, May 31, 1963.

Vice-Minister Tamura, who until then was among those asserting that there was no particular hurry as far as the ILO was concerned, injected a sense of urgency from the International Labor Conference in Geneva; he reported that Japan had been criticized not only by the Workers' Group, as before, but also by several governments.[54]

The ICFTU, in coordination with Japanese unions, probed another source of embarrassment for the Japanese government—the Organization for Economic Cooperation and Development (OECD). In 1963 the Japanese Foreign Ministry and the Ministry of International Trade and Industry were eager to win membership in the OECD as an international status symbol and a bridge to the European economy. Early in 1963 England and France promoted Japan's entry; in July the OECD extended to Japan a formal invitation to join.[55] But the ICFTU exerted pressure through the OECD; it also publicized in Japan the possibility that, because of her labor policy, she would court suspicion at the OECD.[56] This theme was taken up by the Japanese press, and subsequently appeared in exhortations made by the Foreign and Labor ministries in their attempt to hasten the ratification process. Foreign Minister Ōhira Masayoshi even warned the ruling party that the matter might be brought up by the United Nations' Economic and Social Committee.[57]

External pressures became even stronger in November 1963, when the ILO Committee on Freedom of Association proposed that the Governing Body refer the case to the Fact-Finding and Conciliation Commission on Freedom of Association. In February 1964 the Governing Body referred the case to the commission, designated its members, and asked the Japanese government to determine by April 15, 1964, its acceptance or rejection of the commission's visit to Japan.

The Japanese press, the Foreign and Labor ministries, and Prime Minister Ikeda and his close associates all agreed that a commission visit would be a source of grave embarrassment to Japan. The consensus was that such an eventuality should be avoided by a serious effort to settle the issue domestically, thus

54. *Asahi,* July 4, 1963; *Sankei,* July 4, 1963.
55. John White, *Japanese Aid,* pp. 16–17; *Japan Report* 10, no. 9 (May 15, 1964).
56. *RS Undō Shi,* 1963, pp. 747–49.   57. *Asahi,* February 13, 1964.

rendering the visit superfluous. As was indicated earlier, Ikeda was unable to persuade his party to honor the Kuraishi Plan; since he was reluctant to force the original bills on the opposition parties and the unions, he could not settle the issue by April 15. Hence, the government could not avoid making a decision on whether to accept the commission's visit.

Before turning to the factors leading to the government's acceptance of the visit, let us explore the role played by the business community in Japan. In view of the close association of the ruling party, its factions, and the business community [58]—plus the fact that the issue was cast in the context of Japanese economic diplomacy—why did the business community allow the issue to reach that stage?

Officially, the Japan Federation of Employers' Associations (Nikkeiren) did not adopt any resolution on the Kuraishi Plan; it declared itself neutral on the issue.[59] However, Nikkeiren's attitude can be easily inferred from its actions over the years. Its representative on the Labor Problems Advisory Committee, which had initially examined the question of the ratification of Convention 87, supported the government's restrictive interpretations of the committee's recommendations. In 1958 and again in 1962 the association criticized the independent and loosely defined status of the National Personnel Authority, as well as its allegedly irresponsible policies, which tolerated union misbehavior. In 1958 it petitioned the Kishi cabinet to formulate a firm policy in reference to the Japan Teachers' Union (Nikkyōso).[60] In 1961 it criticized Ikeda's "low posture" toward the unions in the public corporations and national enterprises as a symptom of "a growing tendency to make light of law and order." [61] It petitioned the third Ikeda cabinet, expressing regret over the failure of the education system in the realm of "character formation" and the inculcation of moral principles, and asserting that labor-management relations in Japan should take advantage of good Japanese traditions.[62] In 1964, on the other hand, the association revised its official philosophy from "labor-management confrontation" to "labor-management mutual

58. Chitoshi Yanaga, *Big Business in Japanese Politics.*
59. Interview with Mishiro Akio, chairman of Nikkeiren's ILO committee, Tokyo, June 1, 1967.
60. Nikkeiren, *Nikkeiren No Ayumi*, pp. 6, 50–52, 70.
61. *JFEA News*, no. 8, April 1961.
62. For a critique of this approach, see Ōkōchi Kazuo, "Rōshi Kankei No Kyokumen."

cooperation" because of the transformation of Japan into a free-trading, open economic system.[63] Despite this revision, however, the association's consensus continued to be in favor of restrictive legislation on issues related to government employees, and particularly to Nikkyōso.

Reliable informants, such as newspapermen covering the Liberal Democratic party, and staffers of the LDP Policy Affairs Research Council, were unable to determine the role played informally by business groups or influential individuals of the business community. They agreed, however, that the business groups had not tried to press Ikeda into taking drastic measures to settle the issue promptly. One plausible explanation is the fact that from 1963 onward the antagonists over the Kuraishi Plan temporarily ceased to be unions and managements or "progressives" and "conservatives," and were, rather, two elements of the LDP, both with strong ties to the business community, thus neutralizing the latter as a strategic factor in the controversy.

More important, the Japanese business community had been selective in its response to external pressures, carefully weighing punishments and rewards. It was indeed eager to win goodwill and reciprocity in Europe. Hence, Japanese ministries under its influence temporized on the formation of the Organization of Asian Economic Cooperation (OAEC) proposed by the Economic Commission for Asia and the Far East (ECAFE)—apparently in order to avoid complications in Japan's attempts to join the OECD and penetrate European markets.[64]

Japan had been under international pressure to liberalize her trade and investment policies. After prolonged negotiations, Japan responded to pressures from GATT; in 1963 she became an Article 11 nation, denying herself the right to impose controls on the basis of balance-of-payments deficiencies. Similarly, after a grace period of one year, she agreed to deprive herself of the right to impose currency controls without authorization from the International Monetary Fund (IMF). Indeed, Japan had to pay admission to the OECD in the form of an obligation (at first, mostly theoretical) to liberalize restrictions on foreign investments in Japan.[65]

The business community, however, did not perceive any serious

63. *JFEA News*, no. 20 (December 1964); Sumiya Mikio, "Nihon no Kyodai Soshiki," pp. 35 ff.

64. P. L. Singh, *The Politics of Economic Cooperation in Asia*, pp. 158–65.

65. L. Hollerman, *Japan's Dependence on the World Economy*, pp. 230–32.

damage to Japan's economic diplomacy as a result of the ILO issue. It did not consider the issue to be as critical as the Japanese unions, the ICFTU, the Japanese press, and the ministries of Foreign Affairs and Labor had portrayed it. True, Mishiro Akio, chairman of Nikkeiren's ILO Committee and a member of the ILO Governing Body, advocated ratification,[66] and Igarashi Akio, Nikkeiren's secretary-general, advocated swift action on the bills because of his conviction that Japan's failure to ratify "would be misunderstood in Geneva." But, at the same time, Igarashi asserted that no adverse effect on Japanese trade could be expected immediately.[67]

In fact, during the period that the ILO issue was assumed to have threatened Japan with diplomatic damage, Japan had gained considerably in the international arena. The Anglo-Japanese Treaty of Commerce and Navigation was concluded in November 1962; the Franco-Japanese Agreement was signed in May 1963. Moreover, both England and France (joined, shortly after, by Australia) discontinued their application to Japan of the escape clause of GATT's article 35. In the ILO, only two European governments were said to have tried to press the Japanese government into modifying its original position on the issue and accommodating the unions' demands.[68] On the other hand, pressure on Japan to intensify its liberalization programs, and to refrain from flooding foreign markets with cheap, competitive commodities, had been exerted by the United States, Canada, and several European countries; they coupled this pressure with discriminations against certain Japanese export goods. However, these discriminations had been selective, and were not derived from conceptions (or misconceptions) of "social dumping" as in the prewar era, or as related to the abridgement of freedom of association of public employees.[69]

The United States was Japan's foremost trade partner and the

66. *Asahi*, February 27, 1964.
67. *Japan Times*, June 24, 1964.
68. Interviews with Ishii Toru, chief of the Social Affairs Section of the United Nations Bureau of the Foreign Ministry, July 31, 1967, and Haraguchi Yukitaka, Japanese workers' delegate to the ILO, August 27, 1967. Both declined to specify.
69. W. W. Lockwood, "Political Economy," pp. 115–118; M. Kajima, *A Brief Diplomatic History of Modern Japan*, pp. 169–171, 192–93; *Japan Report* 10, no. 7 (April 1964); *Japan Quarterly* 11, no. 2 (April–June 1964), p. 151; no. 3 (June–September 1964), p. 384.

foreign power with the strongest influence on Japanese foreign and domestic policies; yet, significantly, it refrained from pressuring Japan on the ILO issue. At the level of union leaders, the AFL-CIO consistently supported the efforts of the Japanese unions on the issue, both in Geneva and during visits to Japan; but at the *government* level, America was not in favor of sending an ILO mission of inquiry to a member country, primarily because it had burnt its own fingers with such a mission in 1959–1960. At that time the United States had invited an ILO mission of inquiry to survey the extent of freedom of association, with the understanding that the USSR would do likewise, which it did. However, to the chagrin of the United States, the shortcomings pointed in the mission's report were far more embarrassing than those in the report on the Soviet Union—which turned out to be milder than was anticipated—were to the Soviets.[70] What transpired in Geneva over Case 179 could have only a minuscule effect on the attitude of the American government toward Japanese-American trade relations.

70. E. B. Haas, *Beyond the Nation State*, pp. 236–37, 255.

8

The Dreyer Commission

On April 19, 1964, the Ikeda cabinet informed the ILO of its acceptance of the proposed visit of the Fact-Finding and Conciliation Commission (the Dreyer Commission). Aoki Morio, Japanese minister to Geneva, and all the Japanese dailies favored acceptance. But Ikeda's positive response was made in the face of strong opposition from many bureaucrats and LDP Diet members, who were motivated by several considerations. Foremost was the lingering reluctance to recognize the legitimacy of the ILO in dealing with Japanese labor problems; they failed to see the salience of the ILO to the issue, not only in the context of Japanese economic diplomacy, but also in any other context of Japan's foreign policy. Others, while recognizing ILO's legitimacy in principle, objected to the proposed visit for two reasons. First, they were strongly convinced that the Japanese were fully capable of settling their own affairs without external interference. Second, they harbored serious doubts concerning the capacity of foreigners to fully comprehend the presumably unique system of Japanese labor relations—its values, traditions, and functions within the country's cultural, social, economic, and political systems; consequently, they doubted the ability of foreigners to pass a fair judgment. In fact, even the majority of union leaders interviewed harbored the same doubts; their support for the visit, however, was motivated by their conviction that the outcome would be favorable to them.

When the premier came out in favor of acceptance, he advanced a number of arguments. (1) Past contacts with the ILO were reassuring as to the sensitivity of the International Labor Office to the unique Japanese conditions; past experience with a visit of a mission of inquiry to Japan (the Maurette mission and the issue of "social dumping")[1] had served Japan's interests well. (2) The personal integrity and professional background of the commission's members, as well as the commission's terms of reference, were sufficient to dissipate fears of external interference in Japan's domestic politics. (3) Suspicions and misconceptions concerning Japanese labor conditions would be far more serious should the commission be denied admission; only a Communist country could be expected to turn away a mission concerned with freedom of association, whereas the Japanese government could only benefit from such a visit, once the unruly and overly political behavior of Japanese unions was exposed by the commission.

Ikeda's task was a difficult balancing act indeed. Even after notifying the ILO of the government's decision to welcome the commission, he continued to stress the undesirable effects of Japan's failure to ratify the convention prior to the commission's visit. At the same time, he kept reassuring everyone concerned that the visit would not be harmful after all, since Japan's acceptance had already won her the respect of the organization.[2]

Prior to the visit, ill health forced Ikeda to be replaced by Sato Eisaku. At first, Sato moved cautiously and refrained from taking any strong measures. He left the composition of the cabinet intact, replacing only the chief cabinet secretary, a post ordinarily filled by the premier's confidante. Instead of forcing the original bills, Sato met with leaders of Sōhyō and Dōmei for informal talks.[3]

Before the commission's arrival, the LDP agreed upon a new version of a draft legislation. The party claimed that the new draft was based on both the original bills and the Kuraishi Plan. But Sōhyō and the Japan Socialist party (JSP), considering the changes minimal, opposed the new version.[4] When the commission arrived in Japan in January 1965, the Forty-eighth Ordinary Diet had been in session for only twenty days, and the cabinet was still putting the last touches on the revised bills.

THE COMMISSION'S SOURCES OF INFORMATION. Before its arrival, the Dreyer Commission had an enormous store of information on the Japanese case. Most of it had been amassed by the Interna-

1. See chapter 3.
2. See, for example, "Dai-Yonjū-Kokkai Shūgiin Kokusai Rōdō Jōyaku Hachijū-Nana-Go Tō Tokubetsu Iinkai Gijiroku," in Rōdōshō, *Shiryō 87*, p. 232.
3. *Japan Labor Bulletin* n.s., vol. 4, no. 2 (January 1965), p. 1.
4. *Asahi*, November 25, 1964; December 16, 1964.

tional Labor Office under the close supervision of Deputy Director General C. Wilfred Jenks, from unions' complaints, replies by the Japanese government, close association with Minister Aoki in Geneva, and five Japanese nationals on the office's staff. The commission had also received a constant flow of confidential reports from the ILO Tokyo office concerning Diet deliberations, statements of influential persons, and the tone of editorials.[5] Furthermore, the commission had conducted preliminary sessions in Geneva, to which witnesses from Japan and the international labor unions involved were invited.

The commission performed its task in Japan from January 10 to January 26, meeting with cabinet ministers, bureaucrats, and leaders of Sōhyō and its affiliated national unions. The Japan Federation of Employers' Associations (Nikkeiren) did not avail itself of the opportunity to present its views; it pronounced itself "neutral" on an issue concerned with the public sector. Dōmei, Sōhyō's rival in the union movement, was eager to state its position, but because the federation was not one of the complainants, the commission deprived it of this right. During its visit, the commission received several supplementary reports. For two days, its members separated; each paid visits to two prefectures, to enhance the commission's "understanding of Japan as a whole." [6]

THE MISSION'S OBJECTIVE: CONCILIATION. There were very few new facts to be found by the visit of the Fact-Finding and Conciliation Commission, the two days of visits to "Japan as a whole" notwithstanding. Reports of the secret sessions (the content of which became public knowledge in a matter of hours) [7] suggested that the commission concentrated primarily on conciliation. With remarkable mastery of (and sensitivity to) the complexities of the issues, it groped for some area of agreement between the government's latest version and the unions' adamant rejection of anything short of the Kuraishi Plan.

The Dreyer Commission realized that the core problem was

5. Interview with Dr. Takahashi Takeshi, chief, research department, ILO Tokyo branch office, July 6, 1967.

6. For the account of the commission's visit and the summaries of proceedings of its various meetings, see the Dreyer Report pars. 1800–2032.

7. Similarly, although the proceedings in Geneva were also expected to remain secret until the commission chose to publicize them, the February issue of the monthly *Hōritsu Jihō* (Law Review), devoted to the ILO issue, carried detailed accounts of the proceedings.

the lack of mutual trust between the unions and the authorities. Lack of trust underlined Nikkyōso's insistence on legal guarantees for the right to conduct talks with the Ministry of Education. Lack of trust motivated the authorities to insist on restricting the union rights of supervisory employees by law instead of leaving the question to negotiations between labor and management. Meetings with the ministers of education and local autonomy, as well as the director general of the Cabinet Legislative Bureau, convinced the commission that the government had no intention of giving in on the central questions of the issue.

The commission was also concerned with its visit's potential feedback into the future functioning of the ILO supervisory machinery in the area of freedom of association. Missions of inquiry could not be carried out without the consent of the government of the country visited. Since the establishment of the supervisory machinery in 1950, the Japanese government was the first to consent to a request by the ILO for a commission visit. Admission had been refused on two previous occasions—by the governments of Venezuela and the Dominican Republic. Costa Rica and Libya, on the other hand, had *invited* the commission on their own accord in connection with complaints against them.[8] Thus, the visit to Japan was a test case in which the mission could ill afford a rebuff by the Japanese government; such a rebuff might foster the suspicion of other governments—prospective hosts for future inquiries—that accepting a visit could be more damaging than the adverse publicity of refusing to admit the mission.

Consequently, the commission eschewed handing down a "verdict" or presenting a concrete proposal. Instead, it made the following observations:

(1) Early ratification of Convention 87 was indispensable for further progress of the remaining subissues and for Japan's status within the ILO.

(2) The commission refrained from expressing its views on the bills, but noted that certain important points raised by the unions and the commission were taken into account.

(3) Efforts should first be concentrated on sections 4(3) and 5(3), which were directly related to the convention.

8. E. B. Haas, *Beyond the Nation State*, pp. 396–98, 579.

(4) Without specifying the degree of responsibility of either side, it suggested that initiative for change in the attitude of mutual mistrust must come from the highest level of government.

(5) The government should encourage regular exchanges of views between government representatives, employers, and labor on "matters of common concern."

(6) The Diet should be informed of progress made during these exchanges.

(7) The minister of labor and Sōhyō's secretary-general should meet with the commission's chairman and ILO's director general in June 1965 and inform them of the progress made.[9]

Most important to the major question—central negotiations of local employees—were points (4) and (5). As the subjects for the exchanges of views were not specified, they could have led to central negotiations with Nikkyōso through the "back door" without either side's losing face. Yet the government was free to interpret "exchange of views" as *excluding* negotiations.

DOMESTIC REACTIONS. The government indeed appreciated the commission's subtlety and hastened to announce its agreement with the observations. Sōhyō, on the other hand, expressed strong disappointment. Having been convinced that the government was about to ram the revised restrictive package through the Diet, Sōhyō's leaders were anxious to have the commission issue a concrete proposal favoring their position. Sōhyō's expectations for concrete proposals may have been generated in part by two factors: (1) the manner in which the commission conducted its hearings, as if it were a court of law; and (2) the translation of "fact-finding and conciliation" as *chōsa chōtei iinkai,* which in actual practice (although not by law) involves presenting a proposal to both of the concerned parties.[10] Sōhyō pressed the commission until its departure; when the union failed, it adopted the theme usually utilized by the government and the employers—the uniqueness of Japanese conditions. In Iwai's words, the commission's observations were based on "Western common sense rather than due con-

9. Dreyer Report, par. 2013.

10. A "Japanese observer of the proceeding," cited in A. Cook, "The ILO and Japanese Politics," p. 55. For an explanation of this aspect of conciliation in Japanese labor relations, see Kichiemon Ishikawa, "The Role of Government in Labor Relations in Japan," pp. 138–39.

sideration given to the very peculiar situation obtaining in the field of labor-management relations in Japan." [11]

The press welcomed the commission's observations. Prior to their announcement, the press was divided on the question of whether the commission was expected to issue a proposal. However, having been impressed by the commission's ability to understand the crux of the problem, the press was unanimous in accepting the observations as general guidelines. It therefore called upon both sides to follow these guidelines.[12]

The Japan Socialist party asserted that any legislative action had to be preceded by the establishment of mutual trust between the government and the unions. Following the commission's return to Geneva, the government offered to meet union representatives for an exchange of views, but rejected any interpretation of the commission's observations as justifying further delays in the deliberations on the latest version of the bills. The government, according to Labor Minister Ishida, accepted the "spirit" of the observations; but it was not prepared to engage in minute interpretations as if they were a legal, binding document.[13]

THE SPEAKER'S COMPROMISE. On April 15, 1965, when the government was about to ram the bills through the Diet, the opposition promptly paralyzed the proceedings. In the midst of the confusion, Funada Naka, speaker of the lower house, succeeded in persuading the three parties—the Liberal Democratic party (LDP), the Japan Socialist party (JSP), and the Democratic Socialist party (DSP)—to accept the following compromise:

(1) The bill ratifying Convention 87 and the bills amending the domestic laws would be put to a vote after sufficient deliberations in the Diet.

(2) The points still at issue in the bills amending the domestic laws concerned, which were presently awaiting further negotiations between the LDP and the opposition, would be shelved for a year and left to the consideration of the tripartite Advisory Council on the Public Personnel System.

(3) The provisions of the above-mentioned points at issue would be suspended from entering into force until the conclusions of

11. Dreyer Report, par. 2030.
12. *Asahi, Mainichi, Yomiuri,* and *Nihon Keizai,* January 27–29, 1965.
13. Rōdōshō, *Shiryō 87,* pp. 598–603.

the Advisory Council were reached, and such amendments would be made with due regard to these conclusions.[14]

The compromise was practically identical to the proposal that had been consistently advocated by Dōmei (and its predecessors, Dōmei Kaigi and Zenrō Kaigi) and the DSP. It was also in conformity with the "spirit" of the Dreyer Commission. Sōhyō was strongly opposed to the compromise; the JSP accepted the compromise because it considered it inevitable.[15] Both the LDP and the JSP must have been interested in restoring Diet deliberations because of the approaching upper house elections scheduled for July 1965. The JSP was anxious to avoid public criticism of its obstructionist tactics; the LDP was interested in "normalizing" the Diet in order to facilitate the passage of electorally important bills, such as the Farm Land Bill. This compensated 1,600,000 ex-landlords whose lands had been taken by the government (during the occupation-induced agrarian reform) in return for inadequate compensation.[16]

From that point onward, deliberations progressed smoothly in both houses. The package passed the lower house on April 21, and the upper house on May 17, 1965. A day after the ratification, on May 18, 1965, the first regular meeting was held between the government and Sōhyō, and on May 21, between the government and Dōmei. Following the second government-Sōhyō regular meeting on August 12, the road was finally cleared for periodic meetings between the education minister and the Japan Teachers' Union (Nikkyōso).[17]

THE COMMISSION'S FINAL REPORT. The final report to the Governing Body of the ILO was made public on August 15, 1966. It was a voluminous and meticulously perpared document in which the commission presented a lucid analysis of the "jungle" of Japanese labor legislation. This was set against the background of a brief survey of Japanese history, social relations, economic development, and politics, which had been sifted from selected publications available in English. The commission based its judgment on a careful synthesis of the ILO consensus and Japanese processes of

14. The translation largely follows the version in the Dreyer Report par. 2057.
15. Interview with Takaragi Fumihiko, Tokyo, August 25, 1965.
16. About the bill, see N. Ike, "Japan Twenty Years after Surrender," p. 20; H. Fukui, *Party in Power*, chap. 7.
17. *Nikkyōso Nijūnen Shi*, pp. 819, 1094–95.

conflict resolution. It offered detailed criticism of both government and union practices, and a list of recommendations for easing tensions. It also "ventured" to submit certain "observations, recommendations, and suggestions" to the Advisory Council on Public Personnel System concerning the pending questions. The commission emphasized again that a change of attitude was a key to future progress in this field. It also pointed out that although more recommendations were addressed to the government than to the unions, the findings and recommendations qualified each other and had to be read as a whole.

The report received an immediate response in Japan. On the day of its publication, all three parties—LDP, JSP, and DSP—issued public statements to the effect that the findings and recommendations represented a clear vindication of their respective positions. The JSP and Sōhyō played up the parts indicating that the government was subjected to more criticism than were the unions—particularly concerning unfair labor practices, excessive punishments of legal violations, and the absence of adequate compensation for the absolute prohibition of the right to strike (which had been imposed on workers in all public undertakings, irrespective of the degree of their indispensability to the public welfare).[18] Chief Cabinet Secretary Hashimoto Tomisaburo and LDP Secretary Tananka Kukuei emphasized the parts criticizing the unions for excessive engagement in politics (such as their opposition to negotiations with the ROK and to the berthing of nuclear submarines in Japanese ports, and their demands for American withdrawal from Vietnam), and the part asserting that subversion was not a trade union right. The Democratic Socialist party (DSP) and Dōmei, having consistently advocated union rights while opposing political strikes, found the criticism leveled at their two rival camps very agreeable.[19]

The press welcomed the report wholeheartedly. Japanese conditions, it was admitted, were properly stated, and the recommendations were fair (although they could have been more flexible). Yet, while arguing that the spirit of the recommendations should be respected, the press deemed them insufficient by themselves to solve the key question: What is the most adequate method for

18. For statements, see Rōdōshō, *Shiryō 87*, pp. 916–17.
19. *Asahi*, September 3, 1965. *Dōmei News* 1, no. 20; 1–2.

modernizing Japanese labor-management relations to keep them in step with Japan's industrialization? This, said the *Asahi*, was a problem that should and could be solved domestically—by the soon-to-be-established Advisory Council, one could hope.

High regard for the commission's findings was shared by union leaders, politicians, bureaucrats, staff workers of the LDP's Policy Affairs Research Council (Seichōkai), and labor scholars. Only a few added that their evaluation was not absolute, but was predicated rather on the assumption that, being foreign experts, the commission members could not be expected to fully understand the complexities of the issue. This near unanimity of praise may have been a result of sheer politeness, or of sympathy for sincere efforts. But this possibility can be discarded, since criticism of the recommendations was offered freely. Nikkeiren officials and LDP members argued that the recommendations went too far and interfered in internal Japanese politics; this position was admittedly accentuated by their frustrated hopes that the commission would find Japanese unions still "immature," and hence unqualified for the freedoms shared by unions in Western industrialized countries. Union and JSP leaders criticized the commission for being too timid and restrained, but their perceptions of what prompted the restraint varied; the Japan Railways Workers' Union (Kokurō) still clung to the pre–1958 belief that the ILO's weaknesses were inherent in its *tripartite* composition, whereas the others recognized that attempts by any *international* organization to impose its authority on a national government might backfire.

Union leaders, newspaper reporters, editorial writers, and labor scholars considered the most significant recommendation to be the one concerning the right to strike. In the absence of the ILO convention, recommendation, or decision defining the extent of the right to strike in public services, the commission based its recommendation on a series of principles formulated by the Governing Body "which has won general acceptance." These were (1) the need to distinguish, as part of the legal prohibition of the right to strike, between public undertakings "that are genuinely essential because their interruption may cause serious public hardship, and those which are not essential according to this criterion"; (2) the need for compensatory safeguards; and (3) the need for authoritative machinery for implementing these safeguards.[20] While refraining from dealing with the right to strike, the commission nonetheless recommended that a line of demarcation be established between the two types of public undertakings—provided that the unions could reciprocate with a "radical change in attitude and a far greater sense of social restraint and social responsibility." [21] The tobacco monopoly was singled out as an example of a possible nonessential undertaking. Government officials, however, were unofficially reported as having no intention of complying with this recommendation.[22] Moreover, the proceedings of the seventeen meetings of the Advisory Council on the Public Personnel System indicated that it had no intention of following the commission's recommendations concerning the unresolved provisions of the bills, either.

20. Dreyer Report, par. 2139.
21. Ibid., par. 2140–41.
22. *Asahi*, September 1, 1965.

9

The Advisory Council on the Public Personnel System

The utilization of advisory councils in the process of public policy formation became a common practice of Japanese governments in the postwar era. In 1963 one hundred forty councils were deliberating issues that concerned the various ministries.[1] These councils were appointed by and reported to the premier or one of the cabinet ministers. Ostensibly, they were called upon to form a knowledgeable opinion based on a thorough investigation that was shielded, as much as possible, from the disturbing limelight of partisan public scrutiny. Their membership included public figures noted for their expertise in the particular field of public concern, such as constitutional lawyers or professors of public administration.

Advisory councils in other countries (especially in North America and Europe) tend to perform several latent functions. They offer a semblance of representation to the groups affected by the policy being considered, thus lending legitimacy to the policy and the regime. They provide a convenient setting for bargaining among contending groups. They also serve as a delaying device in an intense conflict situation, or as an excuse for government inaction in the face of the opposition's demand for action.[2] In Japan, although advisory councils have often been criticized as smoke screens for the conservative government's policies in the service of

1. C. Yanaga, *Big Business in Japanese Politics*, pp. 73–74.
2. See, for example, H. C. Mansfield, "Government Commissions"; Lyle E. Schaller, "Is the Citizen Advisory Committee a Threat to Representative Government?"; J. C. Courtney, "In Defense of Royal Commissions"; B. C. Smith, *Advising Ministers*, pp. 11–12.

the business community,[3] little systematic study has been made of the composition, operation, and functions of the various councils.[4]

The following examination of the establishment and operation of the Advisory Council on the Public Personnel System in the process of labor legislation should serve to illustrate the overt and latent functions of a Japanese advisory body.

First, it perfomed a representational function; among its members were representatives of the contending labor and management interests, as well as representatives of the general public. Specifically, it included six employers' representatives, six labor representatives, and eight persons of "learning and experience" (*gakushiki keikensha*) representing the public interest. The employers were high officials of national and local administrations and public corporations; labor was represented by five Sōhyō leaders and one Dōmei leader. The public interest members included the president of a semipublic corporation in the field of mass communication, who was the council's chairman; the managing director of a mutual aid society of public personnel, who was vice-chairman; five university professors; and one political analyst.[5]

Second, it served as a council of experts. Not only were the representatives of the contending sides knowledgeable about labor problems, half of the public interest members also fell into that category.

Third, it served as an instrument for bargaining as much as for the collection and examination for expert knowledge. The politicized nature of the council was brought into sharp relief early in the process—at the stage when the eight public interest members were appointed—and prevailed throughout. The appointive authority was invested in Ken Yasui, Director of Administrative

3. C. Yanaga, *Big Business.*
4. For a thorough study of one council, see R. E. Ward, "The Commission on the Constitution."
5. Employers' representatives: Murakami Kōtarō, chief secretary of the Finance Ministry; Furuhata Tokuya, head of the National Mayors Association; Takeuchi Juhei, administrative vice-minister of Justice; Tanaka Yoshio, chairman of the National Council of Prefectural Boards of Education; Soyama Katsumi, head of the Bureau of Personnel of the Postal Ministry; and Abiko Yutaka, former vice-president of the Japan National Railways. Union representatives: Iwai Akira Sōhyō secretary-general; Ayōji Toshichika, Jichirō secretary-general; Takaragi Fumihiko, president of Zentei and chairman of Stōken Iinkai; Makieda Motofumi, Nikkyōso secretary-general; Watarai Sunyo, Zennōrin (Ministry of Agriculture Workers) chairman; and Sugawara Eietsu, Dōmei vice-president. Among the Sōhyō members, nationals in all types of public employment were represented.

Affairs of the Office of the Prime Minister. In the spirit of the Dreyer Report, Ken did not make the appointments at his own discretion; rather, he *negotiated* the matter with Iwai, Haraguchi, and Takaragi, the Sōhyō leaders most prominently involved in the ILO Convention 87 controversy. Simultaneously, he continually consulted officials in the Ministry of Labor and leaders of the Liberal Democratic party. (The Japan Socialist party did not play any role at that stage, since the unions were doing their own bargaining.)

Both sides attempted to assure that a majority of the eight public figures would identify with their respective points of view. Sōhyō initially insisted on the appointment of three labor scholars who had consistently taken Sōhyō's position, had served as its legal advisers, and had refused in the past to cooperate with the government in any capacity.[6] When these were emphatically ruled out, Sōhyō demanded the inclusion of three other labor scholars who, although not consistently identified with Sōhyō, had won the reputation of being sympathetic to the unions and inoffensive to the government. The process ended in a compromise: of the eight public interest members appointed, two were considered pro-Sōhyō, two pro-LDP, and four, including the chairman, neutral. Of the four neutral members, two were expected, on the basis of their former or current professional positions, to be more "neutral" than others (i.e., less readily subject to government pressure).

Fourth, the council demonstrated the two sides' conflicting concepts of what its function should be. The government wanted the council to facilitate a smooth approval of the shelved provisions. The unions, though, conceived of the council as a tool for postponing their enforcement ad infinitum. Therefore, the labor leaders not only bargained hard for the appointment of labor-oriented persons as public interest members; they also complicated matters by making their own participation conditional on the satisfactory solution of several current issues. These included the government's reluctance to comply with a National Personnel Authority recommendation favorable to labor; Sōhyō's insistence on firm assurances for regular meetings between the minister of

6. They were Professors Nōmura Heiji, Matsuoka Saburo, and Nakayama Kazuhisa. Except for the latter on one occasion, they did not participate even in the functions of the scholarly Japan Institute of Labor, a semigovernmental body. See Nihon Rōdō Kyōkai, *Nihon Rōdō Kyōkai Jigyō Nenji Kōkoku,* 1966.

education and the Japan Teachers' Union (Nikkyōso); and the severity of punishment for union members' participation in acts of dispute.

Despite the union leaders' suspicions of government motives, however, they shared the generally optimistic view prevailing among scholars, reporters, and political analysts regarding the prospects for the council's success. Hence, when they were finally confronted (after more than six months of negotiations) with Ken's threat to launch the council without Sōhyō's cooperation, the labor representatives dropped their various demands and gave their consent to the council's composition.

As the council's deliberations got under way on November 1, 1965, it soon became evident that the "spirit of the Dreyer Report" had all but faded. By then, the "high posture" (*kōshisei*) factions of the Liberal Democratic party, which advocated a tough approach in dealing with labor, had a firm grasp of the ruling party. Moreover, the Sato cabinet had strongly antagonized Sōhyō early in November 1965 by forcing through the ratification of the treaty "normalizing" Japan's relations with the Republic of Korea. Sōhyō considered this a step toward an American-dominated Northeast Asian Treaty Organization patterned after SEATO. These events were reflected in the uncompromising positions taken by the labor and management representatives on the council.[7]

The eight public interest members, therefore, became more concerned with reconciling the fixed attitudes of the antagonists than with a thorough examination of the complexities of Japanese labor relations. In order to create a congenial atmosphere, the chairman reached an informal understanding with both sides concerning voting procedures. Although the council was authorized to make decisions by majority vote, it was agreed that no vote would be taken in the absence of one of the groups—thus respecting the Japanese traditional preference for decision making based on consensus. Moreover, in response to a request by a public in-

7. My information on the deliberations is based on the following sources: *Kōmuin Seido Shingikai Gijiroku*, confidential minutes of the proceedings, hereinafter cited as *KSSKG*; newspaper reports; and interviews with three public interest members, three union representatives, a staff member of Sōhyō's Committee for the Recovery of the Right to Strike, a staff worker in the headquarters of a national union affiliated with Sōhyō, having direct interest in the council's recommendations, a member of the executive committee of Jichirō, and an official in the Labor Policy Bureau of the Ministry of Labor.

terest member, the council formally decided to conduct the proceedings in secret.

The process of conciliation was very intensive. The council
members interacted both formally and informally. Formally, deliberations took place in seventeen plenary sessions and in meetings of a steering committee composed of the chairman, the vice-
chairman, a government representative, and a union representative. Informally, negotiations were conducted in conferences of the
public interest members; between union members and single members of the public interest; between union members and government bureaucrats who were not council members; between employers' representatives and public interest members; and between
the union representatives and the management representatives.

Despite the formal secrecy, the mass media (especially the daily
press) played an important role in the process. It faithfully reported the content of the briefing sessions held periodically by the
council chairman, himself a prominent figure in the mass media.
Moreover, reporters and editors diligently tried to piece together
the jigsaw puzzle of shifting combinations of interactions among
and with council members. Reporters regularly assigned to labor
unions and to government agencies represented on the council
utilized their well-cultivated personal relationships with council
members. Others drew on their friendships with the public interest
members. Indeed, the unified picture of the process that the mass
media presented to the general public also assisted the council
members in orienting themselves to new developments in the conciliation process.

Members of the mass media also functioned as a closed-circuit
channel of unpublished information originating with or used by
council members. The personal relationships that developed over
a period of time between reporters and the persons they covered
facilitated a discreet two-way flow of information. Part of the information related informally to the reporters was off the record.
However, although confidential information was not published, it
was passed on to the reporter's editor or colleagues. Since the personalized relationship called for reciprocity, reporters passed back
information picked up confidentially by their colleagues.

On the occassion of the council's inauguration, the prime minister had requested it to perform two tasks: (1) to form an opinion

on matters related to the foundations of labor relations in the public sector, and (2) to report "without delay" on the desirability of enforcing the shelved provisions of the ILO-related laws.[8] But efforts at conciliation were seriously hampered by the deadline of June 14, 1966, for the enforcement of the shelved provisions, which had been set by the Speaker's Compromise of June 15, 1965.

The unions interpreted the council's frame of reference set by the prime minister as necessitating a thorough examination of the complexity of labor relations in the public sector. They urged the council to follow the pattern of the Labor Relations Law Research Committee (Rōshi Kankei Hō Kenkyūkai), a group of twelve lawyers and university professors under the chairmanship of Professor Ishii Teruhisa of Tokyo University. At the request of the Ministry of Labor, this group had been engaged since 1959 in studying the problems of the application of the trade union laws in the private sector.[9] Thus, argued the unions, it was inconceivable that the council could form a sound judgment by June 14.

As a matter of fact, by the thirteenth session on May 11, only two questions had been discussed systematically. These were the composition of employees' associations—centering particularly on problems related to the shelved provisions—and the right of public employees to engage in acts of dispute. From then on, the question whether the June deadline had to be met constantly haunted most of the deliberations in the plenary sessions. The management representatives argued that it was tacitly agreed in the Speaker's Compromise that if the council failed to reach a conclusion, the shelved provisions would be enforced.[10] The union representatives countered that since Diet records did not evidence such an agreement it had no validity.[11]

The government took two measures simultaneously. It tried to divide labor's ranks by placating Dōmei, and it exerted strong pressure on the public interest members to reach a decision by

8. For the prime minister's message to the council, see Rōdōshō, *Shiryō 87*, p. 730.
9. *KSSKG* 1: 136. For the group's report to the minister of labor, see *Rōshi Kankei Hō Kenkyū Kai, Hōkokusho: Rōshi Kankei Unyō no Jitsujō oyobi Mondaiten.* For observations on and criticism of the report, see Ishii Teruhisa, et al., eds. "Rōshi Kankei Hō to Nihon no Rōdō Undō."
10. This fact was clearly recorded in the Dreyer Report, par. 2058. At the time the report was published, neither the unions nor the JSP disputed its authenticity on this point.
11. *KSSKG* 1: 854 ff., 917-20.

June 14 which would legitimize the enforcement of the shelved provisions. As was indicated above, an informal understanding called for decisions based on consensus rather than on majority vote. A semblance of consensus could be created if Dōmei could be persuaded to vote on certain provisions with the management and public interest representatives. Therefore Dōmei was offered concessions in connection with the proposed elimination of the full-time union officer system, in exchange for its support of other provisions. Since Dōmei's affiliates, among which were many small organizations, were more vulnerable to this provision than to the others, it was an attractive offer. Yet Dōmei considered the concessions insufficient and joined Sōhyō in its opposition to the June deadline.

As the deadline drew nearer, government pressures on the public interest members intensified. Their effect was clearly reflected in the chairman's insistence, on the basis of statistics produced at his request by the Office of the Prime Minister, that in contradiction of Labor's arguments, the council had sufficiently considered *all* of the problems relevant to the shelved provisions.[12] This, however, was not the case.

The labor representatives' suspicions of government pressures drastically diminished the element of trust that had initially prevailed between them and the public interest members. Nevertheless, the chairman persuaded them at the last moment to soften their position and agree to a compromise. Under the compromise, two provisions would be recommended for enforcement in June, and the enforcement of the remaining provisions would be postponed for further consideration. However, the government representatives did not reciprocate. All that the chairman could extract from them was an agreement to postpone the enforcement of the restrictions of the full-time union officer system until December 1966. The unions were opposed to such a compromise, and the prospects for a consensus evaporated.

The unions, including the Dōmei representative, decided to boycott the last session (in which the recommendation to enforce all provisions but one was to be adopted); they hoped that their ab-

12. Ibid., pp. 879–80, 890. The statistics concerned the number of times the various problems were touched on while discussing the composition of the employees associations and the right to strike.

sence would prevent the council from taking a vote. However, the chairman decided to adopt the recommendation by a majority vote irrespective of whether the union representatives were present. On June 13 at 3:35 A.M. the recommendation was adopted by the employers and the public interest members. A number of the latter acted in deference to the chairman's request for unanimity, though with great misgivings. The council put a six-month moratorium on the provision concerning the full-time union officer system, and added a number of riders calling for flexibility in application.

During the last stage of the negotiations the JSP and the DSP attempted to influence the outcome by threatening to paralyze the Diet—but the cabinet enforced the provisions just the same. The unions continued their boycott of the council, and the last provision also became law when the six-month moratorium expired in December 1966. It was agreed, however, to leave a grace period of two years before the enforcement of the new regulations concerning the full-time union officer system.

The Speaker's Compromise facilitated the ratification of ILO Convention 87 and the elimination of those legal restrictions on union rights directly related to the convention. Thus, it deprived Japanese labor of a symbolic rallying point and removed a major source of foreign criticism of Japanese domestic legislation. The formation and deliberations of the Advisory Council provided by the compromise had been a domestic affair, with the ILO playing a very insignificant role. The Dreyer Commission report had presented a series of specific recommendations for the consideration of the Advisory Council. The management representatives on the council, however, interpreted the commission's initiative as interference in Japan's internal affairs and preferred to ignore its recommendations. Although the recommendations had been more favorable to the unions than to the government, even the union representatives refrained from pressing their examination by the council. Judging the government's position and the public mood, Sōhyō leaders concluded that an insistence on having outsiders' recommendations followed to the letter would undoubtedly backfire.[13] Only during the council's fourteenth session on May 19, 1966, when breaking the deadline of June 14 became labor's major concern, did one of the Sōhyō representatives demand that the

13. Interview with Haraguchi Yukitaka, Tokyo, August 27, 1967.

recommendations be considered thoroughly,[14] but to no avail.

The Advisory Council, though representative in its composition, was not a successful instrument either for fact finding or for serious bargaining. Hence, it did not secure the legitimacy of government policies in the eyes of labor leadership. It did serve, however, to delay a confrontation between the government and its opposition and to reduce the intensity of the confrontation once it came about, thus making it more manageable for the government.

For awhile it appeared that the Advisory Council would be discontinued in view of union bitterness toward the government and the public interest members. The chairman and several other public interest members let it be known that they wished to resign from the council. Yet, after two years and four months of dormancy, the council was revived at the request of both Sōhyō and Dōmei! The grace period regarding the full-time union officer system was about to expire, and the unions considered it tactically advisable to utilize the council for a reconsideration of the issue. It opened on October 25, 1968, with the understanding that the first priority would be accorded to this issue. By the second meeting, however, both the Local Autonomy Agency and the National Personnel Authority had issued new regulations concerning full-time union officers in the national and local public service, thereby making further extension of the grace period impossible.

The unions chose to continue their participation in the council with an understanding that the new regulations would be taken up during the review of all labor legislation that had come into effect with and after the ratification of ILO Convention 87.[15] In order to strengthen the demand for relaxation of restrictions on union activities, including the right to strike, Sōhyō surveyed the labor legislation of twelve European democracies; in all twelve it found that the right to strike was guaranteed to government workers and that administrative penalties were almost nonexistent.[16]

14. *KSSKG* 2: 928. The representative was M. Makieda, Nikkyōso's secretary-general, who, among Sōhyō's leaders, had been one of the most pessimistic about the capacity of the ILO to interfere on behalf of Japanese unions.

15. *Mainichi Nenkan*, 1969, p. 152; *Japan Labor Bulletin* 8, no. 1 (January 1969): 4.

16. *Asahi Shimbun*, February 12, 1969. The countries were England, France, West Germany, Italy, Belgium, the Netherlands, Denmark, Switzerland, Sweden, Norway, and Finland.

In one sense, the Second Advisory Council on the Public Personnel System was more productive than its predecessor. It spent less time on procedural questions and more time on the various aspects of labor relations in the public sector. The second council took up more subjects and discussed each of them more thoroughly than had the first council. It also dispatched a fact-finding mission to Europe and the United States for a comparative study of labor legislation and practices in industrial countries. Yet it, too, ended in failure; the discussions, although more thorough, had not effected any change in the position of either labor or management, while the public interest members decided to maintain their neutrality, and refrained from reaching any conclusions. On October 17, 1970, the council submitted its final report to the prime minister; it simply presented the conflicting positions of the two sides without taking any unified stand.[17]

A Third Advisory Council on the Public Personnel System was convened in 1971. By October 1971 it had met twice, and the full-time union officer system was again being discussed.[18]

17. Kōmuin Seido Shingikai, *Kōmuin Tō no Rōdō Kankei no Kihon Nikansuru Jikō Nitsuite;* for the council's interim report, see *ILO Kankei Hōritsu Jū Kokkai Shūsei Niyori Shikō O Enki Sareta Kitei Nitsuite (Tōshin)*.
18. *Japan Labor Bulletin* 10, no. 12 (December 1971): 4.

10
Summary and Conclusions

Freedom of association in the public sector was the only political issue in which an international organization responded positively to an appeal by Japanese nongovernmental group for action against the Japanese government.

The fact that the issue-area of labor relations manifested extensive domestic-international political linkages marked a historical continuity. Prior to 1957 the evolution of these linkages had taken several forms: *importation* and *Japanization, socialization, internationalization, attempted imposition, benign transplantation,* and *passive cooperation.*

In the pre-ILO era, Japanese social reformers *imported* into Japan social theories, ideologies, and organizational principles prevailing in the international issue-area of labor policy. Some, such as Marxism, anarchism, and militant trade unionism, with emphasis on conflict and confrontation, were imported unchanged by disaffected elements and failed to take root in Japan. Others, such as an official policy of social welfare, were imported by progressive members of the ruling elite and were given a Japanese cast exemplified in the Harmonization Society (Kyōchōkai). Finally, moderate union leaders imported the principles of democratic unionism and *Japanized* it, by emphasizing cooperation and harmony with management, rather than conflict.

The ILO was founded on the principle of promoting pluralism in member countries and facilitating a bargaining process within that framework. Initially, however, the organization did not succeed in helping Japanese labor unions attain unfettered participation in the policy-making process of their country. The Japanese government had joined the ILO because of its symbolic value—

the prestigious status of a major power in the post-World War I international system—rather than because of the organization's ideology and anticipated programs. Labor was excluded from the highly centralized regime of the rapidly industrializing country; labor policy was dominated by the drive for efficiency and continuity in production, and was concerned more with regulation than with protection. Yet several Japanese individuals—members of the ILO secretariat, scholars, and workers; employers' and even government representatives to the ILO—underwent a process of *socialization* through their association with the organization; gradually, they internalized selective aspects of its ideology and acquired expertise in protective labor legislation. The socialization of one segment of Japan's union leaders into the ILO system precipitated their attempt to promote freedom of association in Japan —by their initiation of and participation in joint moves to promote freedom of association in all member countries.

The socialization of Japanese union leaders was facilitated by the successful *internationalization* of an issue: the selection of the Japanese workers' representative to the early International Labor Conferences. However, in the early 1930s the attempt to *impose* a restrictive trade policy on Japan by domesticating the international issue of "social dumping" failed in the face of a nationalistic labor-management "united front."

The American occupation was probably the most intensive and most complex political linkage in Japanese history. The initial paralysis of management and conservative politicians; the wartime state-induced and state-controlled union organizational experience; and the familiarity of several Japanese individuals with labor policies abroad—all enabled zealous SCAP officials to preside over the *transplantation* of the American and west European systems of labor law into Japan.

The new, extremely liberal labor law system generated new perceptions and new practices on the part of union leaders; SCAP considered these to be inimical to the Japanese political system itself. SCAP decided to avert this eventuality by legally fragmenting the labor movement and prohibiting those union activities that could assume subversive proportions. Against such a background of past repressions and subsequent unfettered freedom, the new restrictions deeply affected the political attitudes of unions.

They further politicized the segment most affected—the unions in the public sector—and gave rise to a new demand which surfaced as a political issue in 1957.

In addition to legal fragmentation, other factors retarded the political efficacy of the labor movement in Japan. The centralization of authoritative decision making in the national centers (or even in the national unions) was hampered by the group-centered social interaction characteristic of Japanese society; the paternalistic labor-management relations in many undertakings, reinforced by modern personnel management techniques; the lifetime commitment system; and the absence of a labor market. The major union federations were plagued by organizational instability. Their leaders were aligned with the ineffective opposition parties of the Left. Public opinion was either indifferent or hostile to union demands. The courts were disinclined to exercise their authority of judicial review to support the unions on constitutional grounds.

Two early attempts to internationalize the demands of Japanese unions failed for several reasons. First, the unions and their mentors at the leftist WFTU made a tactical error in defining their demands in terms of the right to strike rather than in terms of freedom of association; while freedom of association had evolved as a basic right within the framework of the ILO, there was much less consensus within the organization about the right to strike. Second, at that time the ILO imposed strict conditions for accepting complaints against member governments. By the time the Committee on Freedom of Association reviewed the first Japanese complaint, the situation that had given rise to the complaint (i.e., the occupation) had ceased to exist; in the case of the second complaint, the ILO responded by selectively discriminating against Japanese unions on technicalities stemming from the unions' lack of expertise in ILO programs and procedures. Third, most instrumental in the ILO's unresponsiveness was the cool attitude of the ICFTU—the major pressure group within the ILO—due to cold war politics.

The ILO's unresponsiveness resulted in *passive cooperation* by Japanese unions, as well as by employers and government officials —the first because of disillusionment, and the latter two because of defensive indifference.

There were two additional reasons why demands for change in labor policy subsided until 1957. First, managements and unions, especially at the level of the undertaking, were able to make informal adjustments. These accommodations, such as the "full-time union officer system" (*zaiseki senjū*), blunted the sharpness of the legal restrictions. Second, although the restrictions were initially harmful to Sōhyō, since they deposed many of its top officers, at the same time they cleared the way for the new leadership of the Ota-Iwai line. In fact, Sōhyō's leadership of the 1950s *owed* its dominance to the legal restrictions, which eliminated many of its rivals. Only when the position of strategically placed Sōhyō leaders was threatened did Sōhyō finally launch its offensive to eliminate the restrictions.

By 1957 several factors had conditioned Sōhyō's disposition to respond the way it did to the threat to its leaders. First, there had been organizational and policy changes within Sōhyō. Its organization and leadership had stabilized; the number of Sōhyō affiliates in the public sector had increased; Sōhyō had made progress toward multiunion joint economic struggles—the Spring Offensive (Shuntō)—an attempt to go beyond the practice of autonomous settlements in insulated private undertakings and government organizations; concomitantly, it had deemphasized its revolutionary ideology and opted for gradual, legislative struggles against the conservative government. Second, there had been changes in the party system. The strength of the Japan Socialist party, through the financial and organizational support of Sōhyō, had increased; yet the prospects for an immediate socialist access to power had withered away, and the necessity for the unions to engage in pressure politics in both the socialist and the conservative parties had become evident. Third, during the 1957 Spring Offensive public opinion had become overwhelmingly hostile toward the unions because of the major disruptions in public services; these paved the way for an increase in government reprisals. When challenged, Sōhyō was prepared for a political struggle, both organizationally and ideologically. Having been excluded from power, and unable to gain favorable public opinion for its struggle, Sōhyō was forced to appeal to the ILO in order to legitimize its demand within the Japanese political system.

Why did the ILO respond favorably in 1957, instead of dismissing the case as in the past? First, Sōhyō's definition of the issue had changed from the right to strike to that of freedom of association, which was much more congruent with the ILO ideology. Second, the ILO, for reasons unrelated to the Japanese case, had become generally more accessible to complaints against member governments. Third, the ICFTU offered Sōhyō and its affiliates vigorous support and technical expertise. On one hand, the ICFTU hoped to avoid a further drift of the bulk of Sōhyō's leadership away from the ICFTU; on the other hand, since some of the leaders directly threatened by the restrictions were closely associated with the ICFTU despite the general drift, the latter was strongly motivated to come to their rescue.

What were unions' expectations of the ILO? The ILO's quick response to the unions' appeal dissipated whatever doubts many of their leaders harbored concerning the organization's responsiveness. Yet they still varied in their expectations concerning its possible effectiveness. These ranged from grave doubts, at one extreme, to the conviction that the ILO would act as an international tribunal with the authority to compel the Japanese government to modify its domestic policies.

Japanese union leaders not only *had* to internationalize their demand; they also perceived good prospects for a favorable domestic response to international pressures. First, they were aware of the fact that high officials in the Ministry of Labor had recognized the disparity between some of the Japanese restrictions and the legal provisions prevailing in other industrial countries. Second, Japanese influentials and the attentive public had become increasingly sensitive to international criticism because of their deepening desire to augment Japan's role in international affairs (primarily in international trade) and to heighten Japan's prestige abroad. The unions intended to activate a collective sense of shame and to emphasize the restrictions imposed on Japanese trade by some members of GATT because of Japanese labor policy.

The Japanese government indeed offered to cooperate with the ILO on Case 179. Its initial positive response was a result of its narrow interpretation of the scope of the issue, and its consequent leaving of authority to the Ministry of Labor to formulate its position on the issue. The government interpreted the issue as relating to the ratification of Convention 87 and the elimination of employee status as a condition for union membership. By this time, the Ministry of Labor was convinced of the desirability of acting positively on these two components of the issue. The government recognized the ILO *legitimacy* in the case because it did not consider the issue to be strategic (one involving the possible transformation of the general pattern of labor relations in the public sector) and because it did not consider cooperation on the issue to be equivalent to subjection to the ILO's *authority*.

Why did Case 179 (Japan) take so long to resolve? At the international level, two factors were important. First, while the ILO was tending to be more liberal in accepting for review complaints against member governments, this was offset by its tendency to increase the thoroughness of the procedure for collecting evidence. ILO committees and the International Labor Office were bent on postponing offensive decisions as long as formal and informal bargaining (both in Japan and in Geneva) held some promise of success. Once the Japanese government had decided to ratify Convention 87, the ILO refrained from offending it until repeated efforts to solve the issue domestically had failed. Even then the pressures were intensified only gradually, culminating in the visit to Japan of the Fact-Finding and Conciliation Commission.

The second delaying factor was the attitude of the United States, the most influential external factor in Japanese foreign and domestic policies. Because of the United States' own experience with the ILO's involvement in the issue of freedom of association of its own unions, it refrained from pressuring the Japanese government on the issue.

At the domestic level of Japanese politics, several factors contributed to the prolongation of the issue. One was the early transformation of the unidimensional issue focused on the conditions for union membership into a complex issue involving several subissues: the right of public employees to strike and bargain collectively; the full-time union officer system; union membership of managerial personnel; registration of unions; the right of Japan Teachers' Union to conduct talks with the Ministry of Education; and the various ramifications of the legal fragmentation of the union movement. Although the complexity of the issue drew additional unions into conflict, the subissues affected each union differently; this disrupted their unity and thus reduced their effectiveness vis-à-vis the government.

The issue's multidimensionality reflected the high degree of integration within the issue-area of labor legislation. Moreover, it reflected the strong linkage between labor legislation and several other issue-areas of the Japanese political system—primarily those of education and internal security.

The basic question linking these issue-areas was to what extent Japanese unions should be allowed to participate in the process of postwar Japanese democracy. This question was a divisive factor, not only between the government party and the leftist opposition, but also within the ranks of the ruling Liberal Democratic party and its ally, the bureaucracy. There was a wide gap between those taking a restrictive position and those taking a more permissive one. Each side was strongly committed to its own position to such an extent that it reacted disproportionally to the other's moves. Union demands for the elimination of the restrictive membership condition elicited the counterdemands for the abolition of the full-time union officer, heavier penalities for legal violations by union members, and other restrictions of union rights. Similarly, the Fujibayashi Compromise in the Zentei dispute precipitated a sharp increase in union demands, such as for the restoration of the right to strike.

The unions won the first skirmish, but as the conflict spread, the unions realized that they could not possibly end it in victory. The longer it lasted and the more the ILO became involved, though, the better would be the terms the unions hoped to get. The LDP, on the other hand, was prevented by its intraparty divisions from ending the conflict rapidly and conclusively.

A second domestic factor prolonging the issue was the position of the Japan Socialist party. Although Case 179 was a major issue for Sōhyō and the concerned unions, for the JSP it was but a minor part of the "conservative-progressive" confrontation, and one that could be traded for concessions on other, more important issues. General elections, rather than sharpening the differences between the government party and the opposition and bringing the issue into the limelight, actually postponed interparty activities on the issue. It was within the ranks of the ruling Liberal Democratic party that policy disagreements became a major issue. This division within the LDP held the only significant promise for a policy change favorable to the unions, although it was also significant in delaying the solution of the issue.

Another delaying factor was the difference in the way the Japanese participants saw the salience of the international aspect. The participants could be classified into three categories: (1) those concerned with the solution of the issue in accordance with the principles of the ILO; (2) those determined to end the issue independently of the ILO; and (3) those seeking any kind of solution that would have rapidly eliminated the justification (which they recognized) for ILO's involvement in Japanese politics.

The first category, which included Sōhyō, the Japan Socialist party, the premier, and Kuraishi and his group in the LDP and in the Labor Ministry, considered the issue to be both domestic and international. The second, which included the education-internal security group and their allies, considered the issue to be purely domestic. The third, which included Foreign Ministry officials and, to a lesser extent, the Democratic Socialist party and Dōmei, saw it primarily as a foreign policy issue. Those differences in perception of the issue resulted in the consideration of different objectives as possible solutions—and, hence, in different strategies and different propensities to compromise.

The intensification of ILO pressures became significant, not so much in affecting the solution of the various subissues of Case 179 as in finally pressuring the participants to terminate the internationalization of the issue. As a result, it was restored to a temporary state of dormancy. The pressures were least effective when they focused on freedom of association as a basic human right; they were most effective when their scope was broadened to include such freedom as a component in the international image of Japan's foreign trade.

The findings of this case study are congruent with the findings of other recent studies of the dominant role of the Liberal Democratic party in the policy-making process.[1] In the case of the Soviet-Japanese negotiations in 1956, Hellmann found that "this process functioned virtually free from all other major elements in Japanese politics."[2] Fukui and Thayer found strong interdependence and mutual influence between the LDP and its allies—the bureaucracy and the business community. A study by Yanaga illus-

---

1. Hellmann, *Japanese Foreign Policy and Domestic Politics;* Thayer, *How the Conservatives Rule Japan;* Fukui, *Party in Power.*
2. P. 149.

trated the overwhelming role played by the business community in LDP policy making.[3] All agreed on the elitist nature of the process and on the insignificant role played by public opinion despite the fact that in the postwar era public opinion surveys were frequently conducted on various issues (including the ones studied by Hellmann, Fukui, and Yanaga) by the press, government agencies, and private and semipublic polling organizations.

On the issue of Case 179, the government purported to act in the public interest; the unions and the leftist party claimed that public sympathy was with their cause; the press presented its view as public opinion; and people of learning and experience joined advisory commissions as representatives of the public interest. Yet no one conducted a survey to find out the public's opinion on its interest in this case. In the eyes of the participants, the issue was too complex and too technical to merit the involvement of public opinion; it was too remote from the salient issues directly affecting the people's livelihood to stimulate the public to formulate an opinion and make it known to the decision makers.

While the central and crucial position of the LDP was manifest in the policy-making process in this case, the process also involved the active participation of various other elements in Japanese politics. These elements were not only the traditional allies of the LDP—the bureaucracy, business, and other conservative groups—but also opposition elements, such as union leaders and socialist politicians; and neutrals, such as university professors and press commentators. Debate on the issue among these elements took several forms: formal debate in plenary sessions of the Diet and in its committees, and within the institutions of the ILO; formal debate and informal negotiations in advisory commissions; semiformal negotiations between ad hoc committees of the LDP, the JSP, and Sōhyō and between the secretaries-general of the LDP and JSP; and informal talks between union leaders and several LDP Diet members either directly or through the good offices of a conciliator. The opposition elements and the neutrals were as significant in defining the issue and subissues, and in making detailed proposals for their solutions, as were the LDP members and their traditional allies, although the final decisions were made within the "closed circuit," in Fukui's words, of the parliamentary LDP.

3. Yanaga, *Big Business in Japanese Politics.*

The access of Japanese unions to policy making evolved from an early phase of no access until the end of World War II, through representation by socialist parties which dominated the unions until the middle of the 1950s, through representation by socialist parties largely dominated by the unions until the end of the 1950s, to direct access to government and conservative leaders, as well as representation by socialist party leaders and nonparty "men of learning and experience."

The central position of the LDP in the policy-making process and the ubiquity of factions within the LDP stimulated efforts to describe and explain the relationship between factionalism and policy making within the party. All observers agreed that policy differences were not a significant motive for the formation of factions and for belonging to them. Rather, factions served their members' organizational needs (various forms of support for getting elected to the Diet and for gaining leadership positions within the government and the party) and their psychological needs (to belong to a relatively small and intimate group).[4] Still different studies reached different conclusions with regard to the relationship between factions and policy positions. Hellmann found that factions were identified with particular policy positions; however, at crucial points in the decision-making process, inter-factional competition for party leadership overrode the substance of the issue, and policy positions were changed suddenly when the change was necessary for advancing the position of the faction in that competition.[5] Thayer found that members of a particular faction tended to be in one policy group more than in another, but that the policy groups were "supra-factional," cutting across factions rather than forming along factional lines.[6] Fukui found that, since factions were not built on the basis of ideology or policy, they could not function as "units of positive and united action" in a controversial issue; hence, effectively organized action had to be more or less cross-factional. Furthermore, he found that

4. Scalapino and Masumi, *Parties and Politics in Contemporary Japan;* Totten and Kawakami, "The Function of Factionalism in Japanese Politics"; Farnsworth, "Social and Political Sources of Political Fragmentation in Japan"; Leiserson, "Factions and Coalitions in One-Party Japan: An Interpretation Based on the Theory of Games"; Hellmann, *Foreign Policy;* Fukui, *Party in Power;* Stockwin, "A Comparison of Political Factionalism in Japan and India"; and Thayer, *How Conservatives Rule.*
    5. *Japanese Foreign Policy.*   6. *How the Conservatives Rule Japan.*

dominant factions within the party tended to avoid controversial issues, whereas dissident factions tended to use controversial issues to undermine the position of the dominant faction.[7]

On the issue of Case 179, there was still another pattern of relationship between factionalism and policy making. Throughout most of its evolution, the issue involved the participation of a relatively few individuals belonging to various factions. Most interparty and LDP-union talks were not conducted by faction leaders or by their lieutenants; when they were involved, it was in their capacity as party officials, such as the LDP secretary-general, or as *cabinet* members, such as the prime minister. In fact, one of the major participants, especially in the early stages of the issue— Labor Minister Ishida—did not belong to any faction; another major participant—Labor Minister Kuraishi, chairman of the LDP's ILO Sewaninkai—though he belonged to a faction, did not have strong roots in that faction because he had previously belonged to another faction.

Factional considerations became overriding at only one crucial point—a point crucial to intraparty, interfactional competition: the election of the party president.

The number of party Diet members involved had increased disproportionately, and their division into policy groups had been along factional lines; dominant factions supported the position of the president-premier, while dissident factions supported antagonistic positions. As long as party elections were not imminent, the head of the dominant coalition of factions, in his capacity as premier, did not shun involvement in the controversial issue; the dissident factions on their part did not oppose the premier on this issue. But as the elections became imminent, the dissident factions tried to use the premier's position on the issue to undermine his leadership position within the party; consequently, in order to minimize opportunities for such opposition, the premier opted for postponing activities on the controversial issue. At that point the salience of the elections was stronger than that of the pressures from the ILO. In this respect we can accept Hellmann's and Fukui's conclusions that factionalism undermines the leadership of the party president.

7. *Party in Power.*

A corollary to the relationship of factionalism within the LDP to policy making has been the *extent of institutionalization* of policy making within the party. To what extent was the process of informal negotiations among a few faction leaders replaced by studies and debates within the formal party institutions? In Thayer's words, what was the "balance between personality and institution" within the party? [8] Case 179 signified the increasing importance of the party's Policy Affairs Research Council (Seichōkai). Because of the issue's complexity, numerous committees of the council were actively involved. Standing committees included Labor, Agriculture and Forestry, Education, Foreign Relations, Local Administration, and Cabinet; special committees included Transportation and Labor Problems.

These committees were cross-factional. Some were more specific and subissue-oriented than others; some, like the education committee, became the stronghold of one policy group, while others were less homogenous in their policy orientation. A long process of adjustment of different views within and among the committees took place before the Policy Affairs Research Council formulated its recommendations and presented them to the Executive Council. The adjustment centered around the ILO Sewaninkai, which—functioning as an intraparty conciliator, an interparty liaison, and a source of policy recommendation—reflected the *institutionalized informality* that characterized the policy-making process.

The internationalization of the political issue of freedom of association had several consequences which may have affected the participants' attitude toward internationalizing a domestic issue in the future. While the unions were convinced that their struggle with the government had won some legitimacy in public opinion, the ILO's interference had triggered a government counteroffensive that brought measures which the unions considered to be even more repressive than before. The ILO had proved incapable of staving off the counteroffensive, and the union leaders reluctantly admitted that the unions had been defeated in the ILO battle.

Hence, the unions did not look forward to another massive confrontation with the government in the international arena. However, they did not exclude the possibility of utilizing labor legisla-

8. P. 14.

tion and practices abroad as a lever in their own drive for domestic policy changes (as in the comparative study of the Second Advisory Council on the Public Personnel System) and of appealing to international organizations for assistance on specific issues. Even Nikkyōso, initially one of the unions most skeptical of the ILO's responsiveness and effectiveness, modified its position; in May 1969, it presented the ILO and UNESCO with a report accusing the Japanese government of malpractices.[9]

The ICFTU only partially achieved its objective. While its involvement on behalf of the Japanese unions had initiated and gradually increased communication with unions hitherto antagonistic to the ICFTU, it could not convince any of them to formally join its ranks. However, it was successful in averting their affiliation with the WFTU or an Afro-Asian pro-Communist union organization.

Government officials, conservative politicians, and officials of the Japan Federation of Employers' Associations concluded that the ILO had overplayed its role. While ready to admit that the ILO may have been able to comprehend the complexity of Japan's labor problems, they believed it was unable to prescribe the proper measures to tackle these problems effectively. The majority of them are still convinced that Japanese labor problems are and should be a matter of domestic concern.

At the ILO, Case 179 built up the organization's self-confidence in its ability to promote freedom of association in member countries. This attitude may have been reflected in the organization's decision to send a Mission of Inquiry to Greece in 1968 to investigate allegations of repressive practices by the military regime.[10]

What changes have taken place as a result of the involvement of the ILO and Japan's ratification of ILO Convention 87 and the accompanying legislation? Now is probably the proper time for a comprehensive study of these changes. An answer may be attempted by the third Advisory Council on the Public Personnel System. A reestablishment of the council after two frustrating failures was, in itself, an indication that some sense of mutual trust between union leaders and the government, missing through-

9. *Japan Labor Bulletin* 8, no. 7 (July 1969).
10. *Human Rights and International Action*, pp. 105–8.

out the evolution of Case 179, had been created. This sense of mutual trust has lately become all the more important in the face of mounting international pressures (spearheaded by the United States) for a more extensive liberalization of foreign investments in Japan, and for "restraints" in Japan's foreign trade policies, both of which would necessitate large-scale domestic adjustments.

Glossary of Japanese Individuals, Organizations, and Laws

I. Individuals

Aoki Morio 青木盛夫
Minister to Geneva

Araki Masuo 荒木萬寿夫
Minister of Eucation

Ayōji Toshichika 安養寺俊親
Jichirō's secretary-general; member of the Advisory Council on the Public Personnel System

Ayusawa Iwao 鮎沢巌
Former director of the ILO Tokyo branch office; member of the Labor Legislation Council

Fujibayashi Keizō 藤林敬三
Professor at Keio University; chairman of the Public Corporations and National Enterprises Labor Relations Commission; author of the "Fujibayashi Compromise"

Fukuda Takeo 福田赳夫
LDP "high posture" faction leader

Funada Naka 船田中
LDP faction leader; speaker of the lower house; author of the "Speaker's Compromise"

Hanami Tadashi 花見忠
Professor of Law, Sophia University; Research Associate, Japan Institute of Labor

Haraguchi Yukitaka 原口幸隆
Zenkō's president; Japanese workers' delegate to the ILO; Sōhyō's chairman, 1957

Hosoya Matsuta 細谷松太
Sanbetsu's deputy secretary-general; founder of Shinsanbetsu

Igarashi Akio 五十嵐昭夫
Nikkeiren's secretary-general

Ikeda Hayato 池田勇人
"Low posture" Prime Minister, 1960–1965

Ishida Hirohide (Bakuei)
石田博英
Minister of Labor; factionless; member of LDP's "New Right"

Ishii Teruhisa 石井照久
Professor at Tokyo University; chairman of the Labor Relations Law Research Committee; member of the Labor Problems Deliberation Council

Ishikawa Toshihiko 石川俊彦
Head of Kokurō's Legal Department

Iwai Akira 岩井章
Sōhyō's secretary-general, 1955–1970

Kaite Shingo 飼手真吾
Formerly high official of the Ministry of Labor; member, Board of Directors of the Japan Institute of Labor and the Japan ILO Association

Ken Yasui 安井謙
Director of Administrative Affairs, Office of the Prime Minister; in charge of the Advisory Committee on the Public Personnel System

Kishi Nobusuke 岸信介
"High posture" Prime Minister, 1957–1960

Kōno Mitsu 河野密
Prewar leader in the union and socialist movements; JSP Diet member; chairman, JSP Special Committee for the Promotion of the Ratification of ILO Conventions

Kuraishi Tadao 倉石忠雄
Minister of Labor; chairman of the LDP's informal ILO Sewaninkai

Maeda Tamon 前田多門
Permanent government delegate to Geneva in the early 1920s; president of the Japan ILO Association

Maeo Shigesaburō 前尾繁三郎
LDP secretary-general; reached an agreement with his JSP counterpart on the Kuraishi Plan

Makieda Motofumi 槙枝元文
Nikkyōso's secretary-general

Masumoto Uhei 桝本卯平
Government-designated workers' delegate to the First ILO Conference

Matsuoka Komakichi 松岡駒吉
Former president of Sōdōmei; member of the Labor Legislation Council

Mishiro Akio 三城晁雄
Chairman, Nikkeiren's ILO Committee; member of ILO's Governing Body

Nadao Hirokichi 灘尾弘吉
Minister of Education

Nakayama Ichirō 中山伊知郎
Chairman, Labor Problems Deliberation Council; chairman, Japan Institute of Labor; Professor Emeritus, Hitotsubashi University

Nakayama Kazuhisa 中山和久
Professor at Waseda University; adviser to Sōhyō

Narita Tomomi 成田知己
JSP secretary-general; reached an agreement on the Kuraishi Plan

Nikaidō Susumu 二階堂進
Member, LDP's informal ILO Sewaninkai

Nishio Suehiro 西尾末広
DSP's President

Noda Uichi 野田卯一
Member, LDP's informal ILO Sewaninkai

Nōmura Heiji 野村平爾
Professor at Waseda University; adviser to Sōhyō

Ogasa Kōshō 小笠公韶
Member, LDP's informal ILO Sewaninkai

Ōhira Masayoshi 大平正芳
Foreign Minister in the Ikeda cabinet

Ōi Kentarō 大井憲太郎
Founder of the Tōyō Jiyūtō

Ōkōchi Kazuo 大河内一男
Professor and president, Tokyo University; formulator of the *dekasegigata* theory of Japan's labor force

Ōta Kaoru 太田薫
Sōhyō's chairman, 1958–1967; Gōka Rōren's chairman

Saito Kunikichi 斉藤邦吉
Member, LDP's informal ILO Sewaninkai

Sato Eisaku 佐藤栄作
Prime Minister, 1965–1972

Shirai Isamu 白井勇
Member, LDP's informal ILO Sewaninkai

Suehiro Izutarō 末広厳太郎
Professor at Tokyo University; member, Labor Legislation Council

Sugawara Eietsu 菅原栄悦
Dōmei's vice-president; member, Advisory Council on the Public Personnel System

Suzuki Bunji 鈴木文治
Yūaikai's president

Suzuki Mosaburō 鈴木茂三郎
JSP's president

Takahashi Takeshi 高橋武
Research officer, ILO Tokyo branch office

Takano Minoru 高野実
Sōhyō's secretary-general, 1951–1955

Takaragi Fumihiko 宝樹文彦
Zentei's president; chairman, Sōhyō's Special Committee

for the Recovery of the Right to Strike

Toda Yoshio 戸田義男
High official, International Department, Ministry of Labor

Tokuda Kyūichi 徳田球一
Communist leader; member, Labor Legislation Council

Utada Tokuichi 歌田徳一
Official of the Trade Union Section, Ministry of Labor

II. *Organizations and Committees*

Bunkyō-Chian 文教治安
Education–Public Peace, LDP anti-union group

Chikōrō 地公労
Joint Struggle Conference of Unions of Local Public Employees

Chūritsu Rōren (Chūritsu Rōdō Kumiai Renraku Kaigi) 中立労働組合連絡会議
Federation of Independent Unions; Japan's third major union federation

Dai-Nihon Bōseki Rengō Kai 大日本紡績連合会
National Spinning Association; participant in prewar ILO activities

Dōmei (Zen Nihon Rōdō Sōdōmei) 全日本労働総同盟
Japan Confederation of Labor; Japan's second major union federation; supporter of the DSP

Dōmei Kaigi 同盟会議
Japan Trade Union Congress; predecessor of Dōmei

Doryokusha (Kokutetsu Doryokusha Rōdō Kumiai) 国鉄動力車労働組合
Japan National Railways Locomotive Engineers' Union (formerly Kirō); complainant

Eien (Eiga Engeki Rōdō Kumiai Sōrengō) 映画演劇労働組合総連合
Motion Picture and Theater Workers' Union; seceded from Sōhyō to form Zenrō Kaigi

Fusen Kisei Zenkoku Rōdō Dai-Remmei 普選期成全国労働大連盟
National Labor League for the Attainment of Universal Suffrage; founded 1920

Gōka Rōren (Gōsei Kagaku Sangyō Rōso Rengōkai) 合成化学産業労組連合会
Synthetic Chemical Workers' Union; one of the first participants in the "Spring Offensive"

Gyōmin Kyōsantō 暁民共産党
Men of the Dawn Communist Party; an early 1920s leftist group at Waseda

ILO Jōyaku Hijun Sokushin Tokubetsu Iinkai
ILO 條約批准促進特別委員会
Special Committee for the Promotion of the Ratification of ILO Conventions (JSP)

ILO Mondai Yūshi Kondankai
ILO 問題有志懇談会
Conference of the Concerned with the ILO Problem; convened by LDP members opposing the Kuraishi Plan

ILO Sewaninkai ILO 世話人会
Informal Committee on the ILO (LDP)

Jichirō (Zen Nihon Jichi Dantai Rōdō Kumiai)
全日本自治団体労働組合
Prefectural and Municipal Workers' Union; complainant

Jidōsha Rōren (Nihon Jidōsha Sangyō Rōdō Kumiai Rengōkai)
日本自動車産業労働組合連合会
Japan Automobile Workers' Union; a major affiliate of Dōmei

Jimintō (Jiyūminshutō) 自由民主党
Liberal Democratic Party (LDP); the ruling conservative party

Jinjiin 人事院
National Personnel Authority

Jiyūminken Undō 自由民權運動
Popular Rights Movement; Meiji era

Jiyūtō 自由党
Liberal Party; one of the conservative parties

Kaiin (Zen Nihon Kaiin Kumiai) 全日本海員組合
Japan Seamen's Union; a major affiliate of Dōmei

Kaishintō 改進党
Progressive Party; one of the conservative parties

Keidanren (Keizai Dantai Rengōkai) 経済団体連合会
Federation of Economic Organizations; Japan's major "pressure group"

Keieirengō 経営連合
League of Employers' Associations; Keidanren's predecessor

Kempō Chōsa Kai 憲法調査会
Constitutional Investigation Committee

Kenseikai 憲政会
Constitutional Association; prewar conservative party; renamed Rikken Minseitō

Kirō (Kokutetsu Rōso Kikansha Kyōgikai) 国鉄労組機関車協議会
Japan National Railways Locomotive Engineers' Union; complainant

Kōan Chōsa Chō 公安調査庁
Public Peace Investigative Agency

Kokkō Kyōtō 国公共闘
National Employees' Joint Struggle Committee

Kokurō (Kokutetsu Rōdō Kumiai) 国鉄労働組合
Japan National Railways Workers' Union; complainant

Kokusai Rōdō Kyōkai 国際労働協会
Japan International Labor Association; prewar organization supporting progressive labor legislation

Kokusuikai 国粋会
National Essence Society; prewar nationalist organization

Kokutetsu 国鉄
Japan National Railways

Kokutetsu Sōren (Kokutetsu Rōdō Kumiai Sōrengō) 国鉄労働組合総連合
National Railways Workers' Union; predecessor of Kokurō

Kōmuin Kyōtō 公務員共闘
Joint Struggle Conference of National and Local Government Employees; composed of Kokkō Kyōtō and Chikōrō

Kōmuin Seido Shingikai 公務員制度審議会
Advisory Council on the Public Personnel System; established in 1965 to consider

enactment of the shelved bills and to review the system of public employment in general

Kōrōi (Kōkyō Kigyōtai Rōdō Kankei Iinkai) 公共企業体労働関係委員会
Public Corporations and National Enterprises Labor Relations Commission

Kōrōkyō (Kyōdō Senjutsu Kaigi) (公労協)共同戦術会議
Public Corporations and National Enterprises Workers' Unions' Council

Kyōchōkai 協調会
Harmonization Society; government-sponsored labor policy research organization

Mindō (Minshuka Dōmei) 民主化同盟
Democratization League; anti-Communist group of union leaders

Minrōren (Zenkoku Minshushugi Rōdō Undō Renraku Kyōgikai) 全国民主主義労働運動連絡協議会
National Democratic Labor Movement Liaison Council; composed of four Sōhyō affiliates opposing the prolonged strikes in the coal and electric power industries; three of them founded Zenrō Kaigi in 1954

Minshatō (Minshushakaitō)
民主社会党 Democratic
Socialist Party (DSP)

Nihon ILO Kyōkai 日本 ILO 協会
Japan ILO Association

Nihon Kōgyō Kurabu
日本工業クラブ
Japan Industrial Club; a
major prewar industrialists'
association

Nihon Kyōsantō 日本共産党
Japan Communist Party
(JCP)

Nihon Rōdō Kumiai Kaigi
日本労働組合会議
Japan Union Congress; a
prewar organization comprising the right and center segments of labor

Nihon Rōdō Kyōkai
日本労働協会
Japan Institute of Labor

Nihon Shakaishugi Dōmei
日本社会主義同盟
Japan Socialist Federation;
prewar organization

Nihon Shakaitō 日本社会党
Japan Socialist Party (JSP)

*Nikkeiren (Nihon Keieisha
Dantai)* 日本経営者団体
Japan Federation of Employ-
ers' Associations

*Nikkyōso (Nihon Kyōshokuin
Kumiai)* 日本教職員組合
Japan Teachers' Union; com-
plainant

Rikken Minseitō 立憲民政党
Constitutional Democratic
Party; prewar conservative
party

Rikken Seiyūkai 立憲政友会
Friends of Constitutional
Government Association;
prewar conservative party

Rinji Sangyō Chōsakai
臨時産業調査会
Temporary Committee for
the Study of Industry; prewar cabinet advisory body;
reviewed labor policy

Rōdō Hōgaku Kenkyūjō
労働法学研究所
Labor Law Institute

*Rōdō Kankei Kakuryō Kondan-
kai* 労働関係閣僚懇談会
Consultative Council of Bureaucrats Concerned with
Labor Legislation

Rōdō Kumiai Kiseikai
労働組合期成会
Association for the Establishment of Labor Unions;
founded 1897

Rōdō Kumiai Dōmeikai
労働組合同盟会
Labor Unions Federation;
founded 1920

Rōdō Mondai Kondankai
労働問題懇談会
Labor Problems Deliberation
Council; examined the im-
plications of Japan's ratifica-

tion of ILO Convention 87

Rōdō Mondai Tokubetsu Chō-sakai 労働問題特別調査会

Labor Problems Special Investigation Committee; a committee of the LDP Policy Affairs Research Council

Rōdō Rippō Sokushin Iinkai 労働立法促進委員会

Committee for the Promotion of Labor Legislation; a joint committee of labor's right and center; formed in 1928

Rōmu Hōsei Shingikai 労務法制審議会

Labor Legislation Council; drafted the Labor Union Law of 1945

Rōshi Kankei Hō Kenkyūkai 労使関係法研究会

Labor Relations Laws Research Committee; reviewed problems of application of labor laws in the private sector

Saiken Dōmei 再建同盟

Reconstruction League; anti-Communist faction in Zentei

Sanbetsu (Zenkoku Sangyō Betsu Rōso Kaigi) 全国産業別労組会議

National Congress of Industrial Unions; largest pre-Sōhyō union federation

Sangyō Hōkokukai (Sampō) 産業報国会

Industrial Patriotic Society; a national organization, including dissolved unions, that supported the war effort

Seichōkai (Seimu Chōsakai) 政務調査会

Policy Affairs Research Council (LDP)

Seichō Shingikai 政調審議会

Policy Affairs Deliberation Committee; a body of the Seichōkai

Seirei Shimon Iinkai 政令諮問委員会

Government Ordinances Advisory Council; reviewed occupation-initiated legislation; established in 1951

Shakai Minshutō 社会民主党

Social Democratic Party

Shakai Seisaku Gakkai 社会政策学会

Social Policy Academic Association; an association of social reformers founded in the Meiji era

Shinsanbetsu (Zenkoku Sangyō Betsu Rōdō Kumiai Rengōkai) 全国産業別労働組合連合会

National Federation of Industrial Organizations; one of Japan's four major union federations

Shitetsu Sōren (Nihon Shitetsu Rōdō Kumiai Sōrengō) 日本私鉄労働組合総連合

Private Railways Workers' Union; a Sōhyō affiliate

Shuntō 春闘
"Spring Offensive"; national joint wage struggles across industries

Sōdōmei (Nihon Rōdō Kumiai Sōdōmei) 日本労働組合総同盟
Japan Trade Union Federation

Sōhyō (Nihon Rōdō Kumiai Sōhyōgikai)
日本労働組合総評議会
General Council of Japan's Trade Unions; Japan's major union federation

Sōmukai 総務会
Executive Council (LDP)

Stōken Dakkan Tokubetsu Iinkai スト権奪還特別委員会
Special Committee for the Recovery of the Right to Strike; Sōhyō's committee in charge of the ILO struggle

Taisei Yokusankai 大政翼賛会
Imperial Rule Assistance Association; a wartime national organization

Tōitsu Saha 統一左派
Left Unity Faction (Kokurō)

Tōshi Kōtsu (Nihon Tōshi Kōtsu Rōdō Kumiai)
日本都市交通労働組合
Municipal Traffic Workers' Union; complainant

Tōyō Jiyūtō 東洋自由党
Oriental Liberal Party; fore-runner of early Japanese socialist parties

Yūaikai 友愛会
Friendly Love Society; early prewar union organization

Zendentsū (Zenkoku Denki Tsūshin Rōdō Kumiai)
全国電気通信労働組合
Japan Tele-Communication Workers' Union; complainant

Zenkenrō (Zen Kensetsushō Rōdō Kumiai) 全建設省労働組合
Construction Ministry Workers' Union; complainant

Zenkō (Zen Nihon Kinzoku Kōzan Rōdō Kumiai Rengōkai)
全日本金属鉱山労働組合連合会
Japan Metal Mines Labor Union; a Sōhyō affiliate, headed by Haraguchi Yukitaka

Zennichijirō (Zen Nihon Jiyū Rōdō Kumiai)
全日本自由労働組合
Japan Day Workers' Union; a major Sōhyō affiliate, controlled by extreme leftist leadership

Zennōrin (Zen Nōrin Rōdō Kumiai) 全農林労働組合
Ministry of Agriculture and Forestry Workers' Union; complainant

Zenrinya (Zen Rinya Rōdō Kumiai) 全林野労働組合

National Forests' Workers' Union; complainant

Zenrō Kaigi (Zen Nihon Rōdō Kumiai Kaigi)

全日本労働組合会議

Japan Trade Union Congress; Sōhyō's major rival union federation; preceded Dōmei Kaigi

Zenrōdō (Zen Rōdōshō Rōdō Kumiai) 全労働省労働組合

Ministry of Labor Workers' Union; complainant

Zenrōren (Zenkoku Rōdō Kumiai Renraku Kyōgikai)

全国労働組合連格協議会

National Labor Union Liaison Council; founded in 1947; control captured by the Communists; disbanded by SCAP in 1950

Zensanren (Zenkoku Sangyō Dantai Rengōkai)

全国産業団体連合会

National Federation of Industrial Associations; first national employers' association; established in 1930

Zensembai (Zensembai Rōdō Kumiai) 全専売労働組合

National Monopoly Workers' Union; complainant

Zensen Dōmei (Zenkoku Seni Sangyō Rōdō Kumiai Dōmei)

全国織維産業労働組合同盟

Japan Textile Workers' Union; a major Dōmei affiliate

Zensuido (Zen Nihon Suido Rōdō Kumiai)

全日本水道労働組合

Water Supply Workers' Union; complainant

Zentei (Zenteishin Rōdō Kumiai) 全通信労働組合

Japan Postal Workers' Union; complainant; spearheaded the ILO struggle

Zenunyu (Zen Unyushō Shokuin Kumiai) 全運輸省私員組合

Ministry of Transportation Workers' Union; complainant

III. *Laws*

Chian Iji Hō   治安維持法

Peace Preservation Law, 1925; prohibited "extreme" leftist political activities

Chian Keisatsu Hō   地安警察法

Public Peace Police Law, 1900; suppressed union activities

Chihō Kōmuin Hō 地方公務員法

Local Public Service Law, 1950

Chikōrō Hō

地方公共企業体労働関係法

Local Public Corporations and Enterprises Labor Relations Law, 1948

Habō Hō (Hakai Katsudō Bōshi Hō) 破壊活動防止法
Subversive Activities Prevention Law, 1952

Kokkō Hō (Kokka Kōmuin Hō)

国家公務員法

National Public Service Law, 1947

Kōrō Hō (Kōkyō Kigyōtai Rōdō Kankei Hō)

公共企業体労働関係法

Public Corporations and National Enterprises Labor Relations Law, 1948

Rōchō Hō (Rōdō Kankei Chōtei Hō) 労働関係調整法
Labor Relations Adjustment Law, 1946

Rōdō Kumiai Hō 労働組合法
Trade Union Law, 1945

Rōdō Sōgi Chōtei Hō

労働争議調停法

Act for the Conciliation of Labor Disputes, 1926

Rōki Hō (Rōdō Kijun Hō)

労働基準法
Labor Standards Law, 1947

Stō Kisei Hō スト規制法
"Strike Regulation Law," 1952

Bibliography

English Sources

Abegglen, J. C. *The Japanese Factory: Aspects of Its Social Organization.* Glencoe: Free Press, 1958.

Anderson, Ronald S. "Japan," in T. L. Reller and E. L. Morphet (eds.). *Comparative Educational Administration.* Englewood Cliffs, N.J.: Prentice-Hall, 1962.

Ariizumi, Toru. "Historical Outline of the Judiciary in Industrial Relations." In Japan Institute of Labor (ed.). *Changing Patterns of Industrial Relations.* Tokyo: Japan Institute of Labor, 1965.

Ayusawa, Iwao F. *A History of Labor in Modern Japan.* Honolulu: East-West Center Press, 1966.

Bachrach, Peter, and Morton Baratz. *Power and Poverty.* New York: Oxford University Press, 1970.

————. "Two Faces of Power." *American Political Science Review* 56, no. 4 (December 1962): 942–52.

————. "Decisions and Non-Decisions: An Analytical Framework." *American Political Science Review* 57, no. 3 (September 1963); 632–42.

Baerwald, Hans H. *The Purge of Japanese Leaders under the Occupation.* Berkeley and Los Angeles: University of California Press, 1959.

————. "Japan: The Politics of Transition." *Asian Survey* 5, no. 1 (January 1965): 33–43.

————. "Parliament and Parliamentarism in Japan." *Pacific Affairs* 37, no. 3 (fall 1964): 271–82.

Ball, W. MacMahon. *Japan—Enemy or Ally?* New York: John Day Co., 1949.

Barkin, Solomon (ed.). *International Labor.* New York: Harper and Row, 1967.

Bauer, Raymond E., I. Pool, and L. A. Dexter. *American Business and*

Public Policy Making: The Politics of Foreign Trade. New York: Atherton Press, 1963.

Bellah, Robert N. "Continuity and Change in Japanese Society." 1970. Mimeographed.

Bennett, John W., and Iwao Ishino. *Paternalism in the Japanese Economy.* Minneapolis: University of Minnesota Press, 1963.

Bennett, John W., H. Passin, and R. McKnight. *In Search for Identity.* Minneapolis: University of Minnesota Press, 1958.

Borton, Hugh, et al. *Japan between East and West.* New York: Harper and Brothers, 1957.

Brecher, Michael. *The Foreign Policy System of Israel: Setting, Images, Process.* London: Oxford University Press, 1972.

Burks, Ardath W. *The Government of Japan.* New York: Thomas Y. Crowell Co., 1961.

Colbert, E. S. *The Left Wing in Japanese Politics.* New York: Institute of Pacific Relations, 1952.

Cole, A. B., and Naomi Nakanishi (eds.). *Political Tendencies of Japanese in Small Enterprises, with Special Reference to the Social Democratic Party.* New York: Institute of Pacific Relations, 1959.

Cole, A. B., George O. Totten, and Cecil H. Uyehara. *Socialist Parties in Postwar Japan.* New Haven: Yale University Press, 1966.

Cole, Robert E. *Japanese Blue Collar: The Changing Tradition.* Berkeley and Los Angeles: University of California Press, 1971.

Cook, Alice H. *Japanese Trade Unionism.* Ithaca, N.Y.: Cornell University Press, 1966.

———. "Political Actions and Trade Unions: A Case of the Coal Miners in Japan." *Monumenta Nipponica* 22, nos. 1–2; 103–21.

———. "The International Labor Organization and Japanese Politics." *Industrial and Labor Relations Review* 70, no. 1 (October 1965): 41–57.

Courtney, John C. "In Defense of Royal Commissions." *Canadian Public Administration Review* 12 (summer 1969): 198–212.

Crowley, James B. *Japan's Quest for Autonomy.* Princeton, N.J.: Princeton University Press, 1966.

Curry, R. W. *Woodrow Wilson and the Far Eastern Policy, 1913–1921.* New York: Bookman Associates, 1957.

Dahl, Karl Nundrup. "The Role of ILO Standards in the Global Integration Process." *Journal of Peace Research,* April 1968, pp. 309–51.

Dahl, Robert. *Who Governs?* New Haven: Yale University Press, 1961.

Deutsch, Karl W. "External Influences on the Internal Behavior of

States." In R. Barry Farrel (ed.). *Approaches to Comparative and International Politics.* Evanston: Northwestern University Press, 1966. Pp. 5–26.

Dionisopoulos, P. Allan. "Judicial Review and Civil Rights in Japan: The First Decade With an Alien Doctrine." *Western Political Science Quarterly* 13, no. 2 (June 1960): 269–87.

Dōmei News (formerly *JTUC Report*), Tokyo.

Dore, R. P. "The Modernizer as a Special Case: Japanese Factory Legislation, 1882–1911." *Studies in Society and History* 11 (October 1969): 433–50.

Easton, David. *A System Analysis of Political Life.* New York: John Wiley, 1965.

———. "An Approach to the Analysis of Political Systems." *World Politics* 9 (1956–57): 383–400.

Farnsworth, L. W. "Social and Political Sources of Political Fragmentation in Japan." *Journal of Politics* 29, no. 2 (May 1967): 287–301.

Follows, John. *The Antecedents of the ILO.* Oxford: Clarendon Press, 1951.

Fukui, Haruhiro. *Party in Power.* Berkeley and Los Angeles: University of California Press, 1970.

Haas, Ernst B. *Beyond the Nation State.* Stanford, Calif.: Stanford University Press, 1964.

———. *Human Rights and International Action: The Case of Freedom of Association.* Stanford, Calif.: Stanford University Press, 1970.

Harari, Ehud. "The Politics of Labor Legislation in Japan." Ph.D. dissertation, Department of Political Science, University of California, Berkeley, 1968.

Hellmann, Donald C. *Japanese Foreign Policy and Domestic Politics.* Berkeley and Los Angeles: University of California Press, 1969.

Higa, Mikio. "The Japanese Bureaucracy." Ph.D. dissertation, Department of Political Science, University of California, Berkeley, 1968.

Hollerman, Leon. *Japan's Dependence on the World Economy.* Princeton, N.J.: Princeton University Press, 1968.

Holt, Robert T., and John E. Turner. "Insular Politics." In J. N. Rosenau (ed.). *Linkage Politics.* New York: Free Press, 1969.

Ike, Nobutaka. *Japanese Politics: An Introductory Survey.* New York: Knopf, 1961.

———. "Japan: Twenty Years After Surrender." *Asian Survey* 6, no. 1 (January 1966): 18–27.

International Labor Organization (ILO). "Eighth Report to the U.N., Case No. 60 (Japan), Twelfth Report of the Committee on Freedom of Association." Pars. 10–83.

———. "Industrial Labor in Japan." *Studies and Reports*, Series A, no. 37. Geneva, 1933.

———. *International Labor Review* 30, no. 1 (January 1935).

———. *International Labor Review* 57, no. 5 (May 1948).

———. "Japan." *Freedom of Association*, V, *Studies and Reports*, Series A, no. 32. Geneva, 1930. Pp. 401–461.

———. "Minutes of the 65th Session of the Governing Body" (4th sitting). 1934.

———. "Record of Proceedings," 23rd Session, International Labor Conference, 1937.

———. "Report of the Committee of Experts on the Application of Conventions and Recommendations." Geneva: International Labor Conference, 43rd Session, 1959 Report III, Part 4.

———. "Report of the Committee of Experts on the Application of Conventions and Recommendations." Geneva: International Labor Conference, 44th Session, 1960, Report III (Part 4); 45th Session, 1961, Report III (Part 4).

———. "Report of the Committee on Freedom of Employers' and Workers' Organizations" (McNair Report), *Official Bulletin*, vol. 39 no. 9, 1956.

———. "Report of the Director." Geneva: International Labor Conference, 17th Session, 1934. Pp. 17–20.

———. "Report of the Fact-Finding and Conciliation Commission on Freedom of Association Concerning Persons Employed in the Public Sector in Japan" (Dreyer Report). *Official Bulletin*, Special Supplement, vol. 49, no. 1 (January 1966).

———. "Seventh Report of the ILO to the U.N., Case No. 48 (Japan), Sixth Report of the Committee on Freedom of Association." Pars. 737–69, 343–47.

———. "Social Aspects of Industrial Development in Japan." *Studies and Reports*, Series B (Economic Conditions), no. 21. Geneva, 1934. Report by F. Maurette, assistant director, International Labor Office (Maurette Report).

———. "A Survey of Economic and Social Conditions in Japan," *International Labor Review* 60 (July 1949).

Ishida, Takeshi. "Interest Groups in Japan." Unpublished manuscript, 1961.

———. "The Development of Interest Groups and the Pattern of

Modernization in Japan." *Papers of Modern Japan*. Australian National University, 1965. Pp. 1–17.

Ishii, Teruhisa. "The Changing Role of Labor Legislation in Japan." In Japan Institute of Labor (ed.). *Changing Patterns of Industrial Relations*. Tokyo: Japan Institute of Labor, 1965.

Ishikawa, Kichiemon. "Labor Relations Laws Internationally." Address to the American Bar Association, August 8, 1967.

———. "The Regulation of Employer-Employee Relationship: Japanese Labor Relations Law." In Arthur Taylor Mehren (ed.). *Law in Japan*. Cambridge, Mass.: Harvard University Press, 1963.

———. "The Role of Government in Labor Relations in Japan." In Japan Institute of Labor (ed.). *Labor Relations in the Asian Countries*. Tokyo: Japan Institute of Labor, 1967. Pp. 137–44.

Jansen, M. B. "Education, Values, and Politics in Japan." *Foreign Affairs*, July 1957, pp. 666–78.

Japan Institute of Labor, (ed.). *The Changing Patterns of Industrial Relations*. Tokyo: Japan Institute of Labor, 1965.

———. *Labor Relations in the Asian Countries*. Tokyo: Japan Institute of Labor, 1967.

———. *Japan Labor Statistics*. Tokyo: Japan Institute of Labor, 1970.

Japan Labor Bulletin (Japan Institute of Labor), Tokyo.

Japan Quarterly, Tokyo.

Japan Report (Japan's Ministry of Foreign Affairs), Tokyo.

Japan Socialist Review (Japan Socialist Party), Tokyo.

Japan Times, Tokyo.

Jenks, C. Wilferd. *The International Protection of Trade Union Freedom*. London: Stevens and Sons, 1957.

JFEA News (Japan Federation of Employers' Associations), Tokyo.

Johnson, Chalmers Ashby. *An Instant of Treason*. Stanford, Calif.: Stanford University Press, 1964.

———. *Conspiracy at Matsukawa*. Berkeley and Los Angeles: University of California Press, 1972.

———. " 'Low Posture' Politics in Japan." *Asian Survey* 3, no. 1 (January 1963): 17–29.

Journal of Social and Political Ideas in Japan (Center for Social and Political Studies), Tokyo.

Kajima, Morinosuke. *A Brief Diplomatic History of Modern Japan*. Tokyo: Charles E. Tuttle Company, Inc., 1965.

Karsh, Bernard, and Solomon Levine. "Present Dilemmas of the Japanese Labor Movement." *Labor Law Journal* 13, no. 5 (July 1962): 541–48.

Kawada, Hisashi. "The Government, Industrial Relations and Economic Development in Japan." In Arthur M. Ross (ed.). *Industrial Relations and Economic Development.* London: Macmillan & Company, 1966.

Kawai, Kazuo. *Japan's American Interlude.* Chicago: University of Chicago Press, 1960.

Landelius, Torsten. *Workers, Employers, and Governments: A Comparative Study of Delegations and Groups at the International Labor Conference 1919–1964.* Stockholm: Norstedt and Soner, 1965.

Landy, Ernest Alfred. *The Effectiveness of International Supervision: Thirty Years of ILO Experience.* London: Stevens and Sons, 1966.

Langdon, Frank C. "The Making of Political Demands in Japan." *Pacific Affairs* 39, nos. 1–2 (spring–summer 1966): 37–49.

Lange, William. "Some Remarks on the Japanese Press." *Japan Quarterly* 7, no. 3 (July–September 1960): 281–87.

Large, Stephen S. *The Yūaikai, 1912–1919: The Rise of Labor in Japan.* Tokyo: Sophia University Press, 1972.

Leiserson, Michael. "Factions and Coalitions in One-Party Japan: An Explanation Based on the Theory of Games." *American Political Science Review* 57, no. 3 (September 1968): 770–87.

Levine, Solomon B. *Industrial Relations in Postwar Japan.* Urbana, Ill.: University of Illinois Press, 1958.

Lockwood, William W. *The Economic Development of Japan: Growth and Structural Change.* Princeton, N.J.: Princeton University Press, 1954.

———. "Political Economy." In H. Passin (ed.). *The United States and Japan.* Englewood Cliffs, N.J.: Prentice-Hall, 1966. Pp. 93–128.

Lorwin, Lewis L. *The International Labor Movement.* New York: Harper and Brothers, 1953.

Lowi, T. J. "American Business, Public Policy, Case Studies, and Political Theory." *World Politics* 16, no. 4 (July 1964): 677–715.

McAdams, A. K. *Power and Politics in Labor Legislation.* New York: Columbia Univrsity Press, 1964.

Maki, John. *Court and Constitution in Japan: Selected Supreme Court Decisions, 1946–1960.* Seattle: University of Washington Press, 1964.

Mansfield, Harvey C. "Government Commissions." *International Encyclopedia of the Social Sciences* 3 (1968): 12–17.

Maruyama, Masao. "Patterns of Individuation and the Case of Japan." In M. B. Jansen (ed.). *Changing Japanese Attitudes Toward Modernization.* Princeton, N.J.: Princeton University Press, 1965. Pp. 489–531.

Masumi, Junnosuke. "A Profile of the Japanese Conservative Party." *Asian Survey* 3, no. 8 (August 1963); 390–401.

Matsuda, Yoshihiko. "Government Employees in Japan." *Japan Labor Bulletin* 5, no. 10: 4–8; no. 11: 4–8.

Matsushita, Masatoshi. *Japan in the League of Nations.* New York: Columbia University Press, 1929.

Maxon, Yale C. *Control of Japanese Foreign Policy: A Study of Civil-Military Rivalry, 1930–1945.* Berkeley and Los Angeles: University of California Press, 1957.

Mendel, Douglas H., Jr. *The Japanese People and Foreign Policy.* Berkeley and Los Angeles: University of California Press, 1961.

———. "Revisionist Opinion in Post Treaty Japan." *American Political Science Review,* September 1954, pp. 766–74.

Montgomery, John D. *Forced to Be Free: The Artificial Revolution in Germany and Japan.* Chicago: University of Chicago Press, 1957.

Morley, J. W. *Japan and Korea: American Allies in the Pacific.* New York: Walker and Co., 1965.

Ōkōchi, Kazuo. *Labor in Modern Japan.* Tokyo: Science Council of Japan, 1958.

———. "Traditionalism of Industrial Relations in Japan." In Japan Institute of Labor (ed.). *Changing Patterns of Industrial Relations.* Tokyo: Japan Institute of Labor, 1965. Pp. 126–141.

Olson, Lawrence. *Dimensions of Japan.* New York: American Universities Field Staff, Inc., 1963.

———. *Japan in Postwar Asia.* New York: Praeger Publishers, 1970.

Oriental Economist, Tokyo.

Packard, George R., III. *Protest in Tokyo: The Security Treaty Crisis of 1960.* Princeton, N.J.: Princeton University Press, 1966.

Paige, Glenn D. *The Korean Decision.* New York: Free Press, 1968.

Passin, Herbert. *Society and Education in Japan.* New York: Columbia University Teachers College, 1965.

Passin, Herbert (ed.). *The United States and Japan.* Englewood Cliffs, N.J.: Prentice-Hall, 1966.

Polsby, N. W. "Notes on Policy Initiation in the American Political System." 1970. Mimeographed.

Price, John. *The International Labor Movement.* London: Oxford University Press, 1947.

Pye, Lucian W., and Sidney Verba (eds.). *Political Culture and Political Development.* Princeton, N.J.: Princeton University Press, 1965.

Reischauer, Edwin O. *The United States and Japan.* New York: Viking Press, 1957.

Research School of Pacific Studies (ed.). *Papers on Modern Japan.* Canberra: Austrialian National University, 1965.

Richardson, Bradley M. "Japanese Local Politics: Support Mobilization and Leadership Styles." *Asian Survey* 7, no. 12 (December 1967): 860–75.

Rosenau, J. N. "Pre-theories and Theories of Foreign Policy." In R. Barry Farrel (ed.). *Approaches to Comparative and International Politics.* Evanston: Northwestern University Press, 1966. Pp. 27–92.

———. "Toward a Study of National International Linkages." In J. N. Rosenau (ed.). *Linkage Politics.* New York: The Free Press, 1969. Pp. 44–66.

Rosovsky, Henry. *Capital Formation in Japan, 1868–1940.* Glencoe: Free Press, 1961.

Rosovsky, Henry, and K. Ohkawa. "The Role of Agriculture in Modern Japanese Economic Development." *Economic Development and Cultural Change,* vol. 9, no. 1, part 2 (1960), pp. 43–67.

Scalapino, Robert A. *Democracy and the Party Movement in Prewar Japan.* Berkeley and Los Angeles: University of California Press, 1953.

———. *The Japanese Communist Movement, 1920–1966.* Berkeley and Los Angeles: University of California Press, 1967.

———. "The Japanese Labor Movement." Mimeographed.

———. "Japan." In Walter Galenson (ed.). *Labor and Economic Development.* New York: John Wiley and Sons, 1959.

———. "Japanese Socialism in Crisis." *Foreign Affairs* 38, no. 2 (January 1960): 318–28.

———. "The Foreign Policy of Modern Japan." In Roy C. Macridis (ed.). *Foreign Policy in World Politics.* Englewood Cliffs, N.J.: Prentice-Hall, 1962.

———. "Environmental and Foreign Contributions: Japan." In Robert E. Ward and D. Rustow (eds.). *The Modernization of Japan and Turkey.* Princeton, N.J.: Princeton University Press, 1964.

———. "Labor and Politics in Postwar Japan." In W. W. Lockwood (ed.). *The State and Economic Enterprise in Japan.* Princeton, N.J.: Princeton University Press, 1965.

Scalapino, Robert A. and Junnosuke Masumi. *Parties and Politics in Contemporary Japan.* Berkeley and Los Angeles: University of California Press, 1962.

Schaller, Lyle E. "Is the Citizen Advisory Committee a Threat to Representative Government?" *Public Administration Review* 24, no. 3 (September 1964): 175–80.

Schoettle, E. C. B. "The State of the Art in Policy Studies." In A. R.

Bauer and Kenneth J. Gergen (eds.). *The Study of Policy Formation.* New York: Free Press, 1968.

Sebald, William J., and Russel Brines. *With MacArthur in Japan: A Personal History of the Occupation.* New York: W. W. Norton & Co., 1965.

Shotwell, James T. (ed.). *The Origins of the International Labor Organization.* New York: Columbia University Press, 1934.

Singh, Prasad Lalita. *The Politics of Economic Cooperation in Asia: A Study of Asian International Organizations.* Columbia, Mo.: University of Missouri Press, 1966.

Singer, J. David. "The Global System and Its Subsystem: A Developmental View." In J. N. Rosenau (ed.). *Linkage Politics.* New York: Free Press, 1969. Pp. 21–43.

Sissons, David C. S. "Recent Developments in Japan's Socialist Movement." *Far Eastern Survey* 29, no. 1 (March 1960): 40–47, and no. 2 (June 1960); 89–92.

Smith, Brian C. *Advising Ministers.* London: Routledge & Kegan Paul, 1969.

Soukup, James R. "Labor Politics in Postwar Japan: A Study of the Political Attitudes and Activities of Selected Japanese Labor Organizations." Ph.D. dissertation, University of Michigan, 1957.

———. "Labor and Politics in Japan: A Study of Interest Group Attitudes and Activities." *Journal of Politics* 22, no. 2 (May 1960): 314–17.

———. "Japanese Labor: Goals and Political Tactics." *Orient West* 7, no. 3 (March 1962): 15–24.

Steiner, Kurt. *Local Government in Japan.* Stanford, Calif.: Stanford University Press, 1965.

Stockwin, J. A. A. *The Japanese Socialist Party and Neutralism: A Study of a Political Party and Its Foreign Policy.* Melbourne: Melbourne University Press, 1968.

———. "A Comparison of Political Factionalism in Japan and India." *Australian Journal of Politics and History* 16, no. 3 (December 1970): 361–74.

Storry, Richard. *The Double Patriots.* London: Chatto and Windus, 1958.

Sugai, Shuichi. "The Japanese Police System." In R. E. Ward (ed.). *Five Studies in Japanese Politics.* Ann Arbor: University of Michigan Press, 1957.

Supreme Commander, Allied Powers (SCAP). *Summation of Non-Military Activities in Japan and Korea, 1945–1948.* Washington, D.C.: U.S. Government Printing Office, 1949.

————. Government Section. *Political Reorientation of Japan: September, 1945–September, 1948.* Washington, D.C.: U.S. Government Printing Office, 1949.

Taira, Koji. "The Characteristics of Japanese Labor Markets." *Economic Development and Cultural Change,* vol. 10, no. 2, pt. 1 (January 1962), pp. 150–68.

Takahashi, Takeshi. "Social Security in Japan." In Japan Institute of Labor (ed.). *Changing Patterns of Industrial Relations.* Tokyo: Japan Institute of Labor, 1965.

Takezawa, Shinichi. "Social and Cultural Factors in Management in Japan." *International Labor Review* 44, no. 2 (August 1966): 148–74.

Textor, Robert B. *Failure in Japan.* New York: John Day Co., 1951.

Thayer, Nathaniel Bowman. *How the Conservatives Rule Japan.* Princeton, N. J.: Princeton University Press, 1969.

Thorp, Willard L. (ed.). *The United States in the Far East.* Englewood Cliffs, N.J.: Prentice-Hall, 1962.

Totten, George Oakley, III. *The Social Democratic Movement in Prewar Japan.* New Haven: Yale University Press, 1966.

Totten, George Oakley, III (ed.). *Democracy in Prewar Japan: Groundwork or Facade?* Boston: D. C. Heath, 1967.

Totten, George Oakley, III, and T. Kawakami. "The Function of Factionalism in Japanese Politics." *Pacific Affairs* 33, no. 2 (summer 1965): 109–22.

Tsuda, Masumi. *The Basic Structure of Japanese Labor Relations.* Tokyo: Society for the Social Sciences, 1965.

Tsurumi, Kazuko. *Social Change and the Individual.* Princeton, N.J.: Princeton University Press, 1970.

Ward, Robert E. (ed.). *Five Studies in Japanese Politics.* Ann Arbor: University of Michigan Press, 1957.

————. *Japan's Political System.* Englewood Cliffs, N. J.: Prentice-Hall, 1967.

————. "The Commission on the Constitution and Prospects for Constitutional Change in Japan." *Journal of Asian Studies* 24, no. 3 (May 1965): 401–29.

————. "Japan: The Continuity of Modernization." In L. W. Pye and S. Verba (eds.). *Political Culture and Political Development.* Princeton, N.J.: Princeton University Press, 1965. Pp. 27–82.

————. "The Legacy of the Occupation." In H. Passim (ed.). *The United States and Japan.* Englewood Cliffs, N.J.: Prentice-Hall, 1966. Pp. 29–56.

Ward, Robert E., and Dankwart Rustow (eds.). *Political Modernization in Japan and Turkey.* Princeton, N.J.: Prentice-Hall, 1964.

White, James W. "The Sōka Gakkai: Implications of a Mass Movement for Democratic Society." Paper presented to the American Political Science Association Conference, Los Angeles, 1970.

White, John. *Japanese Aid.* London: Overseas Development Institute, 1964.

Wildes, Harry Emerson. *Typhoon in Tokyo: The Occupation and Its Aftermath.* New York: Macmillan Co., 1954.

Windmuller, John P. "International Trade Union Organizations: Structures, Functions, Limitations." In Solomon Barkin (ed.). *International Labor.* New York: Harper and Row, 1967.

Yanaga, Chitoshi. *Japanese People and Politics.* New York: John Wiley and Sons, 1956.

———. *Japan Since Perry.* New York: McGraw-Hill, 1949.

———. *Big Business in Japanese Politics.* New Haven: Yale University Press, 1968.

Yoshida, Shigeru. *The Yoshida Memoirs.* London: Heinemann, 1961.

Japanese Sources

Akahata (Red Flag).

Amazawa Fujiro. "Denden Kōsha niokeru Rōmu Kanri no Mondaiten" (Problems of Personnel Management in the Telephone and Telegraph Public Corporation). *Nihon Rōdō Kyōkai Zasshi* 1, no. 7 (October 1959): 15–25.

Ariga Sokichi. "Kokutetsu niokeru Rōshi *Kankei* no Jissai" (Actual Conditions of Labor Management Relations in the National Railways). *Nihon Rōdō Kyōkai Zasshi* 1, no. 7 (October 1959): 26–31.

Asahi Shimbun, Tokyo.

Azuma Mitsutoshi. *Rōdō Hō* (Labor Law). Tokyo: Aoki, 1950.

———. *Rōshi to Hōritsu* (Labor Relations and the Law). Tokyo: Nihon Rōdō Kyōkai, 1962.

Fujibayashi Keizō. *Rōshi Kankei to Rōshi Kyōgisei* (Labor Relations and Labor Consultation). Tokyo: Dayamondo, 1963.

———. "Waga Kuni no Rōdō Sōgi no Tokushitsu" (The Characteristics of Labor Disputes in Japan). *Nihon Rōdō Kyōkai Zasshi* 4, no. 2 (February 1962): 4–11.

Fujiwara Hirotatsu. *Kanryō: Nihon no Seiji o Ugokasu Mono* (Bureaucrats: Prime Movers in the Japanese Government). Tokyo: Kodansha, 1964.

Goto Kyoshi. *Rōdō Kumiai Hō no Rekishi to Riron* (The History and Theory of the Trade Union Law). Tokyo: Zoshindō, 1948.

Hanami Tadashi. *ILO to Nihon no Danketsuken* (The ILO and Freedom of Association in Japan). Tokyo: Dayamondo, 1963.

————. "Kankō Rōdōsha no Sōgiken" (The Public Employees' Right to Strike). *Nihon Rōdō Kyōkai Zasshi* 9, no. 2 (February 1967): 2–10.

————. "Rōdō Mondai Kenkyū no Hōhōronteki Hansei (Reflections on Methodologies of the Study of Labor Problems). *Nihon Rōdō Kyōkai Zasshi* 9, no. 7 (July 1967): 59–66.

Haraguchi Yukitaka. "Kokusai Jiyū Rōren to Nihon no Kumiai" (The ICFTU and Japanese Unions). *Gekkan Rōdō Mondai* 57 (February 1963): 68–72.

Hōritsu Jihō (Labor Review), February 1965.

Hosoya Matsuta. *Nihon no Rōdō Kumiai Undō: Sono Rekishi to Genjō* (Japan's Labor Union Movement: Its History and Present Conditions). Tokyo: Shakai Shisō Kenkyūkai, 1958.

Ishida Hirohide (Bakuei). "Hoshuseitō no Bijon" (The Vision of the Conservative Party). *Chūō Kōron*, January 1963, pp. 88–97.

Ishida Takeshi. *Kindai Nihon Seiji Kōzō no Kenkyū* (A Study of the Political Structure of Modern Japan). Tokyo: Miraisha, 1956.

————. *Gendai Soshiki Ron* (Modern Organization Theory). Tokyo: Iwanami Shoten, 1961.

Ishii Teruhisa, et al. "Rōshi Kankei Hō to Nihon no Rōdō Undō" (Labor Relations Laws and Japan's Labor Movement). *Juristo* 371 (June 1967): 24–41.

Ishikawa Toshihiko. "ILO no Hannō to Kongo no Tatakai" (ILO's Response to Our Future Struggle). *Hōritsu Jumpō*, February 1962, pp. 18–29.

Jichirō (ed.). *Jichirō no Hata* (Jichiro's Flag). Tokyo: Jichirō Shinsho, 1966.

Jiyūminshutō Kōhō Iinkai (Public Information Committee, the Liberal Democratic Party). *Heiwa to Zenshin no tame ni* (For Peace and Progress). Tokyo: Jimintō, 1966.

————. *ILO Dai-87-go Jōyaku no Hijun to Kankei Kokunai Hō Kaisei Mondai* (Problems of Ratification of ILO Convention No. 87 and Revision of Related Domestic Laws). Tokyo: Jimintō, 1964.

————. *ILO Mondai no Aramashi* (An Outline of the ILO Problem). Tokyo: Jimintō, 1965.

————. *Waga Tō no Kihon Hōshin* (Our Party's Basic Policy). Tokyo: Jimintō, 1967.

————. *Wareware ga Mezasu Shakai no Sugata: Rōdō Kenshō to Sono Kaisetsu* (The Social Conditions We are Aiming At: The Labor Charter and Its Explanation). Tokyo: Jimintō, 1966.

Juristo (Jurist). "Rōdō Hanrei Hyakusen" (100 Labor Verdicts). Tokyo: Yūhikaku, 1962.

Kaigo Muneori, et al. (eds.). "Kyōiku" (Education). *Shiryō: Sengo*

Nijūnen Shi (Materials: Postwar Twenty-Year History). Vol. 5, pt. 1. Tokyo: Nihon Hyōron Sha, 1966.

Kaite Shingo and Toda Yoshio. *ILO: Kokusai Rōdō Kikan* (The ILO: International Labor Organization), rev. ed. Tokyo: Nihon Rōdō Kyōkai, 1962.

Kihata Koichi. "Kokusai Rōdō Undō Monogatari: ITS to sono Soshiki Kankei" (ITS and Their Organizational Relations). *Dōmei*, July 1967, pp. 80–85.

Kikuoka Yaōzō. *Kokkai Binran* (Diet Handbook). Tokyo: Nihon Seikei Shimbun Shuppanbu, 1960–1967.

Kishimoto Eitarō. *Nihon Rōdō Seisaku Shoshi* (A Short History of Japanese Labor Policy). Tokyo: Yūhikaku, 1948.

Kōan Chōsa Chō (Public Peace Investigative Agency). *Nihon Kyōsantō no Rōdō Shintō Kōsaku* (Japan Communist Party Maneuvers in Penetrating Labor Unions). Tokyo: Kōan Chōsa Chō, 1964.

Kōda Yoshio. "*Sōhyō no Hanshuryū no Undō Rosen*" (Sōhyō's Anti-Main Current's Route). *Gekkan Rōdō Mondai* 53 (October 1962): 15–20.

Kokurō (Japan National Railways Workers' Union). *Kokutetsu Rōdō Kumiai 20-nen Shi* (Kokurō's Twenty-Year History). Tokyo: Rōdō Junpōsha, 1967.

Kokusai Jiyū Rōren Tōkyō Jimushō (ICFTU, Tokyo Branch Office). *Kokusai Jiyū Rōren* (The ICFTU). Tokyo: Kokusai Jiyū Rōren Tōkyō Jimushō, 1966.

Kōmuin Seido Shingikai Gijiroku (Proceedings of the Advisory Council on the Public Personnel System). 2 vols. N.p, n.d.

Kōmuin Seido Shingikai (Advisory Council on the Public Personnel System). *ILO Kankei Hōritsu Jū Kokkai Shūsei niyori Shikō o Enki Sareta Kitei nitsuite (Tōshin)* (A Report on the Provisions among the ILO-Related Legislation the Enforcement of Which Was Delayed by the Diet). Tokyo: June, 1966.

————. *Kōmuin Tō no Rōdō Kankei no Kihon nikansuru Jikō nitsuite* (On the Foundation of Labor Relations of Public Personnel and Others). Tokyo, October 17, 1970.

Kōno Mitsu. *Nihon Shakaitō Shi* (A History of Japanese Socialist Parties). Tokyo: Chūō Kōron Sha, 1960.

Mainichi Shimbun, Osaka.

Mainichi Nenkan (Mainichi Yearbook), Osaka.

Masuda Yoneji. *Ō Yakunin* (The Officials). Tokyo: Kobun Sha, 1956.

Matsujima Hiroshi. *Gendai Nihon no Seitō to Seiji* (Parties and Politics in Contemporary Japan). Tokyo: Ōtsuki Shoten, 1966.

Matsumoto Seichō. *Gendai Kanryō Ron* (On Contemporary Bureaucracy). Tokyo: Bungei Shunju Sha, 1964.

Matsushita Keiichi. *Gendai Nihon no Seijiteki Kōsei* (The Political Structure of Contemporary Japan). Tokyo: Tōkyō Daigaku Shuppan Kai, 1964.

———. "Rōso Seiji Katsudō no Rironteki Mondai" (Theoretical Questions of Unions' Political Activities). *Rōdō Hō* 50 (December 1963): 57–69.

Minshushugi Kenkyūkai (Democracy Research Association). *Nihon no Rōdō Kumiai no Seiji Katsudō* (The Political Activities of Japanese Labor Unions). N.p., n.d. (apparently 1964).

Mochizuki Muneaki. *Nikkyōso 20-nen no Tatakai* (Japan Teachers' Union Twenty-Year Struggle). Tokyo: Rōdō Junpōsha, 1967.

Mombu Kisha Kai (Ministry of Education Correspondents Club). *Mombushō* (Ministry of Education). Tokyo: Hobunsha, 1958.

Morita Yoshio. *Nihon Keieisha Dantai Hatten Shi* (History of the Development of Japanese Employers Groups). Tokyo: Nikkan Rōdō Tsushinsha, 1958.

Nagata Masaomi. *Keizai Dantai Hatten Shi* (History of the Development of Economic Organizations). Tokyo: Kofuji Shoten, 1956.

Nakamura Kenji. *Warera ni Sōhyō wa Hitsuyō Ka* (Is Sōhyō Necessary for Us?). Tokyo: Hagi Shobo, 1967.

Nakayama Kazuhisa. *Kankō Rōdō Hō to Rōdōsha no Kenri* (Labor Law in the Public Service and Workers' Rights). Tokyo: Junpōsha, 1964.

Nihon ILO Kyōkai (Japan ILO Association) (ed.). *Nihon ILO Kyōkai no Shiori* (Japan ILO Association Guidebook). Tokyo: Nihon ILO Kyōkai, 1966.

Nihon ILO Kyōkai, Ōsakafu Shibu (Japan ILO Association, Osaka Branch) (ed.). *ILO to Shakai Seigi* (ILO and Social Justice). Osaka: Nihon ILO Kyōkai Ōsakafu Shibu Jimukyoku, 1965.

Nihon Keizai Shimbun, Tokyo.

Nihon Minsei Kenkyūkai (Japan Society for the Study of Democratic Politics). *Kokkai Giin Sōran* (Outline of Diet Members). Tokyo: Hyōron Shinsha, 1965.

Nihon Rōdō Kyōkai (Japan Institute of Labor) (ed.). *Sengo no Rōdō Rippō to Rōdō Undō* (Postwar Labor Legislation and the Labor Movement). Tokyo: Nihon Rōdō Kyōkai, 1959.

———. *Nihon Rōdō Kyōkai Jigyō Nenji Kōkoku* (Yearly Report on the Activities of the Japan Institute of Labor). Tokyo: Nihon Rōdō Kyōkai, 1966.

Nihon Seisansei Honbu (Japan Productivity Center) (ed.). *Seisansei*

Undō 10-nen no Ayumi (Ten Years Progress of the Japan Productivity Center). Tokyo: Seisansei Honbu, 1965.

Nihon Shakaitō (The Japan Socialist Party) (ed.). *Nihon Shakaitō 20-nen no Kiroku* (The Twenty-Year Record of the Japan Socialist Party). Tokyo: Nihon Shakaitō Kikanshi Shuppankyoku, 1965.

Nikkeiren (Japan Federation of Employers' Associations. *Jūnen no Ayumi* (Ten Years' Progress). Tokyo: Nikkeiren, 1958.

————. *Nikkeiren no Ayumi* (Nikkeiren's Progress). Tokyo: Nikkeiren, 1963.

Nikkyōso (Japan Teachers' Union) (ed.). *Nikkyōso Nijūnen Shi* (Nikkyōso's Twenty-Year History). Tokyo: Rōdō Junpōsha, 1967.

Nōmura Heiji. *Nihon Rōdō Hō no Kessei Katei to Riron* (Japanese Labor Law's Process of Formation and Theory). Tokyo: Iwanami Shoten, 1957.

Ogawa Masaaki and Tadenuma Kenichi (eds.). *Gendai Hō to Rōdō* (Contemporary Law and Labor). Tokyo: Iwanami Shoten, 1965.

Oka Yoshitake (ed.). *Gendai Nihon no Seiji Katei* (The Political Process in Contemporary Japan). Tokyo: Iwanami Shoten, 1958.

Okazaki Saburo. *Sōhyō 15-nen: Rōdō Undō no Kōsei Seichō* (Sōhyō's Fifteen Years: The Labor Movement's High Growth Rate). Tokyo: Rōdō Junpōsha, 1965.

Ōkōchi Kazuo. *Sengo Nihon no Rōdō Undō* (Postwar Japan's Labor Movement). Tokyo: Iwanami Shoten, 1961.

————. *Reimeki no Nihon Rōdō Undō* (The Dawn of the Japanese Labor Movement). Tokyo: Iwanami Shoten, 1952.

————. "Rōshi Kankei no Atarashii Kyokumen" (New Aspects of Labor Management Relations). *Chūō Kōron*, August 1963, pp. 34–47.

Ōkōchi Kazuo et al. *Nihon no Union Rida* (Japan's Union Leaders). Tokyo: Tokyo Keizai Shimpo Sha, 1965.

Ōkōchi Kazuo et al. (eds.). "Rōdō" (Labor). *Shiryō: Sengo Nijūnen Shi* (Materials: Postwar Twenty-Year History). Vol. 4. Tokyo: Nihon Hyōron Sha, 1966.

Ōmori Makoto. *Rōdō Kumiai to wa Nani Ka* (What Is a Labor Union). Tokyo: San'ichi Shobō, 1965.

Ōshima Fujitaro. *Kokutetsu* (Japan National Railways). Tokyo: Iwanami Shinsho, 1956.

Ōta Kaoru. *Waga Tatakai no Kiroku* (Record of Our Struggle). Tokyo: Akita Shoten, 1967.

Rōdōshō (Ministry of Labor) (ed.). *Dai-sanjūikkai Sōsenkyo narabi ni Dai-rokkai Tōitsu Chihō Senkyo niokeru Rōdō Kumiai Kakushin Sietō no Senkyo Katsudō nitsuite* (Concerning the Election Activities of Labor Unions and Renovationist Parties in the 31st General Elections and the 6th Unified Local Elections). Tokyo: Rōdōshō, 1967.

————. *Shiryō: Kokusai Rōdō Jōyaku Dai-87-go Hijun Shi* (Materials: The History of the Ratification of ILo Convention No. 87). Tokyo: Nikkan Tsūshin Sha, 1966.

————. *Shiryō: Rōdō Undō Shi* (A History of the Labor Movement). Tokyo: Rōmu Gyōsei Kenkyūjo. Annual.

Rōshi Kankei Hō Kenkyū Kai (Labor Relations Law Study Commission) (ed.). *Hōkokushō: Rōshi Kankei Unyō no Jitsujō oyobi Mondaiten* (The Facts and Problems of the Application of Labor Relations Laws). Tokyo: Nihon Rōdō Kyōkai, 1967. In two parts.

Sakisaka Itsurō. "Tadashii Kōryō, Tadashii Kikō" (Proper Platform and Proper Organization). *Shakaishugi* 88 (December 1958): 45–52.

Sato Susumu. *ILO Jōyaku to Nihon Rōdō Hō* (ILO Conventions and Japanese Labor Law). Tokyo: Hōsei Daigaku Shuppankyoku, 1962.

Shimizu Ikutarō et al. (eds.). "Shakai" (Society). *Shiryō: Sengo Nijūnen Shi* (Materials: Postwar Twenty-Years History). Vol. 5, pt. 2. Tokyo: Nihon Hyōron Sha, 1966.

Shirai Taishiro. *Rōdō Kumiai no Zaisei* (Labor Union Finances). Tokyo: Nihon Hyōron Sha, 1964.

Shūgiin (Lower House) (ed.). *Gikai Seido Shchijūnen Shi: Shūgiin Meikan* (Seventy-Year History of the Parliamentary System: Directory of the Lower House). Tokyo: Ōkurashō Instatsukyoku, 1962.

Shūgiin (Lower House) and Sangiin (Upper House) (eds.). *Gikai Seido Shchijūnen Shi: Kokkai Shi* (Seventy-Year History of the Parliamentary System: History of the Diet). Tokyo: Ōkurashō Insatsukyoku, 1960.

————. *Gikai Seido Shchijūnen Shi: Teikoku Gikai Gian Kenmei Roku* (Seventy-Year History of the Parliamentary System: Registers of Bills in the Imperial Diet) Tokyo: Ōkurashō Insatsukyoku, 1961.

Sōhyō Stōken Dakkan Tokubetsu Iinkai (Sōhyō Special Committee for the Recovery of the Right to Strike). *Kankō Rōdōsha Kumiai Katsudō Hendobukku* (Handbook of Union Activities of Workers in the Public Sector). Tokyo: Union Sabisu, 1966.

Suehiro Izutarō. *Nihon Rōdō Kumiai Undō Shi* (History of Japanese Trade Union Movement). Tokyo: Chūō Kōron Sha, 1954.

Suekawa Hiroshi (ed.). "Hōritsu" (Law). *Shiryō: Sengo Nijūnen Shi* (Materials: Postwar Twenty-Year History). Vol. 3. Tokyo: Nihon Hyōron Sha, 1966.

Sugimoto Hiroshi. "Kokusai Jiyū Rōren no Tainichi Seisaku" (The

Japan Policy of the ICFTU). *Gekkan Rōdō Mondai* 57 (February 1963): 73–78.

Sumiya Mikio. *Nihon Rōdō Undō Shi* (A History of Japan's Labor Movement). Tokyo: Yūshindō, 1966.

――――. *Nihon no Rōdō Mondai* (Japan's Labor Problems). Tokyo: Tōkyō Daigaku Shuppan Kai, 1965.

――――. "Nihon no Kyodai Soshiki" (Japan's Gigantic Organizations). *Asahi Jyanaru*, August 18, 1965, pp. 35–41.

Suzuki Yukio. *Seiji o Ugokasu Keieisha Zaikai no Shisō to Kōdō* (Businessmen Behind Politics; Ideology and Action of the Business Community). Tokyo: Nihon Keizai Shimbunsha, 1965.

Taguchi Fukuji. *Nihon Seiji no Dōkō to Tenbō* (Trends and Prospects of Japanese Politics). Tokyo: Mirai Sha, 1966.

Takahashi Takeshi. "Rōdō Mondai no Kokusaika: Nihon no Keisu" (The Internationalization of Labor Problems: The Japanese Case). *Sekai no Rōdō* 16, no. 11 (November 1966): 2–8.

Tōkyō Shimbun, Tokyo.

Tōkyō Shisei Chōsa Kai (Tokyo Municipal Research Institute). *Maeda Tamon: Sono Bun, Sono Hitō* (Maeda Tamon: His Writings and Personality). Tokyo: Tōkyō Shisei Chōsa Kai, 1963.

Tsuji Kiyoaki (ed.). "Seiji" (Politics). *Shiryō: Sengo Nijūnen Shi* (Materials: Postwar Twenty-Year History). Vol. 1. Tokyo: Nihon Hyōron Sha, 1966.

――――. *Nihon Kanryōsei no Kenkyū* (Studies of Japanese Bureaucracy). Tokyo: Kobundo, 1952.

――――. "Nihon niokeru Seisaku Kettei Katei" (The Policy-Making Process in Japan). *Shisō* 487 (January 1965): 28–37.

Ujihara Shōjiro. *Nihon no Rōshi Kankei* (Japanese Labor-Management Relations). Tokyo: Tōkyō Daigaku Shuppan Kai, 1961.

Ujihara Shōjiro and Nōmura Heiji (eds.). *Chūshō Kigyō no Rōdō Kumiai* (Unions of Small and Middle-Size Enterprises). Tokyo: Nihon Hyōron Sha, 1961.

Ujihara Shōjiro and Rōdō Mondai Bunken Kenkyū Kai (Association for the Study of Labor Problems) (eds.). *Nihon no Rōdō Mondai* (Japan's Labor Problems). Tokyo: Sōgō Rōdō Kenkyūjo, 1966.

Ushiomi Toshitaka. "Sengo no Nihon Shakai to Hōritsuka." In Ushiomi Toshitaka (ed.). *Gendai no Hōritsuka* (Contemporary Jurists). Tokyo: Iwanami Shoten, 1966.

Utada Tokuichi. *Kokusai Jiyū Rōren Sono Soshiki to Katsudō* (The ICFTU: Its Organization and Activities). Tokyo: Nihon Rōdō Kyōkai, 1963.

Watanabe Tōru. *Gendai Rōnō Undō Shi Nenpyō* (Chronology of Contemporary Labor and Agrarian Movements). Tokyo: San'ichi Shobō, 1962.

Watanuki Jōji. *Nihon no Seiji Shakai* (Japanese Political Society). Tokyo: Tōkyō Daigaku Shuppan Kai, 1967.

Yomiuri Shimbun, Tokyo.

Zentei (Japan Postal Workers' Union) (ed.). *Shiryō: ILO Jōyaku Hijun Tōsō Shi* (Materials: The History of the Struggle for the Ratification of ILO Convention No. 87). Tokyo: Zenteishin Rōdō Kumiai, 1960.

Index

democratization, 53, 60, 69–73
Democratization Movement (Mindō), 70–73, 80
Diet: 1890–1930, 13, 14, 40, 42; during occupation, 54–55; and labor disputes, 87–88, 119–120; union leaders elected to, 101; and Dreyer Commission, 154–156; and ILO issues, 4, 120–121, 124–126, 128, 136. *See also* elections; labor legislation; conservative-progressive confrontation; parties
Dōmei (Japan Confederation of Labor), 152, 156, 157, 165–166, 177
Dreyer Commission. *See* ILO Fact Finding and Conciliation Commission

Easton, David, 3
economic nationalism, 43
education: issues, 94–96, 128; legislation, 95–96
education-public peace group (Bunkyō Chian), 133–134, 138, 141, 177
efficiency rating system, 96
elections:
—Diet: 1920, 36; occupation, 59; after occupation, 90, 127, 139
—of LDP president, 139–142, 180
Electrical Workers' Union, 58
emperor, 23, 25, 40–41, 45
employers, 21–22, 76–77, 161. *See also* business community; employers' associations
employers' associations, 21–22, 30–31, 43, 64. *See also* Nikkeiren
enterprise unionism, 68, 98–99, 98 n33

Fact Finding and Conciliation Commission. *See* ILO
factions, 140–142
family, importance of, 16
feedback, to ILO, 8, 43, 153
foreign policy: military control, 46; postwar, 97–98, 104–108, 177
foreign relations: in 1920's, 28–29; postwar, 51, 96, 148. *See also* international involvement
foreign trade: pre World War II, 44, 48–49; occupation and postwar, 79, 97; and ILO, 148, 174, 177
freedom of association: Japanese union pressures, 1, 5, 88, 110–111, 170–171, 177; importance of, to ILO, 3, 81, 110–111; in Japanese constitutions, 40, 78; subissues in Japan, 175. *See also* ILO
Friendly Love Society (Yūaikai), 19, 21, 34

Friends of Constitutional Government (Rikken Seiyūkai), 42
Fujibayashi Keizō, 54, 87, 121–122
Fujiyama Aichiro, 140
Fukuda Takeo, 133
full-time union officer system: explained, 100; as issue in dispute, 125, 130, 135, 137, 138, 166–168
Funada Naka, 155–156

General Agreement on Tariff and Trade (GATT), 97, 147, 148
General Council of Japan's Trade Unions. *See* Sōhyō
genrō, 14
Gompers, Samuel, 34
Government Ordinances Advisory Council, 75–76

Hanami Tadashi, 92 n20
Haraguchi Yukitaka: at International Labor Conference, 1, 85; and ICFTU, 108; and ILO, 111–112, 136; and Zentei dispute, 121
Harmonization Society (Kyōchōkai), 20–21, 39
Hashimoto Tomisaburo, 157
Hatoyama Ichiro, 98
Hoover Mission, 61–64
Hosoya Matsuta, 70, 73

Igarashi Akio, 148
Ikeda Hayato: views as prime minister, 132; LDP presidency, 139–142; and ILO issues, 138, 145–146, 150–151
Imperial Rule Assistance Association, 49
Industrial Patriotic Society, 49
industrialization, 13, 41
Informal Committee on the ILO (Sewaninkai), 133–135
intellectuals, 19–20
International Association for Labor Legislation, 11
International Confederation of Free Trade Unions (ICFTU): aided Japanese unions, 1, 85, 88, 89; relations with Sōhyō, 74–75, 106–112, 174; relations with Nikkyōso, 127–128; pressured Japanese government, 108, 131, 145; Japanese union membership in, 74–75, 106, 182
International Federation of Free Teachers Unions (IFFTU), 127–128
International Federation of Trade Unions (IFTU), 11, 33

220 The Politics of Labor Legislation in Japan

national unions, 99
nationalism, 45, 46
Nichirō, 102
Nikkeiren, 64, 80, 146–147, 152, 158
Nikkyōso (Japan Teachers' Union): complaint to ILO, 77, 127–128, 131, 182;
radical views opposed, 95, 96, 116, 133,
146; negotiation with ministry, 153,
154, 156
Nippon Telegraph and Telephone Public Corporation, 76
Nishio Suehiro, 54, 125
Nōmura Heiji, 110

Ōhira Masayoshi, 145
Ōi Kentarō, 17
Okazaki Kenichi, 35
Ōkōchi Kazuo, 15, 15 n13
Order 18, 146
Oro Rojuichiro, 54
Organization for Asian Economic Co-
operation, 147
Organization for Economic Cooperation
and Development, 145, 147
Oriental Liberal party, 17
Ōsugi Sakae, 37
Ōta Kaoru, 86, 104, 105
Ōta-Iwai line, 105–107, 127

Paris Peace Conference: and formation
of ILO, 10, 11-12; and Japanese government position, 22, 24, 34
parties: pre World War II, 14, 42, 45;
postwar changes, 59–60, 89–90, 173
paternalism, 15, 16, 98
pluralism, 14
police: and labor disputes, 16, 18, 20,
37–38; wartime repression, 50; centralization of, 94–95
Policy Affairs Deliberation Council, 132-
134
Policy Affairs Research Council, 141,
142, 181
"political memory," 9
political system, 12–14, 23
popular rights movement, 13
Postal, Telegraph, and Telephone International (PTTI), 88, 89, 108
Postal Workers' Union. See Zentei
Prefectural and Municipal Workers'
Union, 127
press: in Meiji era, 14; SCAP censorship,
72; on ILO issues, 120–121, 135, 155,
157–158, 164
Printers' Union Fraternal Society, 34

Privy Council, 14
production control (labor tactic), 56
Progressive party, 13
Public Corporations and National Enterprises Labor Relations Commission,
87, 101, 102, 121
Public Corporations and National Enterprises Workers' Unions' Councils,
84–85, 105, 143
public employees: occupation restrictions, 57, 64–67; and ILO Convention,
98, 91–92; in Kuraishi plan, 137–138;
other issues, 1, 100–101, 134. See also
strike, right to
public interest: in MacArthur letter, 66-
67; represented on Adv. Council for
Pub. Personnel, 161–163, 165–166, 168;
on other committees, 76–77, 114
public opinion, 59, 173, 178
Public Peace Investigative Agency, 78

radicals: early, in labor movement, 18,
19, 36; SCAP views, 60, 63–66
Reconstruction League (Saiken Dōmei),
71
Rosenau, J. N., 4, 8 n

Saito, Kunikichi, 86 n, 133 n
Sanbetsu (National Congress of Indus-
trial Unions): formation, actions, and
membership, 61, 63, 68, 69, 73, 80;
anti-communism within, 70–73
Satō Eisaku, 138, 140–141, 151, 163
Seiyūkai, 36
Sewaninkai, 133–135
Shidehara Kijuro, 53
Shiga Yoshio, 56
Shinsanbetsu (National Federation of
Industrial Organizations), 73, 102, 143
Shinyūkai, 34
Shitetsu Sōren, 74
Shuntō. See spring offensive
Social Democratic party (SDP), 17
Social dumping, 43–49, 79
Social Policy Academic Association, 20
Socialists: early organizing attempts, 11,
17; wartime, 49; during occupation,
58, 63; 1950's splits and alignments,
89–90, 94, 104, 125–126. See also Japan
Socialist party
Socialization, 170–171
Sōdōmei (Japan Trade Union Federa-
tion): 1920's, 19, 35, 38, 39; relations
with other federations postwar, 69–70,
73, 102–103
Sōhyō (General Council of Japan's Trade

www.ingramcontent.com/pod-product-compliance
Lightning Source LLC
Chambersburg PA
CBHW021657210326
41599CB00013B/1448